Stan Baldwin

COMPLETE GUIDE TO SALES FORCE COMPENSATION

HOW TO PLAN SALARIES, COMMISSIONS, BONUSES, QUOTAS . . . EVERYTHING NEEDED TO ACHIEVE TOP SALES RESULTS

COMPLETE GUIDE TO SALES FORCE COMPENSATION

HOW TO PLAN SALARIES, COMMISSIONS, BONUSES, QUOTAS . . . EVERYTHING NEEDED TO ACHIEVE TOP SALES RESULTS

James F. Carey

BUSINESS ONE IRWIN
Homewood, Illinois 60430

Sponsoring editor: Cynthia A. Zigmund
Project editor: Rebecca Dodson
Production manager: Irene H. Sotiroff
Jacket designer: Annette Vogt
Designer: Jeanne M. Rivera
Art manager: Kim Meriwether
Compositor: TCSystems, Inc.
Typeface: 11/13 Palatino
Printer: The Book Press, Inc.

Library of Congress Cataloging-in-Publication Data

Carey, James F.
  Complete guide to sales force compensation : how to plan
salaries, commissions, bonuses, quotas : everything needed to
achieve top sales results / James F. Carey.
      p.   cm.
  Includes index.
  ISBN 1-55623-696-4
  1. Sales personnel—Salaries, etc.   2. Compensation management.
I. Title.
HF5439.7.C37   1992
658.3'044—dc20   91-47752

Printed in the United States of America
1 2 3 4 5 6 7 8 9 0 BP 9 8 7 6 5 4 3 2

PREFACE

Each year, one out of three companies changes sales pay plans. Chief executives, marketing and sales executives, human resources executives, and compensation specialists . . . all search for a better way to compensate the sales force. That search can end with the methods presented here.

A practical manual for designing sales compensation, this book fits the needs of any company, large or small. Whether evaluating an existing pay plan or developing a new plan, the reader will find here a complete process to follow, including concepts and techniques to produce a truly effective sales pay plan. This book provides a coherent method for designing sales compensation that gears the principles of human motivation to a company's marketing objectives.

The method of sales pay plan design explained here has proved its value in company after company. Examples of companies achieving high sales force productivity appear throughout the book. However, this is not a collection of "war stories" about unbelievable sales successes. Instead, this book gives the reader practical, step-by-step advice. It tells and shows how to design a pay plan that will get the best from your company's salespeople.

The reader will find in this book practical advice for planning and controlling sales compensation. The book assumes no prior knowledge of sales compensation arrangements—or even of the jargon of sales pay. Draw, split, spiff, windfall, override . . . each is explained, with a discussion of its place in sales compensation. The reader learns where to use and where to avoid various types of pay arrangements. With emphasis on practical how-to-do-it advice, only enough theoretical background is included to explain *why* these methods work.

The first six chapters explain the fundamentals for designing sales compensation. Starting with a review of the principles of human motivation as applied to salespeople, Chapter 1 reviews the important role of sales compensation in a company's marketing program. Both the pay method and the pay amount determine the kind of sales force a company will have and the direction of their selling effort. To establish that direction, the company must identify its marketing objectives, marketing strategy, and sales goals. The well-designed sales pay plan then connects sales force motivation to the company's goals. That connection produces the high sales force productivity that translates to bottom-line profits.

Chapters 2 through 6 take the reader step-by-step through the basic design of a sales pay plan. This systematic approach allows any company to custom-design a sales pay plan to fit the company's own needs and opportunities. The same steps can guide the evaluation of an existing pay plan.

Chapters 7 through 10 explore salaries and draws, bonuses and awards, territories and quotas, and windfall sales. How do draws fit into sales force compensation? Does paying a salary kill incentive? How should you award bonuses and prizes? The reader gets straight answers to these questions and more in Chapters 7 and 8. Chapter 9 tells how to set territories, when to change them, and how to set quotas that the sales force will regard as fair. The issue of windfall sales and whether to limit sales earnings receives a thorough airing in Chapter 10, with description of an approach that will appeal to both the salesperson and the company's controller.

How to analyze the cost of sales compensation is reviewed in Chapter 11, together with advice on methods for controlling costs with least negative effect on motivation of the sales force. Also included is guidance for periodically auditing the cost and effectiveness of the sales pay plan.

Some managers write up the sales pay plan in a brief outline, some don't write at all, and some get a lawyer to write a long and frightening plan document. In Chapter 12 the author tells why each of these is less than ideal. Practical advice on document writing, plus examples of common plan provisions and complete sales pay plan documents, guide the reader to a user-friendly plan document that protects both parties.

Separate chapters on trainee pay, manager pay, and special issues round out coverage of the subject. The book follows a coherent and consistent approach to sales pay plan design. The reader does not have to select and combine pieces from pay plans of other companies and hope that they will function together in a different sales situation. Nor does the reader have to reinvent solutions to old problems. It is all here. This book provides the *Complete Guide to Sales Force Compensation*.

The author, a Certified Management Consultant, shares with the reader over 25 years of experience in designing successful sales pay plans. That experience has included a wide variety of sales situations—from electronic instruments to fertilizer, professional services to shop supplies, airplanes to fresh produce, computer software to burglar alarms. That experience plus motivation research form the foundation for this systematic approach to the complex task of designing a sales pay plan. The reader gets direct advice in plain language, just as though the consultant were in your office guiding every step.

Actual cases demonstrate key points throughout the book. Graphs, tables, and illustrative calculations make it easy to apply the principles of effective sales compensation to any company of any size. Examples of sales pay plan language and compensation reports complete the package of everything needed to design a sales pay plan. There is even advice on how to present the new pay plan to a suspicious sales force. And, how to audit and evaluate the plan after it is in place. Here is the book that can bring the values of more effective sales compensation to your company.

JAMES F. CAREY

ACKNOWLEDGMENTS

This book reflects methods tested and lessons learned in many companies. To those clients, I give my wholehearted thanks.

Also deserving of recognition are my many colleagues in the Institute of Management Consultants. Their advice encouraged me to persevere in the writing and publication of this book.

Special thanks are due to Eunice Massoni, whose assistance in manuscript preparation and office administration made it possible to complete this book while carrying on an active management consulting practice.

CONTENTS

Chapter One

Setting the Course

Plan sales pay to fit marketing objectives.

Top sales force productivity results from a competent sales team working hard to achieve the company's marketing goals. To accomplish that, a company needs to combine several elements, giving motivation top priority in the process. Human motivation provides the power, while marketing strategy provides the direction. Cost takes a secondary but still important place in the order of considerations. The third and last consideration is that of administrative convenience.

Any company can mesh the power of human motivation with marketing strategy by following the systematic approach described here. This method will result in a pay plan that focuses superior sales effort on the things that count most for the company.

A DESTINATION

The airplane backed slowly away from the gate and moved out to the runway. Soon the engines roared and the plane soared into the sky. It landed hours later half a world away. Clearly, the plane had enough fuel and power for the trip, but it had something more—a pilot who knew not only the destination, but also the detailed route to that destination. So it is with sales compensation. To accomplish superior sales results, the company needs a specific idea of where it wants to go. The company needs to set a course and then provide the necessary motive power to reach its objectives.

No company today can afford simply to hope for increased sales. Marketing has become highly sophisticated in most companies at home and abroad. Those other companies are going after your customers. To win your fair share of the market—or just to hold onto what you already have—requires careful planning. Like the airplane pilot, you might have to change course when faced with a storm front, but you should always know your destination. The sales pay plan can help your company get to its destination, but you must first set the course.

Objectives, Strategy, Goals

The course setting begins with business/marketing objectives and strategy, which establish sales goals and, in turn, determine features of the sales pay plan. You can think of business/ marketing objectives as the big picture for a company. Start with the classic question: What business are we in? That question seems elementary, but arriving at an answer may require much debate and deliberation. From that foundation, the company's management can set its broad, long-term objectives and a general plan for reaching those objectives.

Marketing strategy translates the general objectives into a specific plan of action, year-by-year. At this stage, management identifies particular products or services to be offered, the pricing/ profit policy, methods for reaching designated markets (advertising, distribution, sales organization, and selling techniques), and sales goals.

Sales goals are detailed and short-term—usually covering one to three years. These goals should include sales volume, in dollars or units, and gross margin. The goals may be limited to an overall amount if the company sells only one product line with little concern for variations among specific items on the price list. However, if the company sells a variety of products that are not readily interchangeable, sales goals should be established for each such differentiated product or product line. Sales goals should not be a wish list, but a solid business plan. The goals should be carefully researched—or at least thoroughly discussed—so that all employees concerned become convinced that the goals are reachable.

Sales goals may include introduction of new products, changes in pricing policy, and targets for territory coverage and account penetration. The goals may specify a certain mix of products and gross margin. The term *sales goals*, therefore, means more than simply total sales volume.

Some managers balk at the idea of trying to work out a detailed program of sales goals. They may feel that the business contains many unknown factors and intervening elements that will make any plan simply an academic exercise. "That's OK for the business school types, but they need a reality check." Such comments sound a word of warning about the need to recognize tactical as well as strategic considerations.

Whether in military operations or the airplane flying from New York to London, tactical maneuvers may be needed to meet changing or unforeseen conditions. That does not invalidate the objective or the strategy for getting there. Blindly following a long-term strategy can prove as disastrous as trying to cope with day-to-day realities without any sense of direction. The sales pay plan should be designed to support sales goals, but it should permit change when the company needs to respond to new pressures and opportunities.

Plan Design

Your company's sales goals should guide the design of the sales pay plan. In that way you give appropriate direction to the sales effort. If the strategy calls for expanded market penetration, your company should include a special reward for salespeople opening new accounts. For a goal of building sales of high-profit items, you should increase the reward for those sales. In such ways the sales pay plan can direct its motivational power toward sales goals.

When designing or updating a sales pay plan, first examine your company's marketing objectives, strategy, and sales goals.

Although some companies lack a formal definition of such fundamentals, most have a general idea of how they intend to sell their products or services. Sales records plus interviews with executives and field personnel may reveal de facto objectives, strategy, and goals. Put those ideas in writing and get top management's agreement before designing or updating the sales pay plan. You need a destination and a course before starting the journey.

Circular Process

Getting down to the details of a sales pay plan forces you to get specific. You cannot risk being vague about the goals. You must decide where to steer the selling effort and how much motive power to put behind that effort.

What do you want the sales force to work on: volume, profit, penetration, full-line, inventory control, collections, services, or add-on-sales? Exploring such issues of pay plan design inevitably brings about a reexamination of objectives, strategy, and goals. Thus, marketing planning guides the pay plan design, and the plan design feeds back into marketing planning. Each modifies the other. This process continues from initial planning through ongoing sales operations.

No company can afford to freeze any part of the process into a fixed state. Conditions change, and objectives, strategy, and goals, together with the pay plan, should change accordingly.

Each year, one out of three companies changes its sales compensation. My research has shown approximately one-third of companies making major changes in their sales pay plans each year from 1976 through 1991. The search for a better sales pay plan continues in every industry and line of business, in large and small companies alike. Some companies revise sales pay to meet changed marketing conditions. Many change pay arrangements on the whim of an executive or because another company seems to have found something better. Occasionally, a compensation consultant is in the privileged position of knowing that Company A intends to abandon the very pay plan that Company B wants to copy. Instead of arbitrary decisions or a copycat approach, you can follow a rational step-by-step method to design a sales pay plan for your own company's sales goals.

THE PEOPLE FACTOR

How much difference can the right pay plan make? It depends on your company's position in the four Ps of marketing. Those four factors are product, price, promotion, and people. Let us assume that your product and price are satisfactory or better, and your promotion reaches the appropriate market and properly positions the product. The people—your sales force—complete the marketing program. How effectively and efficiently the sales force carries out the marketing program depends upon selection, training, supervision, and compensation. Those four influences shape the people factor and its operation.

Selection

How do you hire? Select no more than one out of five applicants— if you are choosy about who represents your company. Recruit aggressively so you get plenty of applicants. The larger the applicant pool, the better will be your selection. Pick only those who have consistently demonstrated strong achievement drive, high energy, and job stability. For most sales jobs, industry knowledge and the amount of prior sales experience matter less than a demonstrated pattern of achievement. Are you hiring winners?

Training

How do you train? Take advantage of the new employee's eagerness to learn. Work the trainee especially hard for the first month or two. Use formal instruction, planned field exercises, and plenty of homework. After graduation from basic training, the new salesperson should have the tools needed to do the job. Are you preparing and conditioning the sales team for success?

Supervision

How do you guide the sales force? Instruct, evaluate, recognize—only the sales manager can continue to provide these essentials. Certainly, there is more to it than that, but you can never slack off on those basic elements of leadership and development. A professional football team gets to the Super Bowl only with strong coaching. Are you doing the same—guiding your team members toward top performance?

Compensation

How do you pay? Provide enough pay to attract quality applicants and to hold good performers. Provide a sales pay plan fitted to the sales goals of your company and the motivational needs of your people. That means clear criteria and the right risk/reward ratio. A well-designed sales pay plan should mesh with and support the other elements of the people factor—selection, training, and supervision—to help you build and manage a powerful sales team (see Figure 1-1).

SALES GAIN POTENTIAL

If the people factor in your marketing effort is less than optimum, how much better could it be? You can roughly estimate the potential for improvement in total sales force productivity available through the people factor. Consulting experience with many companies suggests that the potential usually equals about one-half of the difference between the median salesperson's sales and the sales of the 80th percentile (top 20 percent) salesperson. Here is the formula:

People Factor Sales Gain = 50% × (80th Percentile
Sales − Median Sales)

Thus, if the median salesperson sells $100,000 per month and the 80th percentile salesperson sells $180,000 per month, you could reasonably expect to increase total sales by about 40 percent through the people factor. Such full improvement of the people factor might require a year or two of intensive management.

FIGURE 1–1
The People Factor

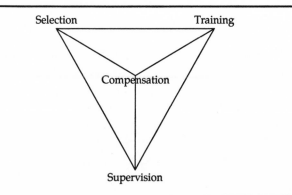

The estimate of sales gain potential assumes sales territories of approximately equal potential. For territories of unequal potential, adjust the sales amounts to what they probably would be in equal territories. If the median and 80th percentile sales differ by less than 20 percent, then either (1) the company already enjoys the advantages of an excellent, well-motivated sales force and no change is needed, or (2) the whole crew performs so poorly that the company has a huge opportunity for improvement.

The people factor operates in conjunction with the other marketing factors of product, price, and promotion. Total sales proceed from the interaction of all four marketing factors. A negative influence in one factor may offset positive values in other factors. However, positive values in all four factors multiply together, and the company gains maximum sales results.

MOTIVE POWER METHOD

The method presented here for planning sales pay might be called the motive power method. Its aim is to mobilize a strong motivational force and direct that force toward the company's sales goals. This method of approaching sales compensation grew out of consulting assignments for companies that wanted a fresh, independent study of opportunities to improve their sales pay arrangements. It has proved its value in diverse types of selling, from sporting goods to electronic components, from computer software to professional services.

There is nothing magic or mysterious about this method. It simply provides an orderly process to follow as you consider each element in the design of a sales pay plan. Most of the advice presented here builds on what you already know about the psychology and economics of sales pay. By assembling the elements properly, you build into the pay plan the motivation values you want at a cost the company can afford.

Motivation First

The motive power method assigns priority to motivation. That should be the first objective of any sales pay plan. Although cost and other considerations are important, motivation comes first. Without strong motivational value, nothing else about the pay plan matters. An otherwise economically rational pay plan that fails to motivate effectively is money lost. Let us review some of what we know about the motivational needs of people and how the pay plan can fit those needs.

Ordinary Salespeople

Any general statement about people may miss the mark when describing an individual. Yet, you must deal with general conclusions about motivation when you design a pay plan for your sales force. Trying to satisfy every individual salesperson can only lead to administrative chaos and charges of discrimination. While you must generalize, you can focus on the sales force you have—or the sales force you want. Within that target sales force, consider primarily the ordinary salespeople, the middle group of satisfactory producers. They constitute most of the players on your team, and they will be more responsive to the pay plan than either the superstars or the marginal producers. You cannot afford to ignore the high and low producers, but you should first give consideration to the middle group. For now, set aside your ideas about the interests of high and low producers and your own personal preferences. Design a pay plan for the center of the target sales force. (We will return to the superstars and the marginal producers later.)

Money's Role

When most people think of motivation and salespeople, they think first of money. We all recognize, however, that salespeople are human and that they respond to a variety of complex and sometimes contradictory motivational needs. Why, then, does money come first to mind when thinking of motivating salespeople? There are two reasons: (1) You can most easily provide and manipulate money and (2) money symbolizes to the salesperson many of the deeper motivational needs.

Money means more than income to buy groceries and pay the rent. The money a person earns by working helps satisfy strong emotional needs. Of the many motivational drives that psychologists list, you can focus your attention in sales pay planning on these:

• Need for achievement
• Need for security
• Need for recognition

The opportunity to satisfy such drives can prompt a person to rise early, make sales calls all day, and spend the evening writing orders and call reports. On the other hand, frustration of such drives may prompt a person to seek alternative sources of satisfaction, perhaps in unproductive behavior or in another job.

Need for Achievement

A vast amount of scientific research on human motivation[1] has shown that the achievement motive is a key factor for success in entrepreneurial and sales occupations. Those people with a high

---

[1] For an in-depth review of the psychology of motivation and the research on need for achievement and other motivations, see David C. McClelland, *Human Motivation* (Cambridge: Cambridge University Press, 1987).

need for achievement work harder and perform better in such occupations than people who scored lower on need for achievement. Therefore, you want to attract and retain the achievement seekers. Here is some background information that forms the foundation for recommendations throughout this book.

A person with a high need for achievement will have the following four characteristics.

1. Sets moderate goals. The achievement seeker wants a 30 to 50 percent chance to succeed at a task. If the goal seems too easy (success almost a sure thing), the achievement seeker loses interest. Not enough challenge makes success an unsatisfying experience. On the other hand, if the goal seems too difficult (failure almost a sure thing), the achievement seeker may not even try. However, achievement seekers will continually raise their sights as they experience successes. Therefore, a difficult goal seems more reachable after smaller accomplishments in the same category of behavior.

2. Takes personal responsibility. The person with a high need for achievement wants to be in control, wants success or failure to reflect his or her own performance. If there is too much random chance or plain luck in the results, the achievement seeker loses interest. If events seem beyond the person's influence, the achievement seeker feels frustrated. Decisions by superiors and sharing responsibility with coworkers weakens the sense of personal responsibility and can cause loss of interest in the task.

3. Uses feedback. The achievement seeker wants frequent information about the results of task performance. Feedback provides satisfaction as a measure of success, and it guides the person toward resetting goals for a reasonable chance of success. For a salesperson, the paycheck often provides the needed feedback, the measure of success.

4. Takes initiative. The person with a high need for achievement tends to search for and try new ways to accomplish goals. The achievement seeker wants minimum restriction on finding more efficient methods for improved chance of success in the task.

The good news for sales managers is that ordinary people can learn to become more achievement-oriented. The sales compensation program and supervisory practices can go a long way toward awakening the achievement motive.

In sales pay planning, experience supports theory in showing need for achievement as most important. In contrast, need for security (emotional security) opposes need for achievement in some elements of pay plan design. Need for recognition relates closely to need for achievement, but it deserves special consideration, especially in designing award programs.

Salespeople come to the job with varying levels of the need for achievement, from strong to weak. Let us assume that you want a sales force characterized by a moderately strong need for achievement. Perhaps you might like one stronger than that, a team of tigers, but you doubt that you can afford the cost and aggravation of such a sales force. Whether you design the pay plan for a moderate or for a strong degree of need for achievement, you should provide three essentials: goals, rules, and rewards.

Goals

First, the salesperson with a moderate-to-strong need for achievement wants to know the goals. What is necessary to win? The criteria must be understood and achievable. The salesperson must believe that the goals can be reached through the salesperson's own efforts. Therefore, territories and quotas should be assigned impartially, based on criteria the salesperson understands. Sales success should depend largely on the performance of the salesperson. Random chance—whether good luck or bad luck—may influence the results but should not be seen as a major factor in sales success.

Rules

Second, the achievement-oriented salesperson wants clear, consistent rules of the game. Rules help to ensure that the person's own performance will determine the rewards received. Rules reduce the salesperson's risk of losing through intervening variables beyond the salesperson's control. Therefore, the pay plan should be understandable and well documented. A salesperson may try to work around the rules or bend them, but the company must never cheat. If the company appears to renege or reinterpret a rule, the salesperson's reaction will likely reflect sheer frustration and outrage. Such an insult to the salesperson's sense of self-determination may stir deep emotions—far beyond any rational basis or financial impact of the situation.

Rewards

Third, the salesperson hungry to satisfy the need for achievement wants a substantial risk/reward opportunity. When results are very good, the paycheck should be very good. When results are disappointing, the paycheck should reflect that condition also. The greater the sales-related variance in pay from month to month, the greater the motivational impact. Rewards must track goal results to satisfy the need for achievement. That feedback answers the question, "How am I doing?"

The achievement-oriented salesperson wants prompt and clear reward for results. When the salesperson accomplishes the intended sales results, the paycheck should reflect that—without undue delay. Like applause for an entertainer, or cheers for an athlete, the paycheck nourishes the salesperson by satisfying the need for achievement. If, for some compelling reason, payment must be deferred more than one month beyond the sale, a monthly statement of sales results and earnings may partially satisfy. The company that delays paying commissions and bonuses robs the salesperson of much satisfaction and, in turn, deprives the company itself of full value for its payroll expenditure.

Combining those three essentials—goals, rules, and rewards—in a pay plan means that you must consider both the amount and the method of pay, together with the company's sales goals. Following chapters show how to design a pay plan that will provide the amount that you want to pay while applying pay methods that motivate with the power and direction you need. The motive power method can guide you to a sales pay plan that will fit your company and your sales force.

THE STEPS

The motive power method is not a cookbook formula. You design the sales pay plan. You apply your knowledge and your judgment to produce a plan that is custom designed for your company and your salespeople.

When designing a pay plan, you start with the advantage of advance knowledge about your company, its selling methods, and its past pay practices. That knowledge provides clear values for the task of pay plan design. However, that same intimate knowledge may blind you to opportunities or prompt you to jump to something new without thorough investigation and testing. That is why the motive power method follows a definite series of steps, the same steps that a compensation consultant would follow in designing a sales pay plan for your company. Complete each step as outlined and you will save the time of exploring many blind alleys—or of missing a valuable opportunity. Do not rush ahead to find the best pay formula, but follow these five steps in conducting your study of sales pay:

1. Fact-finding
2. Defining objectives
3. Developing plan elements
4. Testing, revising, retesting
5. Documenting, communicating

The following is a summary of each of the five major steps.

Fact-finding

Get the facts—not hunches, or hearsay. You want as much factual information as you can get. After reading this book you will better understand the information you need and why you need it. Some information may come readily to hand, some may require digging into records. You may need to reorganize data that were programmed into the computer differently from the way you now want them. If possible, compile historical sales data for every salesperson who has been on the payroll over the past three years. Note past changes (products added, prices changed) and changes projected for the next year or two. Numbers are not the only information you need. Also compile ideas and opinions through interviews. The main categories of information to assemble, with illustrative items, appear in Table 1–1.

When it comes to fact-finding, it may help to remember Will Rogers's comment: What everybody knows ain't necessarily so. Here is an example. The Vice President of Marketing and Sales for a software company told the consultant that they had changed their sales pay plan "about every three months." The consultant remarked that the salespeople must be less than happy about that. When the consultant interviewed salespeople as part of the fact-finding step, one salesperson said that the company had changed the sales pay plan "every month." "It couldn't be that bad," thought the consultant, so he checked into the records. The longest the company had gone between changes was three months, the shortest time was three weeks!

Management statements about how much salespeople sell and earn frequently vary from the facts. In spite of detailed monthly reports, top executives and sales managers often recall obsolete or extreme figures. The president may report that "our salespeople earn about $50,000," when only a few earn that much and most actually earn $30,000 to $35,000. Fact-finding takes time. However, it provides the foundation you need for designing an effective sales pay plan—and for convincing others that you know what you are talking about. Memory can store errors, but the file cabinet stores facts. Get the facts.

Defining Objectives

Some people leap into sales pay planning by asking, "Which is the best formula to use?" That is like asking, "Which is the best way out of this city?" In either case, you have to decide where you want to go before you can make an intelligent decision about how to get there. If you rush the definition of objectives in sales pay planning, you will likely pay the price later in reworking the plan.

The President and the Vice President of Sales for a manufacturer of computerized process controls agreed on added sales volume as the main objective for a new sales pay plan. However, the consultant noted that company earnings had declined while sales increased slightly. The President dismissed this as a temporary condition caused by unusual research expenditures and some large-volume, low-margin orders. Further fact-finding by the consultant disclosed that the salespeople were free to negotiate price and product features within a wide range on their own authority—and an even wider range with approval of the Vice President of Sales. Up to that point, the senior executives had given no thought to including gross margin in the sales pay plan objectives. However, establishing gross margin improvement as a major objective of the plan resulted in reorienting the whole company away from sales for the sake of sales and to sales for the sake of profit.

Defining objectives involves refining the company's marketing objectives and strategy into a set of specific sales goals for the sales pay plan. Here is a simple technique for imposing some discipline to the process. Start by writing at the top of a page: "We will have a good sales pay plan when we get these results." Then list the objectives that you expect to achieve with the sales pay plan. Note that the following examples of goals include target times as well as target results.

- Increase sales force productivity (dollars sold per dollar paid) by 20 percent within 18 months.
- Increase full-line selling until none of our three product lines is selling less than 20 percent of total, with total sales at budget for next year.
- Cut turnover of salespeople to industry average within 12 months.
- Increase next year's gross profit dollars 15 percent over this year's, without additional salespeople.
- Introduce new product, building to $100,000 monthly sales by year-end, with no drop in other products below budget.
- Get new reps up to adequate sales volume within six months of hire.
- Reduce average age of accounts receivable to 45 days.

The more specific the goal, the greater its usefulness in planning and evaluating a sales pay plan. You might end with a long list of

TABLE 1–1
Fact-finding Questions

Where are we in the market? (Status and trends in marketing)	*Where do we want to be? (Marketing objectives, long-term and near-term, quantified where possible)*	*How will we get there? (Marketing/ sales strategy)*	*How are sales made? (Selling process and the role of the salesperson)*	*What are the characteristics of our salespeople?*	*What is the competitive labor market?*
• Products, and/or services: features, quality	• Higher sales volume	• Increase sales force productivity	• Finding prospects	• Education and experience at hire	• Sources for hiring new salespeople
• Prices: how set, profit margins, changes, deals	• Higher profit margin percent	• Redirect selling effort	• Getting to the buyer	• Length of service for each salesperson	• Destinations of departing salespeople
• Competition: products, quality, prices, marketing methods	• Higher profit dollars	• Expand sales force	• Qualifying	• Training for new salespeople	• Sales pay survey for your industry
• Customers: type, size, location	• More customers	• New products	• Presenting	• Supervision provided	• Sales pay survey for industries you hire from and lose to

- Company's share of market

- Bigger orders
- Full-line selling
- Larger share of market

- Pricing changes
- Distribution changes
- Advertising

- Closing
- One-shot or continuing relationships
- Repeat orders
- Sales cycle time
- Follow-up sales and services

- Monthly sales by product or product group, by salesperson
- Salary for each salesperson
- Incentive earnings: when and how much?
- Draws taken
- Salesperson's attitudes toward incentive pay
- Sales force turnover (Frequency? When? Why? Cost?)

- Availability of the kinds of people you want to hire

goals, especially if a committee develops them. In that case, the committee should establish an order-of-importance for the goals. You may have to omit goals that are contradictory in plan design or low in importance. Four, perhaps five, seems to be the maximum number of goals that can function effectively in a sales pay plan. The more goals that are included, the less valuable, less important, and less memorable each becomes.

Take the time to write out the goals. Get agreement from those concerned: chief executive, marketing/sales executive, field sales manager, finance executive, human resources executive . . . whoever will be involved with the operation and results of the new pay plan. Facts and philosophy, dreams and reality—all merge in this most intimate and vital aspect of planning a company's future. Give it the full time and attention it deserves.

You may find that you need to modify some goals as the study progresses. However, by formalizing them early you are likely to establish specific, realistic goals that will survive. In the process, you will have set the stage for acceptance of the pay plan that finally emerges.

Developing Plan Elements

Once you have identified where you are and where you want to go with the pay plan, you are ready to develop the pay plan elements. You will need to decide upon four major elements:

1. Type of pay plan—the general pattern of fixed pay (salary) and variable pay (commissions, bonuses) that you want to provide.
2. Target pay—the amount you want salespeople to earn at various levels of performance.
3. Incentive criteria—the results you want to reward.
4. Pay formula—the rate at which you will pay for results.

Later chapters review each of these elements and how they mesh to produce a motivationally powerful pay plan.

Testing, Revising, Retesting

Designing a sales pay plan, like other complex design tasks, involves the cut-and-try process. Your first outline probably will not survive into the final draft of the plan. As you assemble the plan elements, you may find that some conflict with others. So you make changes. It means balancing or compromising among the objectives that you most want and dropping those of lesser importance. Everyone concerned with designing the sales pay plan should understand that each part must be subject to change until the total plan is completed and approved.

There are some common problems that can prompt a change in plan design. For example, you rough out a pay formula using annual figures, but you find that the formula does not work the same way when applied to monthly sales results. Or—you design a pay plan around one salesperson, perhaps a real or hypothetical top producer, then you find that the plan does not pay enough for the majority of the sales force. Look for such problems by testing the plan on a spreadsheet of realistic individual sales results. When testing the plan, examine the motivational effects as well as the cost and payout under varied conditions (as explained in Chapter 11, "Costing and Auditing the Plan"). Accept the plan as final only after you have tested it against realistic sales data across the full range of salespeople and territories. Even then, you should test the plan against extreme sales results—the kind that have never happened but that might happen.

The importance of testing the extremes was illustrated when a consultant received a telephone call from a chief executive who said, "You have to change that sales pay plan you designed for us three months ago. It's not working right."

No consultant wants to get that kind of a call. "What's the trouble?" the consultant asked.

The president replied, "One of our salespeople earned $30,000 this month, and he will earn that much in each of the next two months under your rolling-average formula."

"How did that happen?"

"He sold 10 units this month, at full list price, all to one customer." No one had ever sold more than one of those expensive
machines in one month.

"But, you got full price and a huge order. What's the problem?"
the consultant asked.

"Well . . . $30,000 is more than I earn in a month as president.
It doesn't seem right to pay that much to any salesperson."

It is certainly better to explore the what-ifs while they are only
theoretical. When those in authority accept both the normal and
extreme examples, you are ready to launch the plan.

Documenting and Communicating

You are finally ready to convert from a draft outline to a finished
document. The document itself reflects the care and concern that
management has given to designing the sales pay plan. Let the
document look as important as it is. Complete, clear, precise—
those words should describe the plan document that your salespeople will turn to for information about their pay.

Beyond the written document, your salespeople deserve a personal explanation of the new sales pay plan. They know that their
compensation has been under study. They have some anxiety
about what the new pay plan will do for them—or *to* them. Clear
up questions and concerns with an open presentation that demon-
strates top-management endorsement. You might even turn up
some issue that had been overlooked. It is certainly preferable to
accomplish those things when you launch the plan, rather than
later.

You begin the planning process with fact-finding and progress
through the several steps—with some inevitable looping back.
You end with an explanation of the plan to the sales force. Their
initial reaction may seem cautious, even skeptical. In three to six

FIGURE 1–2
Sales Pay Plan Development

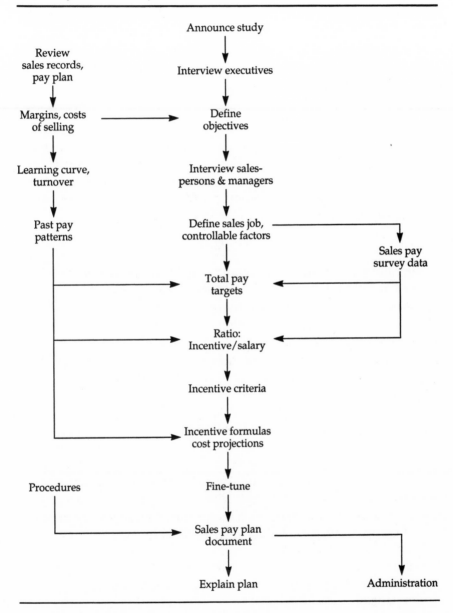

months, however, you should start to see positive results. By the end of the first year, you will know whether you have an effective pay plan in place. Figure 1-2 shows the steps in the motive power method for developing a sales pay plan to fit your company.

TERMS USED

The following chapters examine each part of the pay planning process in detail. They include advice on how to design sales pay plan features for the motivational effect that you want. Before proceeding, however, you might find it helpful to review the following list of terms that appear frequently—just to ensure that we are speaking the same language. (A longer glossary of sales compensation terms appears at the end of this book.)

- **Sales**—a general term meaning whatever you are paying the salesperson to accomplish. You may define sales as bookings, shipments, or billings. You may measure sales in dollar volume, gross profits, units, percent increase, percent of quota, and so on.
- **Salary**—regular base pay. Usually paid weekly, biweekly, or semimonthly.
- **Draw**—an advance against future commission earnings. A regular amount paid weekly, monthly, biweekly, or semimonthly—or it may be paid on request.
- **Commission**—variable incentive pay based on some measure of sales results. Usually paid weekly, monthly, or quarterly.
- **Bonus**—incentive pay based on some special or sustained performance. Usually paid quarterly, yearly, or upon achievement of a special goal.
- **Incentive pay**—a general term meaning a variable element of compensation based on sales results; includes commission and bonus.
- **Total pay**—salary plus commission and bonus. Does not include cost of benefits, automobile, or reimbursed expenses.
- **Company**—any organizational unit with common marketing objectives. May be the total corporation, a subsidiary, division, or product group.

For convenience, this book presents material as though a company has only one sales force with one set of sales goals. However, you may apply the same principles in developing sales pay plans for separate sales teams, such as field sales, telemarketing sales, or different product-group sales teams.

CHECKLIST FOR SETTING THE COURSE

√ Design the sales pay plan from marketing objectives to marketing strategy to sales goals.

√ Plan for sales force productivity improvement based on the potential of the "people factor" of your marketing program.

√ Put motivation first in your planning.

√ Plan for the ordinary salespeople.

√ Recognize that money symbolizes several important motivational drives, especially the need for achievement.

√ Consider both method and amount of pay in plan design.

√ Follow the prescribed steps; do not jump to premature decisions about pay plan features.

√ Expect to loop back in the design process and modify parts until the whole plan is final.

Chapter Two

Pay Plan Types

One of four types fits each sales team.

Even a widely experienced sales manager or compensation specialist can benefit from reviewing all four types of sales pay plans: straight commission, commission-with-draw, salary-plus-incentive, and straight salary. Recognizing where each type of plan fits best and the characteristics of each can provide perspective and a fresh view of existing plans in the company and industry. You need not select a plan type by the default of traditional practice. Instead, you can consider the alternatives impartially and select the one that best fits your company's style of management, selling process, and risk assignment. This chapter gives the information needed for an informed choice. That choice provides the framework within which pay plan elements will fit as the planning proceeds. Any plan type can be used in any kind of selling: field, inside, telemarketing, and so on.

STRAIGHT SALARY

Many people find it hard to believe that any company pays salespeople only a base salary. No direct incentive for sales results! However, that is the case in some companies. For example, transportation companies—air, rail, and highway—usually pay straight salaries to their representatives who solicit freight and passenger business. Many pharmaceutical companies pay straight salaries to the detailers who present their drug products to physicians, hospitals, and pharmacies.

With a straight salary pay plan, the company accepts the full risk. The salesperson receives the same pay each month, whether sales are large or small. Some managers claim that the salesperson risks losing the job if sales are not satisfactory. Experience shows, however, that companies using straight salary often operate under a benevolent, protective style of management. The company rarely fires anyone, just as it rarely rewards anyone. The salesperson accepts no significant risk; the company carries it all.

A straight salary plan gives the company a fixed cost of selling. The company spends the same number of dollars for selling whether sales are up or down. This appeals to some financial planners who like predictable budgets. When sales rise, the fixed dollar cost of selling helps boost profits. The opposite also applies. In a period of declining sales, the company's dollar cost of selling remains constant, cutting into profits—unless the company reduces its sales force.

Salary and Motivation

Motivationally, a straight salary plan provides substantial satisfaction to those who have a strong need for security. The pay is steady and predictable. Salespeople with a strong need for achievement, however, are likely to find little satisfaction in a straight salary plan. Some salespeople refuse to consider a straight salary job, even at a high salary. They may recognize their own motivational needs. "I want to be paid for what I accomplish, not what somebody in the home office happens to think I should get." Such comments reveal that the salesperson does not belong in a straight salary plan. On the other hand, those who find security more satisfying than achievement say things like, "I'm glad to have a paycheck I can count on with no worries about hitting a streak of bad luck or slow business conditions."

Straight salary provides no scoreboard by which the salesperson can measure accomplishment. Therefore, the company paying straight salary should provide other measures to help satisfy the need for achievement. Weekly or monthly reports of new leads, bids and proposals, new accounts, sales volume, gross profit trends . . . all such data can help the salesperson gain some sense of success on the job. The achievement motivation thrives on tangible results—good and bad. When the paycheck delivers no such feedback, management must provide it unless information about results is inherent in the nature of the work. For most straight salary sales jobs, management should work overtime to keep each salesperson or sales team fully and promptly informed of their results. For people with a high need for achievement, nonfinancial feedback can be as effective as cash incentives. Those with less built-in achievement drive respond more to the extrinsic rewards of incentive pay.

Straight salary is less than ideal for motivating and directing sales effort, however it may be necessary or even preferable in a company facing one of the following conditions.

Sales Credit not Traced

The company may be unable to determine sales credit among the salespeople. For example, the pharmaceutical detailer calls on a physician who then prescribes the medicine. The final purchase by the patient, however, may be made in any drugstore—perhaps in a city remote from where the detailer made the presentation. The drugstore may purchase through a central buying office or wholesaler in another state. The pharmaceutical company knows only the sales to the central distribution point and cannot tell how effective the individual detailer has been—hence straight salary, no incentive pay. (This does not apply to all pharmaceutical companies; many now track sales to local territories with reasonable accuracy.)

Sales Role Unclear

A solicitor for XYZ Air Freight, Inc. calls on a prospect regularly for many months. The prospect ships nothing. At long last the prospect needs to ship by air, and he chooses XYZ Air Freight, Inc. What triggered the sale—advertising, competitive rates, service, or the solicitor? The freight solicitor's contribution to the sale seems unclear. Straight salary, no incentive pay.

Team Selling

Team selling may produce a situation where management cannot clearly distinguish the contribution of each team member to the sales results. Straight salary is used in some such situations; however, many companies provide group incentives for team selling.

Long-term Orientation

Concern for long-term customer relationships and emphasis on consultive selling have led some companies to provide straight salary instead of incentive pay. A major commercial insurance brokerage firm prides itself on paying straight salary to its salespeople. The customers know that the advice they receive is not colored by any prospect of short-term commission income for the representative. Teamwork and mutual cooperation among the firm's salespeople is encouraged by straight salary, avoiding the what's-in-it-for-me style of some commission-based insurance firms.

Order Taking

Selling is by bid or almost totally beyond the influence of the salesperson. Some managers describe this as "order taking" and argue that it should not be classified as a sales job. The salesperson does little to locate and interest the customer or to influence the decision to buy. The job may require substantial technical knowledge, but the selling process is largely beyond the control of the salesperson. Inside salespeople often fit this category. Many companies, however, find that order-takers can create add-on sales when they are offered incentives to do so.

Infrequent Sales

When the sales cycle is long (several months or even years), straight salary may seem to be the only practical pay method. One-year or multi-year supplier contract selling often fits into this category. Some people selling packaging materials, newsprint, and ingredients for food or chemical processes are paid straight salary. Such salespeople spend much of their time solving problems of delivery or quality and maintaining good will for the next contract renewal. The salary pays for that service. The company offers no incentive pay. Some companies, however, provide incentive pay for achieving milestones along the course of a long sales cycle. For example, an architectural products company pays an award for getting the company's product designated as the standard in specifications on large projects.

No Sales Forecast

When bringing a new product to market, a company may be unable to estimate sales. In such a situation the company may elect to pay straight salary—at least until the product gains market acceptance and management can establish reasonable sales expectations. A straight salary enables the salesperson to survive during the early missionary period. It also avoids the risk of setting an incentive pay rate that may prove to be too low or too high for the eventual pattern of sales.

Reluctant Salespeople

This condition differs from lack of sales forecast. Here the salespeople, rather than management, decide how they will be paid. This may reflect personality characteristics of the salespeople as much as it does the actual risk of sales failure. Some engineers, for example, are willing to participate in selling only if they receive a substantial regular salary.

Trainees

Some companies pay only a salary to trainees, and more companies should consider doing so. The idea is to encourage trainees to complete their formal training by paying them an adequate base salary. Trainees get no incentive pay until they complete their initial training. After the person graduates from trainee status, the company may reduce or eliminate the salary as incentive earnings build. Without such a salary program, trainees may start selling before they learn the product line and develop basic selling skills. Premature launching of trainees can lead to unbalanced sales presentations, a negative image of the company, and discouragement of trainees. The salary keeps trainees in training until they are ready to enter the field with a high probability of success. More on this subject in Chapter 14, "Trainee Pay."

Straight salary for salespeople usually is administered within the company's regular system of job evaluation, salary ranges, and merit increases. Other types of sales pay plans usually are administered apart from regular salary management because of its major emphasis on incentive pay and its unique volatility. Incentive-based sales pay rarely meshes comfortably with conventional salary management.

A recent survey of over 558 companies found 18 percent paying straight salaries to their field salespeople (excluding trainees).[1]

STRAIGHT COMMISSION

One hundred eighty degrees opposite from straight salary, straight commission provides only incentive pay—no salary or draw. Companies pay straight commission for direct (in-home) selling of cosmetics, plastic containers, food supplements, soaps, and encyclopedias. Insurance, real estate, and securities salespeople, as well as independent manufacturer representatives and sales agents, also earn straight commission.

Minimum Wage

When the government extended minimum wage and overtime pay requirements to inside (store) salespeople, many retail establishments abandoned their traditional straight commission pay plans. Most stores today provide combination pay plans that in-

---

[1] *1991/92 Sales and Marketing Personnel Report* (Fort Lee, N.J.: Executive Compensation Service, Inc., 1991), p. 35.

clude a base wage rate for hours on the job plus incentive pay for sales.

Field sales jobs generally remain exempt from the minimum wage and overtime pay requirements of the Fair Labor Standards Act under the Act's provisions for "Outside Salesman." However, some field sales jobs fall into a gray area requiring analysis of the job as a whole to determine whether it qualifies as being exempt under the Act. Such gray-area jobs include (1) those that largely involve promotion rather than obtaining orders, (2) those in which service and repair work constitutes a substantial part of the job, and (3) those requiring substantial delivery, shelf-stocking, and display work. This is a complex matter, requiring careful analysis of job duties and interpretation of governmental regulations. For more information on this subject, obtain WH Publication 1281, *Regulations, Part 541: Defining the Terms "Executive," "Administrative," "Professional" and "Outside Salesman"* from

U.S. Department of Labor
Employment Standards Administration
Washington, D.C. 20210

Some states have similar but not identical laws governing minimum wages and overtime pay. If there is a question about exempt/nonexempt status, consult an attorney who is expert in labor and employment law. Some employer associations also provide advice in these matters.

Risk

The help wanted columns of newspapers regularly advertise opportunities in commission selling with unbelievable earnings opportunities. That is part of the problem; the claims are unbelievable. Many people doubt that such earnings are achievable. The company offering straight commission today faces skepticism bred of promises unfulfilled, inadequate training, and poor field support. Fewer people today will accept a big risk, even if a big earnings potential exists. Increasingly, companies that once paid straight commission are switching to combination plans such as commission-with-draw and salary-plus-incentive. Such companies often cannot find enough competent salespeople willing to work on straight commission, and they do not want a sales force made up of beginners and those desperate for any employment.

The salesperson takes the full risk in a straight commission pay plan. If the salesperson fails to sell, the company has no cost—except the lost opportunity. That makes straight commission attractive to companies with small financial reserves, unproven or hard-to-sell products, and limited supervision for the sales force.

Commission and Motivation

For salespeople who are strong on need for achievement, straight commission seems ideal. Such people like to earn rewards for what they accomplish, and may be willing to forego security for opportunity. They may show only a nominal identification with or loyalty to the company. For example, the top sales representative for a wholesale grocery distributor refused to attend his company's sales meetings with this explanation: "They sell less than I do, so I have nothing to gain. I do not intend to share my know-how with them." He worked an intensive 60 hours a week, operating from his home. He kept a complete stock of samples on shelves in his garage to save the time and annoyance of visiting headquarters. The garage looked like a small grocery store. He came into the company office only upon the strongest demand from the president. Impossible to supervise, totally uncooperative, and a lone wolf—he produced 30 percent more sales volume than the second ranking sales representative. He and others like him thrive on straight commission. However, they are few.

Straight commission may seem the most powerful source of sales motivation, but it usually fits best where one or more of the following conditions exist.

Salesperson not Controlled

The company provides little supervision, guidance, and support for the salesperson. Both company and salesperson see the job as essentially an independent business affiliation. Management may not even care whether the person works full time or how much the person sells. Even if management does expect full time selling effort and a reasonable volume from the territory, the salesperson may receive little communication, help, or encouragement. Straight commission fosters a jungle survival philosophy in management and salespeople alike. It is totally at odds with the protective, controlling philosophy seen in straight-salary companies.

Salesperson Determines Sales

The product is a commodity or hard to differentiate from competitors. Advertising, name, and price are not positive sales factors, and sales are difficult to make. Such conditions place the full sales burden on the salesperson. If a sale is made, it is the salesperson who controls it. Such conditions are often associated with straight commission.

No Salary or Draw Expected

Industry tradition sustains straight commission in residential real estate sales, even though a combination plan might better fit some companies. Independent industrial and wholesale sales representatives typically expect no salary or draw.

Company Resources Limited

A small company or one with a weak financial foundation may see no alternative but to pay straight commission. Some stronger companies, however, pay straight commission under the notion that unless a sale is made there will be no money to pay the salesperson. One wonders how the company continues to pay salaries to the president, the secretary, and the accountant.

For effective sales pay planning, look beyond one sale or one salesperson. Examine the cost, efficiency, and effectiveness of the total sales force. Consider the effects on the total sales force before you decide whether straight commission is right for your company.

COMMISSION-WITH-DRAW

A draw is an advance, or loan, to be subtracted from subsequent commission earnings. A draw against future commissions enables salespeople to weather ups and downs that they would not tolerate under straight commission. A slow month is not a disaster; the draw lets the salesperson pay the rent and buy groceries. It provides an income cushion on the downside while leaving in place the opportunity for higher earnings when sales turn up.

This kind of pay plan leaves most but not all of the risk with the salesperson, who is expected to pay back the draws out of future commissions. The company, however, shares in the risk by advancing money with some possibility of loss. If the salesperson's employment terminates while a negative balance exists in the draw account, the company absorbs the loss. The company also absorbs the cost of any negative draw balances that it may forgive.

Under a commission-with-draw plan, the cost of selling remains largely a variable cost. The dollar cost of selling fluctuates as sales fluctuate. The company can forecast the cost of selling as a percent of sales. The only distortion is the effect of draw balances that the company absorbs.

Draw and Motivation

Commission-with-draw plans partially satisfy the need for security while also satisfying the need for achievement. Such plans, however, can have negative effects. If the draw balance grows too large, the salesperson may become discouraged, feeling that there is little chance of getting out of the hole. Less recognized is the potential negative effect of reducing pay variance. If the draw becomes too large in relation to total earnings, pay variance may decline below the level for adequate motive power. These issues are reviewed in Chapter 6, "Pay Variance," and Chapter 7, "Salaries and Draws."

Survival Pay

Companies in a wide variety of industries use commission-with-draw plans. They generally fit the categories described for straight commission companies; however, companies offer a draw when they recognize a need to provide survival pay. This helps to attract and retain the number and kind of salespeople they need. A company using this type of pay plan should analyze the cost and cash flow aspects of providing draws. Accountants often treat draws as loans until earned, not as compensation. Draws not paid back to the company may end up on the company's books as "bad debts," not charged to the cost of selling. The president of an office equipment company was surprised to learn that draws were costing his company 10 percent over the reported "total commission" cost. Most commission-with-draw plans, however, produce only a modest added cost over straight commission.

A survey of industrial companies showed 8 percent paying straight commission or commission-with-draw.[2]

SALARY-PLUS-INCENTIVE

The most popular type of sales pay plan among industrial companies pays a base salary plus incentive pay for one or more criteria. The salary provides for the survival needs of the salesperson, while the incentive pay offers reward for achievement. In such plans, the company and the salesperson share the risk. Companies offering salary-plus-incentive typically exercise greater care in selecting, training, and supervising the sales force than do companies offering either straight commission or commission-with-draw. This type of pay plan can foster a spirit of mutual interest between company and salesperson, corresponding to the shared risk.

---

[2] *1991/92 Sales and Marketing Personnel Report* (Fort Lee, N.J.: Executive Compensation Service, Inc., 1991), p. 35.

The company accepts a fixed cost for the salary and a variable cost for the incentive pay. Just how variable the total pay cost will be depends on the salary/incentive ratio and the incentive formula.

Salary, Incentive, and Motivation

The salary satisfies the salesperson's need for security to some degree. Certainly, the salary should cover minimum survival needs. That is its primary purpose in the pay plan. Survival means the ability to get by—uncomfortably—on that income for a month or two. It differs for people with different standards of living. The incentive pay steers sales effort and helps to satisfy the salesperson's need for achievement. The negative features of a straight commission plan may be reduced in a salary-plus-incentive plan. Both the salesperson and management are less likely to feel that the salesperson is in business independent of the company. The company typically provides more control and more support to the sales force than is common in commission or commission-with-draw situations. The salespeople typically display greater identification or loyalty to the company, with correspondingly lower turnover of the sales force.

Some companies provide a draw against future commissions while also paying a base salary. Such arrangements occur where the sales cycle is long or where something in addition to the regular salary is needed to attract a well-qualified job applicant. In providing a draw, the company smoothes its own cash flow and the salesperson's income. However, such arrangements may dampen pay variance excessively and deprive the salesperson of the deeper satisfaction of earnings that closely reflect sales results.

Widely Used

Many salespeople today refuse to consider jobs that do not provide a reasonable base salary plus incentive pay. Such people refuse to answer ads offering only straight commission or commission-with-draw. Although many companies have grown dissatisfied with the problems of draws and switched to salary-plus-

TABLE 2–1
Sales Pay Plan Characteristics

Plan	Characteristic			
	Risk	*Cost*	*Security*	*Achievement*
Salary	Company	Fixed	High	Low
Commission	Employee	Variable	Low	High
Commission-with-draw	Employee	Variable	Little	High
Salary and incentive	Shared	Mixed	Moderate	High

incentive plans, rarely does a company change from salary-plus-incentive to any other type of sales pay plan. The popularity of salary-plus-incentive plans continues to increase steadily. Three out of four industrial companies now pay salary-plus-incentive, and the number continues to grow.[3]

Table 2–1 summarizes the characteristics of the four types of sales pay plans.

BONUS

An electrical equipment manufacturer pays a $500 award to the salesperson when a new account orders $5,000 of equipment within three consecutive months. That award fits the definition of a bonus: an infrequent or irregular payment for a special or sustained achievement. Bonus plans usually provide for a payment opportunity at three months, six months, one year, or at some event such as completing a transaction. The new-account bonus described here is paid when the defined result is achieved.

Although listed here with the four basic plan types, bonus plans do not stand alone as a plan type. They *always* supplement some other type of sales pay plan. You can add a bonus to any type of

---

[3] *1991/92 Sales and Marketing Personnel Report* (Fort Lee, N.J.: Executive Compensation Service, Inc., 1991), p. 35.

plan from straight salary to straight commission. No clear dividing line separates bonuses from commissions or from special awards and contests. They overlap in concept and in practice.

You can add a bonus to steer effort toward special objectives—particularly those that do not fit neatly into a regular incentive formula. Some examples are new accounts, sustained high sales, consistently high gross profit, collection of slow-pay accounts, and special service at trade shows.

Bonus and Motivation

A bonus opportunity can help to satisfy the need for achievement when the bonus criteria meet these standards:

- Salespeople understand and accept the criteria
- Salespeople know that their results will be evaluated objectively

Bonuses can have a negative side. They can create dissatisfaction or simply waste money, if one of these conditions exists:

- Salespeople do not know the criteria in advance. It is a surprise reward. Such "retroactive expectations" provide no direction of effort and little satisfaction of the need for achievement.
- Bonuses seem to be at the whim of the boss. Such a bonus equates to a handout. It places the salesperson in a dependent role and evokes ambivalent feelings at best. The salesperson may assume favoritism and lack of planning by management.

Choose one of the four types of sales pay plan, based on your company's characteristics and your marketing strategy. If your marketing objectives include something out of the mainstream of selling, add a bonus. If you have an objective that is best measured at infrequent intervals, add a bonus. Just make sure that you design the bonus opportunity carefully and communicate it clearly. Chapter 8, "Bonuses, Contests, and Awards," discusses the uses of bonuses in further detail.

CHECKLIST FOR PAY PLAN TYPES

√ Review each plan type against the company's characteristics.

√ Select the plan type best fitted to the company's needs, with attention to recruiting, retention, and motivation.

√ Consider each of the four plan types: straight salary, straight commission, commission-with-draw, and salary-plus-incentive.

√ Any plan type other than straight salary can be designed to deliver strong motive power based on the need for achievement.

√ Consider adding a bonus to any plan, including straight salary, to reward special achievement.

Chapter Three

Pay Targets

Start with three answers.

How much should your salespeople earn? Answer that question and you have completed an important part of the pay plan design. An effective sales pay plan produces no surprises. By starting with defined pay targets, the plan designer can develop plan features that produce the desired results. Three pay targets are needed for normal, high, and marginal sales results. Target total pay includes the sum of salary, commission, and bonus that you intend for each of the three levels of sales results.

Some common approaches to targeting and evaluating sales pay amounts may seem sound but are flawed. Regardless of the approach you select, you will want to give consideration to competitive pay levels. This chapter reviews four approaches to setting pay targets and then provides specific advice for setting each of the three pay targets: normal, high, and marginal.

WHICH APPROACH?

Consciously or unconsciously, managers usually follow one of four approaches when determining the amount of pay for salespeople. You will be in a position to consciously select the approach that best fits your company after you review each of these four approaches:

- Affordability
- Super reward
- Uniformity
- Balanced

Affordability

Under the affordability approach, the company pays what it can afford for each person's sales. This financial approach gears the cost of selling to the company's ability to pay. Although that may sound reasonable, it falls short of being ideal for most companies. Under this approach, a weak company struggling to establish itself in the market will pay too little. Sales are low, pay is low. The sales force grows weaker with high turnover and low-caliber hires. Such conditions fail to produce the market penetration that the company needs. Introducing a new product from an unknown or second-tier company is a difficult sales challenge best handled by competent, experienced sales representatives. They cost more. Added selling cost may be necessary for the company's survival in the market.

Unlike the weak company that pays too little, a strong company that follows the approach of paying what it can afford may pay more than is needed to get the job done, perhaps wasting money. Grossly overpaying salespeople can demoralize managers, sales-support people, and other employees who do not receive such open-handed generosity. You cannot heal their disaffection by saying, "If they do not like it, they can quit" or " . . . they can try selling." Such a response fails to answer the universal employee expectation of fair treatment by management.

If you focus the affordability approach on the single sale, you lose sight of other critical issues. Consider instead (1) overall productivity of the entire sales force, (2) survival needs of salespeople, and (3) motivational aims of the pay plan. The most successful companies do not pay what they can afford. They pay what it takes to get the job done—not much less and not much more.

After you design a pay plan to fit your marketing strategy, analyze the total cost under varied conditions. Then decide whether (1) you can live with the cost of the pay plan, (2) you need to modify it, or (3) you need to consider using other selling methods. Alternative methods might replace or supplement field selling with telemarketing, independent reps, direct-response advertising, catalog, or even abandonment of thin territories. Cost is an important consideration, but marketing objectives and sales-person motivation should come first in your planning.

Super Reward

The super reward approach calls for paying plenty to top producers, little to others. This philosophy of sales pay planning has two aims: (1) to attract and retain high producers and (2) to inspire others to become high producers. The motivational aims may seem desirable; however, few companies ever reach those objectives. Reality gets in the way.

Superstars stand out for their individual productivity. The manager wishes the other salespeople performed as well. However, in most companies the ordinary people produce most of the sales, not the superstars. There will always be more ordinary people than superstars, and you need those competent, if not remarkable, producers. A pay plan that generates extreme pay differences may hurt overall sales force productivity. While lavishly rewarding the few superstars, the pay plan offers little to attract and hold ordinary salespeople. Those who can produce satisfactory but not outstanding sales results become discouraged and leave. Rarely can a company find enough superstars to offset the cost of excessive turnover among satisfactory producers.

Another problem with the super reward philosophy is that extremely high pay for superstars may interfere with their promotion to management positions. A company with few management openings may find no difficulty in this; however, an expanding company may need to consider promoting salespeople into management.

Uniformity

Under the uniformity approach the company pays a reasonable amount to everyone, but no one earns much above average. This approach reverses the super reward philosophy. The aim here is to attract and retain an ordinary sales force at reasonable cost. The company seeks to avoid pay compression with managers and overpayment of a few high producers. This approach assumes that the individual salesperson exercises only a modest effect on sales. Product, advertising, brand, price, and distribution may exert greater influence over sales results than does the work of the salesperson. If your sales force operates primarily as order-takers, shelf-stockers, or good-will promoters, the uniformity approach may fit your needs.

The manager following this approach should remain alert to an important risk. The relatively flat profile of sales pay can lead to a sheltered workshop atmosphere in which management tolerates poor performance. Such an environment encourages migration of the best producers out of sales and into management or to other companies.

Balanced

Companies following the balanced approach provide adequate pay for survival, better pay for satisfactory sales results, and higher pay for high production. Pay balance results. This approach aims to attract and retain a strong sales force. The company assumes some risk as it hires new salespeople and carries them over low periods with survival pay. The company also accepts the risk of losing some superstars. Overall, however, it expects to build a much-above-average total sales force.

The balanced approach provides adequate survival pay when sales results are marginal. This may be in the form of salary, draw against commissions, or a base of commission income from steady sales. In addition to survival pay, this approach scales the incentive pay (commission and bonuses) to results. Satisfactory results produce attractive total pay. When sales results are high, the pay is also high—but not extravagant.

This approach to sales pay focuses management attention on the sales force. It encourages careful selection, initial training, ongoing coaching, and weeding out of low producers who do not respond to coaching. When the company has an investment at risk, management gives more attention to the sales force. This alone pays off in improved overall sales force productivity.

The balanced approach applies widely in businesses of all types. Even if you are in doubt about which approach is best suited to your company's selling situation, you can safely plan sales pay on the balanced approach. You won't go far wrong.

Whichever approach to sales pay you select, keep it clearly in mind as you get down to the details of setting target pay.

COMPETITIVE PAY

You can develop an effective pay plan only after you decide where you want it to take you. One major part of that answer is target pay—how much you want your salespeople to earn. The other part is sales goals. For most companies, target pay relates closely to competitive pay. If other companies generally pay about $3,000 per month for the kind of salespeople you need, you will probably want to pay around $3,000 also. A pay survey can tell you what other companies pay.

Anyone who talks with salespeople hears stories about how much other companies pay. Those other companies always seem to pay more than your company! Since the earliest days of selling, no salesperson has ever told the boss about a competitor who pays less. Such hearsay information does not constitute a pay survey. It is worthless—except for one thing. An increasing amount of such talk from your salespeople may signal a loss of confidence. The salespeople may suspect that you are not keeping up with competitive pay. The rumors serve as a plea for you to look at the pay. To do that, you need a pay survey. The survey should compile data from many companies that compete for the kind of salespeople you hire.

SURVEY SOURCES

Sales pay surveys fall into three categories:

- Published surveys
- Do-it-yourself surveys
- Consultant surveys

Each has its advantages and disadvantages. You might need more than one survey to learn what you want to know about the competitive labor market.

Published Surveys

Commercial surveys of sales pay are published regularly by various organizations at a cost of $200 to $1,000 or more. Even the expensive surveys are a modest cost if the data prove useful to you. These surveys offer the advantages of being quickly available and of being based on a large sample of companies. Job matching is a problem with published surveys. Rarely do they report enough detail to let you decide how closely the survey jobs match the content of your jobs. If you hire from a broad labor market and lose salespeople to a wide variety of other companies, a published sales pay survey may be all you need.

Commercial publishers of surveys try to get large numbers of participants, rather than closely matched companies and jobs. Indeed, some surveys reflect little understanding of the industries they purport to cover. For example, one prominent survey includes companies selling packaged grocery products under "food products industry," as you would expect, but they also include companies selling wine, beer, soft drinks, and animal feed. That may constitute a single industry in some economic statistics, but it certainly is not a single category in terms of sales pay. That survey also fails to distinguish among salespeople selling to the retail trade (grocery stores), institutions (restaurants, schools, hospitals), and industrial users (food processors)—even though sales pay differs substantially among those three categories.

Some published surveys are limited to selected, participating companies. Only those companies may buy the survey report. In addition to the general data, the survey publisher may provide a customized report comparing your company's salaries to a composite of other participating companies selected by you. Thus, you get the advantage of a large data base plus the opportunity for analysis of a precisely targeted group of companies. Organization Resource Counselors, Inc., and Radford Associates publish such surveys with much careful attention to job matching and data collection. Their elaborate reports may extend to one or more thick volumes of data. Some users find the reports difficult to understand and use because of the extensive statistical treatment. The cost of these excellent, but elaborate, surveys may range from several hundred dollars to $2,000 or more, plus your time to complete the survey participant's report.

It pays to acquaint yourself with published surveys. They can give you some perspective on the general pattern of pay among many companies. Ask the publishers to send you information about their sales pay surveys. Select one or two surveys that provide information related to your company. Here are some sources:

Abbott, Langer & Associates
548 First Street
Crete, IL 60417
(708) 672-4200

Dartnell Corporation
4660 Ravenswood Avenue
Chicago, IL 60640
(312) 561-4000

Wyatt Data Services/ECS
Two Executive Drive
Fort Lee, NJ 07024
(201) 585-9808

Organization Resource Counselors, Inc.
1121 Avenue of the Americas
New York, NY 10036
(212) 719-3400

Radford Associates
Alexander & Alexander Consulting Group, Inc.
2540 North First Street, Suite 400
San Jose, CA 95131
(408) 954-0900

Survey Sources (A directory of hundreds of surveys,
including some on sales compensation in specific
industries.)
Personnel Systems Associates
2227 Cliff Drive
Newport Beach, CA 92663
(714) 548-9900

Do not overlook your industry trade association as a possible
source for sales pay survey data. If the trade association serving
your industry does not offer a sales pay survey, encourage them to
sponsor such a service to members. Some trade associations retain
a compensation consulting firm to design and compile their
surveys.

Do-It-Yourself Surveys

You can conduct your own pay survey by contacting several companies and asking them to submit pay data. Then compile the data
into a survey report. It is customary to provide each participant
with a copy of the survey report. More than a courtesy, the offer of
a free survey report provides the needed inducement to get others
to participate.

A do-it-yourself survey lets you select appropriate companies
and match jobs carefully. You get up-to-date pay data from the
companies of most interest to you—those you compete with for
salespeople. A disadvantage of the do-it-yourself survey is the
time you devote to designing and conducting the survey. Another
disadvantage is that top management and salespeople may be
skeptical of the survey's accuracy and objectivity. Such surveys
often end with only a few companies participating, and you may
get only a limited picture of the competitive labor market. Some
executives may refuse to participate in direct exchanges of pay
data between companies because of concern about confidentiality
of the data or about possible exposure to antitrust or conspiracy
charges. Your corporate legal counsel can advise you about the
degree of legal risk in a direct exchange of pay data among companies in your industry.

Consultant Surveys

If you lack the time and resources for a survey of your own, you may consider retaining a consultant to conduct a specialized survey among selected companies. A management consulting firm experienced in conducting customized pay surveys can provide several advantages. The specialists know how to design and conduct a pay survey to fit your needs. With your initial guidance, they can match jobs and include those other touches that will help provide a survey that applies directly to your company. They know how to encourage companies to participate in a survey, and the consultant's role as an independent third party helps ensure confidentiality in handling the data and objectivity in reporting them. The participating companies cannot be accused of a direct exchange of pay data if the survey report shows only combined data. For maximum legal protection, the survey report should show no individual company data, not even company-coded data. The consultant's survey report will be impartial, helping you to sell the results to those concerned.

The major disadvantage of a consultant-conducted sales pay survey is the cost. Consultants may charge from $5,000 to $10,000 or more, depending upon the size and complexity of the survey. If a trade association sponsors the survey, the member companies share the cost through their dues or by a modest charge for the survey report. Association sponsorship helps encourage broad participation. Most often, however, a special survey conducted by a consultant is sponsored by a company that wants the information for its pay planning. Such a survey becomes part of the total cost of a professionally designed sales pay plan.

USING A SURVEY

Some managers open a sales pay survey report, find an average pay figure, and conclude that they have found **THE ANSWER.** Compensation professionals, however, take a more careful approach. They first read the notes accompanying the survey report to find such information as:

1. Date the survey was conducted, not the publication date. When were these pay rates in effect?
2. Geographic area covered. Where are the companies and the employees located?
3. Companies surveyed. What size and kinds of companies? Enough companies for a reliable estimate of the industry pay patterns?
4. Number of employees in each job. How large a sample of the universe does the survey represent? Enough to be statistically meaningful?
5. Pay data reported. Salary, draw, commission, or total pay? Bonuses included? Are auto and other expenses included or excluded as part of pay?
6. Scope data. Average sales per salesperson? Correlation of pay to sales?
7. Pay plan types. How many companies use each type of plan? How does pay differ in each type of plan?

First decide whether the survey fits your company, then study the pay data. Here are some terms you will find in the surveys:

Mean. The pay of all employees divided by the number of employees. Also called weighted average.

Median. The middle pay. Half of the employees earn that amount or more, and half receive that or less. The median is not affected by pay extremes, and is therefore more reliable than the mean. Use the median for your analysis if it is reported. Otherwise use the mean or weighted average.

Simple average. The company average; the total of company average pay amounts divided by the number of companies. Each company counts equally, regardless of the number of employees. The simple average is not a useful figure for pay planning because it reflects average pay among companies, not among people.

High 25% or 75th percentile or third quartile. The upper limit of the middle 50 percent of all data reported; 25 percent earn at or above this amount.

Low 25% or 25th percentile or first quartile. The lower limit of the middle 50 percent of all data reported; 25 percent earn at or below this amount.

Middle range or interquartile range. The low 25 percent to the high 25 percent, includes the middle 50 percent of employees. This gives an idea of the spread of pay around the median.

Four precautions will help you use pay surveys effectively:
- Select
- Equate
- Beware
- Adjust

Select

Choose a survey that matches your labor market. You want to know the pay offered by companies that compete with your company for the same salespeople. Few companies compete for labor only among their sales competitors. Does your company hire from outside your industry or lose people to companies outside your industry? If so, you should learn about that broader labor market also. Make sure that the survey matches your jobs reasonably well. Consider qualifications required, type of selling, sales volume, and so on. The earnings of high school graduates selling $25,000 per month should not be compared to the pay for a job requiring a degree in engineering and average sales of $150,000 per month. If you cannot find a close match to your jobs, note the differences that may add to or subtract from the value of your jobs. If the survey does not report enough information to answer your questions, do not assume that the survey fits your needs. Get another survey.

Equate

Make sure you are using consistent pay data, not a mixture. For sales jobs, that usually means total pay—salary, commissions, and bonuses—exclusive of auto and expense reimbursements. If possible, use median pay, the pay earned by the middle salesperson in the survey. With some surveys, however, you have to settle for the mean (weighted average) pay because that is the only figure reported. The mean can be distorted by a few extremely high or low pay rates. That makes it less reliable than the median as an indicator of the center of all pay rates. You will find use also for the pay rates at the top quartile (highest-paid 25 percent) and at the low quartile (lowest-paid 25 percent). Few surveys report the full frequency distribution of pay rates, but it is interesting when you can obtain it.

If you have to adjust pay data from different sources to a common measure, use the conversions shown in Table 3–1.

Beware

Watch for errors. People complete survey questionnaires, people process and report survey data, and people make mistakes. A survey covering fewer than 6 companies and 30 employees provides a weak statistical foundation for any conclusions about competitive pay. Try to get a broader survey. If you see crazy numbers in the survey results, get another survey. If it doesn't look right, it probably is not right. When in doubt, throw it out.

Adjust

Every survey is obsolete when published. The data may have been collected several months before publication, and pay continues to change. You want to build a pay plan for the future, not the past. Therefore, you should correct for the time difference between when the survey was compiled and when you want to apply it. The process of estimating is called aging the survey data.

Professional compensation planners usually estimate the general rate of pay increase (not the Consumer Price Index) from the survey date to the middle of the next pay year. They adjust the survey data to estimate competitive pay at that future target date.

TABLE 3–1
Pay Rate Conversions

Per Month & Year	*Per Week & Month*	*Per Hour & Week*
$ Year ÷ 12 = $ Month	$ Year ÷ 52 = $ Week	$ Year ÷ 2080 = $ Hour
$ Month × 12 = $ Year	$ Month ÷ 4.333 = $ Week	$ Month ÷ 173.333 = $ Hour
$ Week × 52 = $ Year	$ Week × 4.333 = $ Month	$ Week ÷ 40 = $ Hour
$ Hour × 2080 = $ Year	$ Hour × 173.333 = $ Month	$ Hour × 40 = $ Week

This puts the adjusted or aged survey data slightly above market at the start of the year, at market by midyear, and slightly below market at year-end. Some companies adjust survey data to the end of the next pay year. That practice helps to ensure that their pay will be above market all year.

You can get information about the general rate of pay increases from articles on the subject that appear from time to time in *The Wall Street Journal*. Look in the "Labor Letter" column that appears on *The Wall Street Journal*'s front page each Tuesday. Some trade association surveys and published salary surveys include pay increase trend information. A comprehensive survey of pay increase data, past and projected, for all major industry categories, is published annually by

American Compensation Association
14040 N. Northsight Blvd.
Scottsdale, AZ 85260-3601
(602) 951-9191

Some consulting firms publish surveys of projected pay increases and many compensation consultants will freely tell you on the telephone their best estimate of the rate of pay change.

Apply the estimated rate of pay increase to the survey data for the time between the survey collection date and your target date. For example, assume that the survey was conducted in March and you are using it in November to design a pay plan that will go into effect in January. You need to estimate the general rate of pay change between March of one year and July of the following year, a period of 16 months. You estimate that pay is increasing at, say, 5 percent per year. You should increase the survey median pay by 6.722 percent (5 percent annual rate compounded for 16 months). That calculation estimates the level of competitive pay as of your future target date. Later discussion of "adjusted survey median" refers to this adjustment for aging from the survey to your target date. Table 3-2, "Survey Aging Factors," can help simplify your calculation of the necessary adjustments of survey data.

TABLE 3–2
Survey Aging Factors

Months Survey to Target Date	Rate of Pay Change per Year							
	3.5%	4.0%	4.5%	5.0%	5.5%	6.0%	6.5%	7.0%
4	1.0115	1.0132	1.0148	1.0164	1.0180	1.0196	1.0212	1.0228
5	1.0144	1.0165	1.0185	1.0205	1.0226	1.0246	1.0266	1.0286
6	1.0173	1.0198	1.0223	1.0247	1.0271	1.0296	1.0320	1.0344
7	1.0203	1.0231	1.0260	1.0289	1.0317	1.0346	1.0374	1.0403
8	1.0232	1.0265	1.0298	1.0331	1.0363	1.0396	1.0429	1.0461
9	1.0261	1.0299	1.0336	1.0373	1.0410	1.0447	1.0484	1.0521
10	1.0291	1.0332	1.0374	1.0415	1.0456	1.0498	1.0539	1.0580
11	1.0320	1.0366	1.0412	1.0457	1.0503	1.0549	1.0594	1.0640
12	1.0350	1.0400	1.0450	1.0500	1.0550	1.0600	1.0650	1.0700
13	1.0380	1.0434	1.0488	1.0543	1.0597	1.0652	1.0706	1.0760
14	1.0410	1.0468	1.0527	1.0586	1.0645	1.0703	1.0762	1.0821
15	1.0439	1.0502	1.0566	1.0629	1.0692	1.0756	1.0819	1.0883
16	1.0469	1.0537	1.0604	1.0672	1.0740	1.0808	1.0876	1.0944
17	1.0499	1.0571	1.0643	1.0716	1.0788	1.0861	1.0933	1.1006
18	1.0530	1.0606	1.0683	1.0759	1.0836	1.0913	1.0991	1.1068
19	1.0560	1.0641	1.0722	1.0803	1.0885	1.0966	1.1049	1.1131
20	1.0590	1.0676	1.0761	1.0847	1.0933	1.1020	1.1107	1.1194
21	1.0621	1.0710	1.0801	1.0891	1.0982	1.1074	1.1165	1.1257
22	1.0651	1.0746	1.0840	1.0936	1.1031	1.1127	1.1224	1.1321
23	1.0682	1.0781	1.0880	1.0980	1.1081	1.1182	1.1283	1.1385
24	1.0712	1.0816	1.0920	1.1025	1.1130	1.1236	1.1342	1.1449

To estimate competitive pay at a future target date, multiply the survey median pay by the appropriate aging factor. Find the estimated Rate of Pay Change per Year and go down that column to the number of months between the survey date and the target date. Example: survey median pay for a job is $40,000. The estimated Rate of Pay Change per Year is 5.0%, and there are nine months from survey to target date. Thus: Factor 1.0373 × Survey $40,000 = $41,492 at Target Date.

NORMAL PAY TARGET

Once you have compiled and adjusted the survey data, you are ready to set targets for total pay. You need three target pay amounts for three levels of sales results: normal, high, and marginal. Start with the big issue—normal pay for normal, satisfactory sales results, as defined in your sales goals.

At Survey Median

Most executives want to provide total pay near the competitive median for comparable sales jobs. That is, they want the pay for normal sales to be in the middle of the market. This keeps the cost of selling in line with other companies while offering enough pay to attract and retain competent salespeople. If you set the normal pay target at the adjusted survey median, the job will offer financial appeal to somewhat fewer than one-half of the potential applicants. One-half of the people working in similar jobs already earn as much or more than the median pay; your pay will not interest them. One-half of the alternative job opportunities probably pay as much or more than the survey median.

Above Survey Median

Set the normal pay target above the adjusted survey median if you want access to a larger pool of sales applicants or if you want to reduce the risk of losing good producers. Most pay surveys show quartiles as well as median pay. Twenty-five percent of the people covered by the survey earn at or above the top quartile amount. The difference in pay between the median and the top quartile may be as little as 10 percent or as much as 30 percent.

For example, a survey shows the median pay for sales representatives in an industry as $4,000 per month and the top quartile as $4,600. That is a 15 percent difference. In that case, 15 percent higher pay would provide access to 25 percent more salespeople. Thus, by setting target pay 15 percent above the median you could gain access to about three-fourths of the available labor supply and your salespeople would find few alternative job opportunities that pay as well as yours.

You can set your target pay somewhere other than at the median or at the top quartile. Pay that is only five percentage points above the median might give access to 60 percent or more of the available applicants. The recruiting advantage of slightly higher pay can be substantial.

Setting target pay above the adjusted survey median may be worth the added cost for another reason. Higher pay itself can help to attract and retain a higher caliber sales team. In addition, when a company pays more, the managers tend to expect more. One sales supervisor, when told of a new pay schedule for salespeople said, "Great! Now I can hire really good, experienced people. But, if I have to pay that much to my present sales force, they are going to have to shape up or ship out." Certainly, any company can obtain the benefits of top-quality selection, training, and supervision—even at relatively low pay levels. Among most companies, however, those that pay more also give closer attention to what they get for their money.

Below Survey Median

Not every company needs to pay at or above the adjusted survey median. After all, about half of all those salespeople surveyed earn below the median. Some of the lower-paying companies succeed quite well. If you are not planning to hire experienced salespeople and you are willing to risk higher turnover, you might wish to pay below the adjusted survey median. The low quartile reported in a pay survey tells you the amount at the lowest-paid 25 percent of the survey population. Generally, you should not set target pay for normal sales results below that amount. Some of your salespeople will be selling below the normal target amount, and you would risk losing too many of them.

Company Current Pay

Before you decide on the target pay amount for normal sales results, examine the recent earnings of your sales force. Regardless of the cost or effectiveness of your present pay plan, it establishes a base of employee expectations. You ignore those expectations only at your own peril. If the pay survey you are using was compiled during the past year, compare your company pay data to the survey data for the same period. If, however, the survey data are older than one year, adjust the survey data to approximate the same time period as your company data.

TABLE 3–3
Comparative Pay Analysis Example (Total pay [salary + commission + bonus] in thousands per year)

	Pay Survey	Our Company	Difference (%)
Trainee Sales Rep (0–1 yr.)			
Low 25%	$19.0	$18.3	−4%
Median	20.0	20.0	0
High 25%	22.0	24.5	11
Sales Rep (2–4 yrs.)			
Low 25%	$23.0	$19.5	−15%
Median	26.0	22.8	−12
High 25%	31.0	28.0	−10
Sr. Sales Rep (5+ yrs.)			
Low 25%	$27.5	$22.0	−20%
Median	32.0	27.6	−14
High 25%	43.0	35.0	−19

Survey: National Consultants, Inc., "Sales Compensation Survey." Nationwide survey of total pay for sales reps in bland industry. Data for year ended March 1991.
Company: Our company's total pay for sales reps, April 1991 to March 1991.

Sort your salespeople according to their experience and sales volume, corresponding to the categories used in the survey. For each category, compute total pay (salary, commissions, and bonuses) at your company's median, high quartile, and low quartile. Enter your company data and the survey data in a comparative pay table like the one shown in Table 3–3.

If your company's current pay is low compared to the survey data, as in the Table 3–3 example, you can select any target pay amount from the low quartile to any higher figure. Employee expectations will be less of a concern than will be the cost of higher target pay. If, however, your company's current pay exceeds the survey median, you face a more difficult problem. Target pay much lower than current pay risks alienating the sales force. Therefore, the survey data may influence your pay targets less than your company's current pay. You could set target pay even higher than the already high current pay, but there is little value in continuing to raise payroll costs in such conditions. Management's fiduciary obligation to stockholders would not be well served by paying $10,000 to get a $4,000 job done.

A comparative pay table such as that shown in Table 3–3 will help as you review these additional considerations:

1. What caliber of sales force do we want?
2. How difficult is it to recruit suitable candidates?
3. What is a tolerable rate of sales force turnover?
4. How difficult is the selling task?
5. What contribution does the salesperson make?
6. What is the quality of initial and ongoing training?
7. What is the quality and closeness of supervisory guidance?
8. What is the degree of sales support provided through advertising, promotion, leads, brand name, price, and customer service?
9. What cost-of-selling do we want?

No one can tell you the right target pay for your company. That remains a matter of management judgment. You may base the decision partly on the nine rational considerations listed here and partly on your company's sales compensation philosophy. Some leading companies, for example, pay above the median of their industry. They follow this policy even though they have the advantage of superior brand, advertising, market position, supervisory structure . . . everything that could justify paying less. Do such companies pay more because they are successful or are they successful because they pay more? It is probably some of each.

Next, you will want to plan pay for the high producers and the marginal producers. Those target pay amounts are as important as the target pay for normal sales performance. You need all three to arrive at a suitable pay formula, as discussed in Chapter 5, "Incentive Formulas."

HIGH PAY TARGET

How much should high producers earn? Not the all-time top producer, but the top 80th percentile—the salesperson who outsells 80 percent of the sales force. Pay surveys can provide some idea of where you may want to set the target for high pay. You could, for example, set the target at the adjusted top quartile shown in the survey. Or, you could set it where you estimate the top 20 percent of competitive salespeople are paid. Or, you could set the target at some other amount based on your judgment.

High Pay and Motivation

For reasonable motivation, set the high pay target no less than 25 percent above the normal pay target. A 50 percent differential is more common, and some companies even plan the pay for top producers at two or three times the normal pay amount.

The aim is to provide "good" pay for good sales results, and "good" depends upon the perception of the salesperson. Deciding upon the high pay target, like the normal pay target, requires your good judgment. Consider (1) competitive pay patterns, (2) motivational aims—what will seem reasonable to the sales force, (3) and cost effects on your company.

The role of the salesperson in making sales also warrants attention when setting pay targets. The greater the salesperson's influence in the selling process, the greater should be the difference between the normal pay target and the high pay target. If your company enjoys a steady sales momentum and most salespeople differ little in their productivity, you do not need to set the high pay target more than 50 percent above the normal. If the normal pay target is $4,000 per month, the high pay target might be $5,000 to $6,000. At the other extreme, if yours is a company in which high producers sell several times the volume of average producers, you may consider a high pay target 100 percent or more above the normal pay target. With a normal pay target of $4,000, the high pay target might be $8,000 to $10,000—or more. Remember that you will test and cost the pay plan later, and you may decide then to reset the pay targets.

MARGINAL PAY TARGET

Where should you set the target pay for marginal producers? This question also calls for management judgment, but it is not difficult to answer. The marginal producer's results are slightly above poor. Further training, closer supervision, or more experience probably can bring the salesperson's performance to a satisfactory level. At this step in pay planning, you need to think about the marginal producer, not the poor producer. The marginal producer is a person you want to retain—at least for several more months.

Survival Pay

Set the target pay for marginal sales at a level that will permit the marginal producers to survive and become better producers. That means uncomfortable subsistence. The pay should not provoke despair but should stimulate hard work for improvement. Forget about your own personal standard of living, and consider what pay your salespeople need to get by. Do not consider at this point whether part of the pay will be a draw or salary. Write down your best estimate of the lowest monthly survival pay for your marginal producers.

The target pay for marginal results should equal or slightly exceed survival pay, that is, the lowest pay level that meets the salesperson's immediate economic needs (food, rent, car payments). That income figure depends upon the accustomed earnings of the typical salesperson in your organization. Table 3–4 shows estimates, based on the author's experience, of the lowest marginal pay that most salespeople will tolerate for a few months. You might wish to set your marginal pay target higher than the amount shown in the table to meet the financial and emotional needs of your own salespeople as you understand them.

TABLE 3–4
Marginal Pay Guidelines

Normal Pay	Marginal Pay
$ 2,000	$1,700
3,000	1,950
4,000	2,200
5,000	2,550
6,000	2,900
7,000	3,350
8,000	3,800
9,000	4,350
10,000	5,000

Estimated lowest pay that most salespeople will
tolerate for up to three consecutive months,
compared to their normal, accustomed pay.

Now you have set three target pay amounts, such as:

Results	Total Pay
High	$6,000 per month
Normal	4,000
Marginal	2,500

Avoid confusion by working consistently in monthly amounts, or weekly if that is your pay period. Do not mix annual and monthly amounts in the planning process. If you think of an annual amount, convert it immediately to the monthly equivalent.

SALARY

If your pay plan will include a base salary, estimate the typical salary to be paid. If you will pay the same salary to all salespeople, that is the figure to enter. If you will offer a range of salaries, enter a figure from the middle of the range. In any case, the salary should be no more than the target pay for marginal results. The salary is survival pay, and that should be close to the total pay target for marginal results.

Subtract salary, if any, from total pay to determine the target incentive amounts, such as:

Results	Pay Targets		
	Total	Salary	Incentive
High	$6,000	$2,000	$4,000
Normal	4,000	2,000	2,000
Marginal	2,500	2,000	500

SALES TARGETS

Once you reach a tentative decision about where to set your pay targets you must then decide what will be considered as high, normal, and marginal sales results. What level of sales performance will be required to produce the target pay?

Normal Sales

Some managers define normal sales results at a level above expected performance. They set higher sales goals for the salesperson, thus providing a stronger economic justification for the intended pay. That approach, however, can easily be overdone. If so, it will result in below-average pay for satisfactory sales results.

Your objective, after all, is to provide reasonable target pay for a reasonable level of sales results. For most companies, that means median pay for median performance. The median salesperson in a median month will earn the amount that you have designated as normal target pay. That happens because you design the sales pay plan to make it happen. You start with the answers, target pay and normal sales results. You design the plan to produce the pay results that you intend. This approach requires that you forecast median sales results for the coming year. Statistical trend analysis can help, but the final decision rests upon your good judgment.

Marginal and High Sales

Analyze the frequency distribution of monthly sales results in your company. Identify the median. Decide where, in your judgment, "poor" leaves off and "marginal" begins and what you consider to be "high" results. Perhaps for your company marginal results will be the low 20 percent of monthly sales, and high results will be the top 20 percent. Those reference points could be the top and bottom 15 percent or 10 percent amounts—or any amounts based on your good judgment about what to expect next year. Table 3–5 shows the frequency of various monthly sales volumes over a 24-month period for 20 sales representatives in one company.

Remember that the term *sales results* here means whatever measure of results you wish to reward. It could be gross margin, units, dollars, market share, sales as percent of quota, and so on. For now, the example uses only one criterion for incentive pay, sales volume.

When setting the sales amounts that will characterize high, normal, and marginal sales results for the coming year, adjust for any increase in sales projected over the prior year. Keep it realistic, not optimistic.

Drawing upon the past pattern of monthly sales, as shown in Table 3–5, and adjusting for an expected 10 percent sales increase next year, the monthly sales and pay targets in the example might look like this:

Results	Sales	Pay		
		Total	Salary	Incentive
High (top 20%)	$187,000	$6,000	$2,000	$4,000
Normal (median)	149,000	4,000	2,000	2,000
Marginal (low 20%)	88,000	2,500	2,000	500

TABLE 3–5
Frequency of Monthly Sales Volumes: An Example

Monthly Sales Volume ($000)		Rep-months	Rep-months (Cumulative)	Cumulative Percent
0 to	9	2	2	0 %
10	19	0	2	0
20	29	1	3	1
30	39	6	9	2
40	49	10	19	4
50	59	16	35	7
60	69	16	51	11
70	79	18	69	14
80	89	25	94	20 (low 20%)
90	99	23	117	24
100	109	27	144	30
110	119	33	177	37
120	129	40	217	45
130	139	43	260	54 (median)
140	149	42	302	63
150	159	35	337	70
160	169	28	365	76
170	179	20	385	80 (high 20%)
180	189	12	397	83
190	199	14	411	86
200	209	21	432	90
210	219	17	449	94
220	229	13	462	96
230	239	8	470	98
240	249	6	476	99
250	259	4	480	100

Data from 20 reps for 24 months. 20 × 24 = 480 rep-months.
Examples: 20 percent of rep-months were below $80,000 sales, 20 percent were above $170,000 sales, and the median rep-month was about $135,000 sales.

In this example, we have defined three key levels of sales results and the corresponding pay target for each, using a single criterion, sales volume. When you develop the incentive pay formula, you will know how well it fits your targets. In fact, you will make the formula fit your targets.

Multiple Criteria

If the sales goals call for more than one incentive pay criterion, you will need to divide the target incentive pay among those multiple criteria and define the high, normal, and marginal results for each criterion—just as in the example above. Here is an example, assuming that the company wants to reward separately for sales of products A and B and for opening new accounts. The following table shows a division of incentive pay among those three criteria.

Results	Product A		Product B		New Accounts		Total Incentive
	Sales	*Pay*	*Sales*	*Pay*	*No.*	*Pay*	
High	$141,000	$2,000	$85,000	$1,200	4-5	$800	$4,000
Normal	93,000	1,000	56,000	600	2-3	400	2,000
Marginal	43,000	300	29,000	200	0-1	0	500

The next chapter discusses how to select the criteria for your sales pay plan. After deciding upon the criteria to reward, you might want to return to this chapter and refine your pay targets. Those pay targets will then help you develop a pay formula for your plan.

CHECKLIST FOR PAY TARGETS

√ Follow the "balanced" approach, unless another better fits your situation.

√ Study sales pay surveys among companies that compete for the same salespeople.

√ Note competitive total pay at median, high 25%, and low 25%.

√ Adjust survey data to target date, such as middle of planned pay year.

✓ Set pay targets for normal, high, and marginal sales results.

✓ Divide target pay into salary (if any) and incentive pay.

✓ Set sales targets for normal, high, and marginal results.

✓ Set incentive pay target for normal, high, and marginal results in each sales criterion.

Chapter Four

Incentive Pay Criteria

Pay for what you want to accomplish.

You get what you pay for. If you want increased dollar sales volume, make it a criterion for incentive pay. If it is increased gross profit that you want, then make that a criterion. If your strategy calls for full-line selling, include that as a criterion for incentive pay. The incentive pay criteria steer selling effort. This element of pay plan design connects motive power compensation to sales goals, and hence to marketing strategy and marketing objectives.

The criteria listed in this chapter are those most often used in sales compensation. Each has its place, but not all in one place. Highlights of each criterion indicate the most appropriate sales situations. Guidelines for measuring each criterion include consideration of absolute versus relative measures and dollar measures versus percentage measures. For each criterion included in the pay plan, identify three levels of expected results: normal, high, and marginal. Those three results levels correspond to the three target pay amounts. Together, they guide development of the incentive pay formula.

A company selling micrographic services (microfilming, microfiche, etc.) paid its salespeople on total dollar sales volume. Half the sales force were not selling the company's new laser printing service. Investigation showed they had little reason to try. They could make more money by selling the old, familiar services to the old, familiar customers. A change of incentive pay criteria put new emphasis on full-line selling. Total earnings of the sales force changed little. However, company profit strengthened as the salespeople sold more high-profit laser printing.

Some managers fail to give enough attention to selecting incentive pay criteria. A manager may concentrate on one objective, such as total sales volume, and overlook others. Or the manager may adopt another company's plan, assuming that the criteria will fit the manager's current company. You must custom-tailor the incentive pay criteria to the marketing strategy and sales goals of your company. That is the way to direct motive power toward the right objectives.

When designing your sales pay plan, consider each possible criterion separately. Match each against your marketing strategy and sales goals. A single criterion, such as sales volume or gross profit, may be enough to meet your sales goals. If you need more criteria, include them—up to four. If you use more than four criteria, the plan becomes confusing and the effect on pay becomes trivial for one or more of the criteria. You need no more than a few strong links between pay and your sales goals. No company can benefit from a clutter of insignificant criteria.

SELECTING THE CRITERIA

What do you want the salesperson to accomplish? Answering that question may prove more difficult than the question seems. Think it through, talk it through. Then decide which incentive pay criteria to include in your sales pay plan. You may need one, two, three, or four criteria to match your marketing strategy and sales goals. To identify which might fit your company, review each of these most widely used incentive criteria:

- Dollar sales volume
- Unit sales
- Gross profit
- New accounts
- Product mix

Dollar Sales Volume

Total dollars of sales volume continues as the most commonly used criterion. It fits a wide variety of sales situations. If a company sells many different products at various prices, dollar sales volume may be the only useful measure of sales performance. (Dollar sales volume is used in most of the examples throughout this book. However, you can substitute in those examples other criteria such as unit sales or gross profit.)

Unit Sales

Widely used in commodity-type selling, unit sales measures results by the quantity sold, not dollar value. Distributors of grocery products, for example, usually credit sales to the salesperson in cases or case equivalents. Others measure sales in dozens (clothing), tons (fresh produce), cubic yards (concrete), and so on. Using unit sales as a criterion insulates the salesperson's pay from changing prices and profits. It does not invite the salesperson to steer the customer to high-profit items. Use unit sales as a criterion where the customer's needs determine what will be sold or the company sells only one item. The salesperson's task is to get the order for the company. The salesperson does not influence product mix, price, or profit.

Gross Profit

The difference between cost and selling price is called gross profit or gross margin. It can serve as a useful criterion where the salesperson can influence profit, either by directing sales effort toward higher-profit items or by negotiating for the best price. A special feature of gross profit as a sales pay criterion is that it provides automatic adjustment of the salesperson's pay for orders taken at other-than-normal selling price. The greatest value of gross profit as a criterion, however, is that it directs sales effort toward profit rather than toward sales volume at any price. If your salespeople could invest their time and effort in a more profitable mix of products or customers, you should consider including gross profit as a criterion in your sales pay plan. Also consider using gross profit if your salespeople can negotiate price, trade-ins, product features, or "extras." Even if salespeople have no authority over price concessions, they can become avid pleaders on behalf of their customers. However, a gross profit criterion can change their orientation away from price selling and toward value selling.

Some managers avoid using gross profit as an incentive pay criterion because they are unsure about the gross profit of each item sold. Others do not want to reveal the gross profit to the salespeople. Even so, you can get all the motivation value of gross profit as an incentive pay criterion by using an *assigned* gross profit (GP). Simply designate a GP value to each product or product group. Use a GP that is near the actual or estimated gross profit. It does not have to be accurate.

You can group together products of roughly equal gross profit into a single GP category for easy recall and calculation by the salesperson. You can also adjust for motivational effect. Raise or lower the assigned GP according to the sales push you want to provide for that product or product group. For example: Product A has an actual gross profit of $100 and product B has a gross profit of $150. You want to encourage sales of B, but B requires greater selling effort than A. So, you assign a GP of $200 for B, giving it greater push than the actual gross profit would provide. The assigned GP is used only for calculating incentive pay. It has no effect on the company's cost accounting practices.

New Accounts

The opening of new accounts provides an appropriate criterion for the company with a special interest in broadening its customer base. With new accounts as an incentive criterion, the salesperson sees a clear value in going after new accounts instead of spending full time in more comfortable surroundings. If all or most sales already are made to new accounts, or if added sales volume must come from new accounts, the general criterion of sales volume may be sufficient without adding new accounts as a special criterion.

Product Mix

The product mix criterion is used less often than it should be. Many companies overlook the opportunity to encourage selling the complete line of products or the high-profit items. Does your marketing strategy call for a full-line selling effort to achieve sales cost efficiency, operating efficiency, or market control? To encourage full-line selling, offer premium pay (either a bonus or a higher commission rate) for those months or those orders with more than a designated minimum in each of several product lines. Positive incentives for reaching product mix objectives work better than do penalties for failing to sell the designated product mix.

If you sell many products, group them into three, four, or five noncompeting categories. Here is an example from an office supplies distributor:

- Papers—Writing, typing, drawing, copier
- Pencils and pens—Wooden, mechanical, colored, disposable pens, quality pens
- Implements—Staplers, punches, paper cutters, binding machines
- Miscellaneous—Binders, report covers, page dividers, calendars, printed forms, glue.

Using only a few categories makes it easy for the salesperson to remember to present all categories. Establish the criterion for premium pay at a moderate, not high, level of sales for all or most categories. Set the standard so that about half of the salespeople can reach it in most months. The aim is to get every salesperson into the habit of presenting the full line every time, even if the effort results in only modest sales for some product lines.

Beyond the five common criteria of dollar sales volume, unit sales volume, gross profit, new accounts, and product mix, companies use many other criteria to meet specific marketing and motivational aims. Five less-common criteria include:

- Multi-item orders
- Special-item sales
- Consistently high results
- Market share
- Milestones

Multi-Item Orders

The criterion of multi-item orders is much like full-line sales. The objective is to encourage the salesperson to try for add-on sales while the customer is in a buying mood. Retailers use multi-item sales incentives more than wholesale or industrial sales organizations do. Often established as the basis for a bonus, a contest, or a premium commission rate, this criterion can be especially effective to encourage inside salespeople or order-takers to suggest related items to customers for inclusion in orders.

Special-Item Sales

A separate criterion may be used to encourage the sale of certain products for their high profit margin or for some other reason. Designated items receive extra incentive credit. This is applied frequently in retailing as a bonus or premium commission rate—called a spiff. Retailers often use spiffs to help clear the shelves of obsolete, odd size or color, last few, or slow-moving merchandise. Only rarely do retailers use spiffs to reward high-profit sales, but perhaps they should do so more often. You can apply the special-item sales criterion as a temporary device or as a regular continuing incentive criterion.

Consistently High Results

A criterion based on high sales results over an extended period recognizes the true superstar. It does not reward the salesperson who occasionally gets lucky. This criterion can apply to dollar sales volume, unit sales, gross profit, or other standard criteria—but the key is consistently high results. Measure performance over a long enough period to be sure that results are consistent. You can establish the criterion as a certain sales result to be achieved over a three-month or longer period, with no single month below a stated minimum. Consider using the rolling three-month average sales as the base, which provides a monthly incentive opportunity based on three-month sales results. The rolling average lets you pay high rewards for continuing strong sales results—without overpaying for a lucky windfall or for bunching sales into one month.

Market Share

Perhaps the most reasonable measure of success in selling is market share. However, few companies use market share as an incentive pay criterion, because most are unable to measure their market share rapidly and accurately in each salesperson's territory. For grocery and drug items, however, market share data are available through reporting services. A few other businesses likewise keep tabs on market share and could apply it as a sales pay criterion. Note, however, that market share as an incentive criterion could increase incentive pay while company sales decline. This could occur if the total market shrinks faster than the company's decline. If top management can accept that concept and a fair measure of market share is available, consider it as an incentive criterion.

Milestones

Intermediate progress toward a sale may apply as a useful criterion in special situations. A milestone is a significant step toward a final sale, such as developing a qualified lead or getting the prospect to test the product. When a milestone is reached, the salesperson qualifies for a bonus or partial commission. The salesperson earns this reward even though the sale has not yet been made—and may never be made. Companies have used milestone criteria effectively in long-cycle, big-ticket selling. Examples include selling airplanes, large power generators, mainframe computers, and construction services. In such selling, the salesperson's task is to locate a qualified buyer and develop the relationship to some point, such as becoming accepted as a qualified bidder. Technical and financial people may complete the final arrangements. It makes sense in those circumstances to reward the salesperson for reaching the specified milestone. The reward comes promptly after the accomplishment. When used for incentive pay, however, the milestone criterion is usually one of two or three criteria, not the sole basis for incentive pay.

SUBJECTIVE CRITERIA

Most companies use only objective sales pay criteria, such as those just discussed. Both management and salespeople like the impartiality, the economic relevance, and the measurability of such criteria. For some companies, however, marketing strategy and sales goals call for results in a criterion that is not objectively measurable. Such subjective or qualitative criteria may include training dealers, handling customer problems, and serving at trade shows.

A subjective criterion can be an effective motivator if it meets certain standards.

Job-Related

Be sure it makes good business sense. Avoid possible charges of favoritism or discrimination (sex, race, etc.) by using only criteria that are clearly job-related. "Resolving customer complaints promptly and efficiently"; that is job-related, but not objectively measurable. It must be evaluated subjectively.

Results or Behavior

Include only what is observable. Avoid using effort, attitude, personality characteristics, or traits as criteria. You cannot see them. You cannot prove they are job-related. You cannot discuss them without stirring up emotional turmoil with or within the salesperson. Use only results or behavior as a criterion. "Make effective presentations at distributor meetings"; that is observable behavior even though you will subjectively judge the quality of the presentations.

Specific

Define the subjective or qualitative criterion as narrowly as possible. Put your definition in writing so the salesperson can know what you will consider in your evaluation. "Train four dealers per month in how to demonstrate the new product effectively." Such a goal is specific, although a qualitative rating of the training may apply.

Defined Rating

Use a simple rating scale with two to five levels of rating. If possible, define what will be required to reach each level. Both the manager and the salesperson should know in advance what will be considered as outstanding, satisfactory, and below standard.

Many sports events, such as figure skating and diving, are rated subjectively. Apply the same kind of definition and discipline if you expect to achieve acceptance for a subjective criterion. Do not confuse a subjective or qualitative incentive criterion with a discretionary bonus.

DISCRETIONARY BONUS

Few companies include a discretionary element in sales pay. Where it does happen, a senior manager awards a bonus based only on the manager's judgment. Discretionary means that the manager defines no criterion in advance. No previously defined achievement produces the award. It comes as a pleasant surprise to the recipient. It is like finding money—but not like earning money.

The salesperson does not know in advance what to do to win a discretionary bonus. The bonus opportunity therefore provides no direction to job performance. At the most, the salesperson knows only the vague objective of trying to keep the boss happy. A discretionary bonus does nothing to satisfy the need for achievement in either the winners or the nonwinners. The winners like receiving the money, but they may also feel some loss of self-determination as they are placed in a dependent relationship to the person providing the handout. The nonwinners are spared such ambivalence. They can hold unmixed feelings toward the manager who decided not to reward them. Discretionary bonuses primarily satisfy the person in control, rather than the person receiving the bonus.

If you still think that you may want to grant an occasional bonus outside the regular incentive criteria, get some motivational value for the money. Think ahead to the kinds of situations that would warrant such a bonus. Then put it in writing. Tell the salespeople how they might qualify for one of these special Presidential Awards. Now you have moved it away from the category of a handout decided after the fact. You have created a planned special award program. See Chapter 8 for more on special awards.

GROUP CRITERIA

Salespeople want to be paid for what they do. Most have a strong need for achievement, and the paycheck is their scoreboard for measuring what they accomplish. Managers generally recognize these characteristics and design sales pay around criteria that reward each salesperson for individual results. However, you might consider using group or shared criteria to fit one of the following conditions.

Team Selling

For example, one salesperson locates the prospect and qualifies him, then a second salesperson closes the sale. Automobile dealers and real estate firms have used prospectors and closers in such team selling. In another example, the salesperson works as a team member with technical and financial specialists to arrange the sale of large capital equipment or complex systems. Consider using group results as criteria wherever two or more people must work together to make the sale.

Luck of the Draw

Customers are assigned randomly, and occasionally a large sale occurs. The company may provide that the lucky windfall be shared among all salespeople. A few companies share all sales among the group, regardless of differences in individual performance.

Sales not Credited

When sales cannot be clearly credited to one salesperson, group criteria may apply. For example, a company manufacturing hospital supplies could trace sales only to its distributors. Three or four company representatives called on hospitals in the area served by one distributor. Because the company could not determine how much each hospital purchased from the distributor, they shared sales credit among all representatives in the area. (The company later developed a method for tracking sales to individual hospitals, and switched from the group criteria to individual criteria.)

Group criteria encourage cooperation and teamwork among the members of the group. If that is a major marketing strategy for your company, consider using group criteria. Recognize, however, that group criteria submerge individual performance in the pool of group results. The loss of individual recognition may frustrate the salesperson who lives and breathes for personal achievement. If you make group criteria a major part of the pay program, be prepared for a different personality in the sales force.

CRITERION BASE

After you select incentive pay criteria that support your marketing strategy and sales goals, you must decide how to measure results in each criterion. To select an appropriate criterion measure, follow this two-question decision process:

- Absolute or relative?
- Percent-variable or dollar-variable?

Absolute Measure

If you want to reward for every sale, starting with the first, use an absolute measure. If you pay commission on every unit or sales dollar or gross profit dollar, you are using an absolute measure: total sales results. This often applies in one-shot selling. Each sale stands as a unique event, no matter how many sales the salesperson makes. The salesperson enjoys little or no sales momentum, no ongoing flow of business, few repeat orders. If the salesperson doesn't work at selling, the company books no orders from that territory. Differences in territory potential may show little effect on sales where the salesperson's skill and effort largely determine results. Such selling characteristics generally fit consumer-direct selling (door-to-door), insurance, real estate, big-ticket items (autos, appliances, machine tools), and many others. Select an absolute measure of the incentive criterion if it fits your sales situation. Otherwise, consider a relative measure.

Relative Measure

If sales performance is best evaluated against some standard, such as a quota, use a relative measure. If you pay commission on sales compared to a quota, you are using a relative measure. Other relative measures include past sales of the territory or, rarely, average sales of other salespeople, or market share. Relative measures find wide use in wholesale selling and industrial selling where a momentum of repeat sales exists. If you can identify a reasonable level of expected sales results, you can use a relative measure for the incentive criterion. Consider using relative-measure criteria where (1) territory differences exert a large effect on sales, (2) repeat orders or an established volume are almost certain, or (3) you can forecast territory sales with reasonable accuracy. These situations define satisfactory performance in relative terms, such as "making quota" or "exceeding last year."

TABLE 4–1
Test of Absolute versus Relative Measures of Results

	Salesperson A	*Salesperson B*
Quota	$150,000	$100,000
Sales	$140,000	$130,000

Assume this is your company and the quotas shown are reasonable.
1. Which salesperson performed better this month?
2. Which salesperson should receive the higher commission?

There is a simple way to examine the issue of absolute versus relative measures. Set up a test like that shown in Table 4–1. Use a criterion and amounts that seem familiar in your company. Answer the questions yourself. Then ask other interested executives in your company to give their answers. You might get agreement or a lively debate, but you should explore this issue before deciding which kind of measure to use with each criterion in your pay plan.

In the Table 4–1 test, Salesperson A sold more volume than B, but A sold less than quota for the territory. Salesperson B sold less volume than A, but B sold well above quota. If you answered A to both test questions, you favor an absolute criterion measure. If you answered B to both questions, you selected the relative measure. There is no right or wrong answer to this test. Your answers will be influenced by your company's sales situation and your experience with quotas.

Many companies use an absolute criterion measure, such as total dollar volume, total gross profit, or total units sold. Such companies typically pay a direct commission on that criterion, such as a percent of sales volume or dollars per unit.

If you have decided that your company needs an absolute criterion measure, you can ignore the next issue. However, if you think that a relative criterion measure fits your company, you must now decide the second issue: percent-variable versus dollar-variable measure. That is, how will you measure results compared

TABLE 4–2
Test of Percent-Variable versus Dollar-Variable Measures of Results

	Salesperson B	Salesperson C
Quota	$100,000	$200,000
Sales	$130,000	$240,000
Amount over quota	$ 30,000	$ 40,000
% over quota	30	20

Assume this is your company and the quotas shown are reasonable.
   1. Which salesperson performed better this month?
   2. Which salesperson should receive the higher commission?

to quota? To explore this issue, try another simple test, as in Table 4–2, adapted to your company.

Percent-Variable versus Dollar-Variable Measures

The test of percent versus dollar variable in Table 4–2 shows that Salesperson B sold a larger percentage above quota than did Salesperson C. However, C sold more dollars above quota. If you answered B to both questions, you favor a percent-variable for measuring results relative to quota. If you answered C to both questions, you believe that a dollar-variable is the appropriate measure of results compared to quota. Again, neither answer is right nor wrong, but one may better fit your company than the other.

If you gave mixed answers in either of the tests, Table 4–1 or Table 4–2, you should further consider your company's selling situation and motivational aims before proceeding with the sales pay plan. "Better" performance normally should mean higher pay. If results perceived as better do not produce higher pay, the salesperson will receive mixed instead of clear signals about achievement on the job.

Companies that use a percent-variable relative measure for a criterion apply a wide variety of incentive pay arrangements. Some develop the incentive pay as a percentage of the salesperson's salary. For example, for every 1.0 percent of quota sold, the salesperson earns 0.5 percent of salary. Another arrangement pays a percentage of sales related to the percent of quota sold. Yet another arrangement pays a percentage of a target award amount. The percentage may vary for sales above and below quota. For example, for every 1.0 percent that sales exceed quota the salesperson adds 1.0 percent to the target award, but for every 1.0 percent that sales fall short of quota the salesperson loses 2.0 percent from the target award amount.

Companies using a dollar-variable relative measure for an incentive criterion often pay a direct commission on sales or gross profit in excess of a minimum amount. The minimum may be some percentage of quota. For example, the salesperson receives 3.5 percent of sales in excess of 50 percent of quota. If quota is a realistic expectation of sales, set the minimum low enough to ensure that at least 80 percent of salespeople will earn some incentive pay each month. You want to encourage performance, not discourage it by setting the minimum too high.

Instead of the dollar-variable relative measure, the percent-variable measure fits situations where extra effort or skill is likely to produce added sales proportionate to the territory potential. For an example of the territory-percent response, assume that hard work in a small territory would produce 50 percent more sales; the same hard work in a large territory would produce 50 percent more sales there also. In contrast, the dollar-variable fits situations where extra effort produces additional dollars of sales, with little regard to territory potential. If quotas vary among territories by less than 25 percent, the difference between a percent-variable and a dollar-variable measure will not be significant. Choose either one.

Did the answers to the tests in Tables 4–1 and 4–2 result in uncertainty about which criterion base best fits your company? If so, you might analyze sales records to find which patterns most often characterize your company's selling situation. Sales records, however, do not always yield a clear answer. The analysis can be confused by conditions such as: (1) the best salespeople get the best territories, (2) substantial turnover of the sales force, or (3) territories have changed several times in recent years. Besides, real life seldom fits neatly into the categories shown in a book. If your company falls between the types shown, use your best judgment to pick one of the three alternatives for each incentive:

- Absolute measure
- Dollar-variable relative measure
- Percent-variable relative measure

POINT SYSTEM

Some companies assign point values to products and pay a certain commission per point. This method can be used to reflect unit sales, dollar sales, gross profit, or other criteria. Reductions in selling price can be reflected in lower point values.

A point system gives the company some flexibility in designing and managing its sales pay plan. For many salespeople, however, the point system may seem a confusing layer of abstraction between sales results and pay. If you can operate in another way, clarity of pay arrangements argues for avoiding a point system for incentive pay.

Points can be useful for crediting a variety of different kinds of results into one program, such as a contest. In that case the company may award points for high sales volume, opening new accounts, and keeping accounts receivable at an acceptable level.

This discussion of criteria and measurement emphasized the motivation of salespeople toward the objectives of your marketing strategy. The cost of the sales pay plan was put aside for later consideration. After you draft the pay plan and test it, you can then make any adjustments needed to meet your cost objectives. For now, continue to concentrate on the motivational goals that you want to accomplish. The next chapter provides detail on selecting a pay formula to fit your pay targets. For now, identify each incentive criterion to be used and the measure of results for each.

CHECKLIST FOR INCENTIVE PAY CRITERIA

√ Select one to four criteria based on marketing strategy and sales goals.

√ Consider using an assigned gross profit instead of actual gross profit as a criterion.

√ Waste no money on discretionary bonuses.

√ Use group criteria for shared selling or where individual results are not measurable.

√ Select a suitable criterion measure: Absolute, dollar-variable relative, or percent-variable relative.

Chapter Five

Incentive Formulas

Select a formula that matches your targets.

Management has agreed tentatively to the pay targets and to the sales results criteria. Knowing where you want to go makes it possible to select the best route. The incentive formula provides the route to intended pay for expected sales results.

This chapter shows how to combine the normal, high, and marginal pay targets with the corresponding three levels of sales results to develop an incentive pay formula. A simple graphic method can help the plan designer select the appropriate plan type to fit the company's aims. The mathematical details then fall into place. A review of incentive formulas describes how each works and where it works best.

FLAT-RATE FORMULA

A constant commission rate or incentive for all sales is the simplest and most common type of incentive pay formula. For example, one company pays 2.5 percent of dollar sales volume; a second company pays 5 percent of gross profit; a third company pays 50 cents per case sold, and a fourth company pays 0.5 percent of salary for each new account. Each of these is a flat-rate formula. The company pays a constant incentive on every sale. With a flat-rate formula, the company knows in advance the cost for every sale. The salesperson also knows the pay for every sale. It is easy to plan, easy to remember.

FIGURE 5–1
Flat-Rate Formula (Commission = 2.5% of all sales)

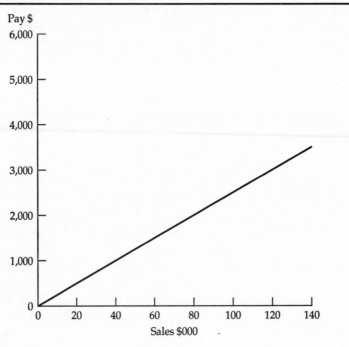

Figure 5–1 illustrates earnings under a flat-rate formula based on 2.5 percent of sales. When sales reach $80,000, the incentive pay equals $2,000. Sales at half that amount produce incentive pay of one-half, or $1,000. Higher sales bring higher pay directly proportional to the sales increase. The flat-rate formula rewards the same for every sale from first to last.

SET-ASIDE FORMULA

The second most common type of sales pay formula is the set-aside formula—also called quota-based or minimum or threshold formula. It pays incentive only on sales above an assigned minimum. For example, one company pays 4 percent of sales over

$30,000 in a month. Another company pays 20 percent of gross profit that exceeds 50 percent of quota. A third company pays $200 for each new account beyond three in a month. Such set-aside formulas require the salesperson to pass a threshold before the incentive pay begins. The salesperson gets commission only for sales above the minimum, no commission on sales below minimum.

Retail stores often establish the minimum at a level that offsets the cost of the base salary. The plan designer may think in terms of straight commission, with the minimum set at a level equivalent to the base salary. When commissions exceed the salary minimum, the company pays the excess commission to the salesperson.

Another approach matches the minimum to the sales momentum of the territory. The pay plan encourages sales beyond the lowest expected volume. There is no reward for the early, easy-to-get sales. Where reorders and unsolicited sales make up a significant part of sales volume, the set-aside formula can provide strong motivation to build sales above that "given" amount. By paying no commission or incentive on sales up to the minimum, the company can pay a higher rate on sales above the minimum. That increases the excitement and reward values in the normal range of sales results above the minimum.

For a motivationally effective set-aside formula, establish the minimum at an amount that is easy to reach. You want to encourage marginal performers by giving them a taste of success. Set the minimum at a level that your salespeople will exceed in at least 80 percent of their sales months.

The graph in Figure 5–2 shows payments of a set-aside formula that pays 4 percent of sales in excess of $30,000 in a month. Note that this formula pays $2,000 when sales reach $80,000. That is the same pay produced by the 2.5 percent flat-rate formula in Figure 5–1. The set-aside formula, however, provides a more exciting reward opportunity for high sales. When sales reach $120,000 the

FIGURE 5–2
Set-Aside Formula (Commission = 4.0% of sales over $30,000)

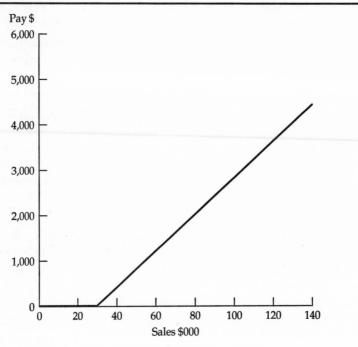

flat-rate formula pays $3,000 but the set-aside formula pays $3,600—20 percent more. The set-aside formula also provides more risk for low sales. At $40,000 sales, the flat-rate formula pays $1,000 but the set-aside formula pays only $400. More risk, more reward.

PROGRESSIVE-RATE FORMULA

The progressive-rate formula is also popular with many sales executives. It pays higher commission rates on higher sales. The salesperson's earnings increase at an accelerating rate as sales increase. The graph in Figure 5–3 illustrates earnings under this progressive-rate formula:

FIGURE 5–3

Progressive-Rate Formula (Commission = 1.5% of sales to $40,000 + 3.5% to $80,000 + 5.5% over $80,000)

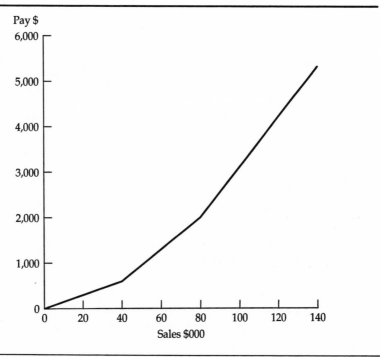

- 1.5% of sales up to $40,000, plus
- 3.5% of sales from $40,000 to $80,000, plus
- 5.5% of sales over $80,000

Note that each segment of the formula adds to the lower segments. Include the word *plus* in the formula or you could find yourself paying larger-than-intended commissions under a step-rate formula.

In the progressive-rate example, sales of $80,000 again produce $2,000 commission. The salesperson earns commission from the first dollar of sales. The earnings grow substantially larger at higher sales volume. Compare earnings under the prior three formulas at three levels of sales:

	Sales		
	$40,000	$80,000	$120,000
Flat-rate formula	$1,000	$2,000	$3,000
Set-aside formula	$400	$2,000	$3,600
Progressive-rate formula	$600	$2,000	$4,200

The progressive-rate formula is based on the concept that early, easy-to-get sales deserve some commission but at a lower rate. Added sales at high volume require more effort and skill—and justify a greater reward. The formula ties the level of reward to the perceived degree of difficulty. It pays more for those difficult sales to encourage the extra time and effort required.

You can combine a progressive rate with a set-aside formula. Such an arrangement provides zero commission until sales reach a minimum; above the minimum the commission rate increases as sales increase.

Top salespeople often argue for a progressive-rate formula. However, the manager must remember that the pay plan needs to serve ordinary producers also. Added sales volume and increased commission rate multiply together and can raise pay to a high level. Some managers justify the added cost by noting that the added sales provide greater gross profit and net profit. Therefore, the company can afford to pay more for those added sales. Chapter 3, "Pay Targets," dealt with the affordability argument, but here it arises again. The most effective sales pay plans are those built on a foundation of motivational aims, not on economic considerations such as affordability. Just because the company can afford to pay more does not mean that it should do so. The motivational issue is whether the salespeople and managers perceive higher sales results as being substantially more difficult to achieve and therefore worth a compounded commission rate.

FIGURE 5–4
Step-Up Formula (Commission = 2.5% of sales if $20,000 or over, zero if below $20,000)

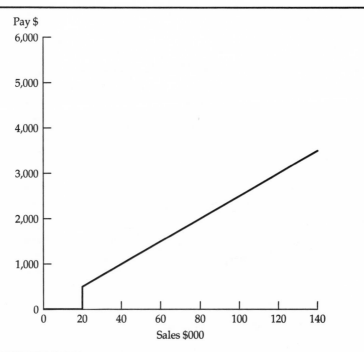

STEP-UP FORMULA

Companies use the step-up formula and the following two formulas much less frequently than the three preceding formulas. One of these, however, might fit your pay objectives. The step-up formula applies a constant commission rate to total sales, provided sales exceed an assigned minimum. It differs from the set-aside formula by paying commission on all sales, not just on those sales that exceed the minimum. This arrangement creates an abrupt increase in pay when sales pass the minimum, hence the name step-up formula.

The graph in Figure 5–4 illustrates earnings under a step-up formula: 2.5% of total sales if sales equal or exceed $20,000. The company pays no commission if sales fall short of $20,000. Once that minimum is reached, the 2.5 percent commission applies to all sales—including the first $20,000. This pay pattern is identical to the flat-rate formula in Figure 5–1, except for the pay step at $20,000 sales.

In the example, the $1 of added sales that brings total sales from $19,999 to $20,000 produces $500 in added commission. That kind of attention-getting importance prompts some companies to use a step-up formula. However, the frustration of a salesperson falling just short of the minimum prompts others to seek a pay plan with less of a do-or-die character.

If you set the minimum very low, it has no significant motivational effect. Everyone easily exceeds the minimum and thereafter follows a flat rate. Some companies use the step-up formula with a low minimum as a device for disposing of residual sales credits when a salesperson terminates.

STEP-RATE FORMULA

Closely related to the step-up formula, the step-rate formula carries the concept further. The step-rate formula pays higher commission rates on total sales when sales exceed various assigned amounts. This produces sharp increases in pay at several points as sales increase. The formula may pay commission from the first dollar of sales or from an assigned sales minimum. It then provides steps at higher sales amounts, as in the example shown in Figure 5–5 which pays commission at:

- 2.0% of all sales if sales are less than $60,000, or
- 2.5% of all sales if sales are $60,000 to $90,000, or
- 3.0% of all sales if sales are $90,000 or more

Note that the formula segments are connected by *or* in the step-rate formula, while the progressive-rate formula used *plus* to create a smooth progression without steps.

FIGURE 5–5
Step-Rate Formula *(Commission = 2.0% if below $60,000, or 2.5% if $60,000 to $90,000, or 3.0% over)*

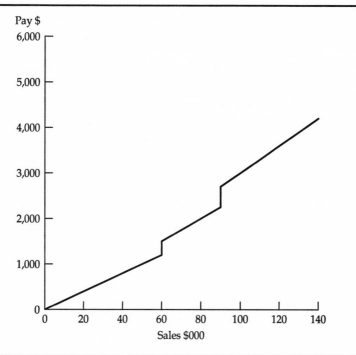

Again in this example, sales of $80,000 provide pay of $2,000. Sales below $60,000 are paid at a lower rate. When sales exceed $90,000, total pay rises significantly. At sales of $120,000, the commission is $3,600.

The concept behind the step-rate formula is to make achievement of certain sales goals a special, exciting event. It functions something like a special bonus at each designated step. For full motivational value set the steps at achievable sales levels, but at levels that differentiate among salespeople. In the preceding example, the steps will be motivationally meaningful if about 20 percent of the salespeople reach the top step while perhaps 20 percent fall short of the first step. The first step signals graduation from the lowest sales category. The second step acknowledges progress into the top-producers category. The pay steps should provide at least a 10 percent increase in pay, preferably 20 to 25 percent, as in the example. Otherwise, the steps will seem too small to be worthy rewards for achievement.

The top commission rate in a step-rate formula may be less than the top rate in a progressive pay formula or the regular rate in a set-aside formula. Applying the top commission rate of a step-rate formula on total sales is costly. That cost might limit your opportunity to pay higher rates for added sales.

If you are considering a step-rate formula with more than two steps, a progressive-rate formula might better fit your aims. As an alternative to the step-rate formula, consider offering a lump-sum bonus as a reward when the salesperson reaches certain sales goals.

DECLINING-RATE FORMULA

A declining-rate formula operates as the reverse of a progressive-rate formula. It pays lower commission rates on added sales. As sales increase the pay increases—but at a slower rate. The graph in Figure 5–6 illustrates this example of a declining-rate formula:

- 3% of sales up to $40,000, plus
- 2% of sales from $40,000 to $90,000, plus
- 1% of sales over $90,000

Why would any company offer lower commission rates for added sales? The very idea is enough to send some salespeople toward the exits; therefore few companies use such a sales pay formula. However, some companies use declining commission rates as a control on windfall sales (see Chapter 10, "Windfall Sales"). There are other applications as well.

An equipment supply company with branches nationwide uses a declining-rate formula. In the smaller branches the salespeople usually sell in the first commission level. In midsize branches they

FIGURE 5–6

Declining-Rate Formula *(Commission = 3.0% of sales to $40,000 + 2.0% to $90,000 + 1.0% above $90,000)*

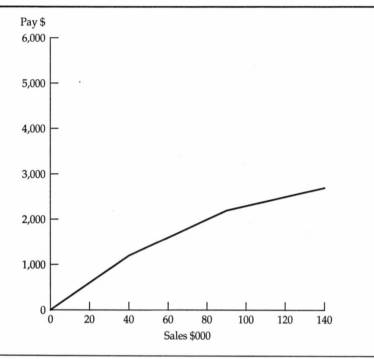

sell in the middle of the pay schedule. In a few large branches the salespeople sell in the upper part of the schedule. No salesperson experiences the entire range of commission rates. Each salesperson operates within a small part of the total pay schedule. Each salesperson experiences essentially a flat rate within that person's normal month-to-month sales pattern.

The declining-rate formula lets this equipment supply company use one formula for all branches. Top management in this company also wants to curtail earnings of top producers. Otherwise, the top salespeople might not accept promotion to branch manager in small branches. The declining-rate formula fits the special needs of that company. In most companies, however, if you an-

TABLE 5–1
Example Formula Payouts (as in Figures 5–1 through 5–6)

			Formula Payout ($)			
Sales ($000)	Flat Rate	Set Aside	Progressive Rate	Step Up	Step Rate	Declining Rate
0	0	0	0	0	0	0
10	250	0	150	0	200	300
20	500	0	300	0	400	600
30	750	0	450	750	600	900
40	1,000	400	600	1,000	800	1,200
50	1,250	800	950	1,250	1,000	1,400
60	1,500	1,200	1,300	1,500	1,500	1,600
70	1,750	1,600	1,650	1,750	1,750	1,800
80	2,000	2,000	2,000	2,000	2,000	2,000
90	2,250	2,400	2,550	2,250	2,700	2,200
100	2,500	2,800	3,100	2,500	3,000	2,300
110	2,750	3,200	3,650	2,750	3,300	2,400
120	3,000	3,600	4,200	3,000	3,600	2,500
130	3,250	4,000	4,750	3,250	3,900	2,600
140	3,500	4,400	5,300	3,500	4,200	2,700

nounce a declining-rate pay formula, do not expect the salespeople to stand up and cheer.

Any type of formula can be used to produce normal target pay at normal sales. All six of the formula examples in this chapter pay $2,000 at $80,000 sales. Differences among those formulas appear in the incentive pay for sales below and above that normal target. Selection of a formula depends upon the pattern of pay intended through the range of expected sales results. Table 5–1 shows pay under the six example formulas.

FORMULA DEVELOPMENT

Developing a sales pay formula involves working backward. Start with the answers—target pay and target criteria. Develop a formula that produces the desired target pay at the three designated sales levels—normal, high, and marginal. To start, lay out a graph like the examples in this chapter, and plot your three sales/pay targets for an incentive criterion. Then visualize the kind of pay curve that would most closely fit the three target points.

Working Backward

Once you have an idea of the type of formula that might fit your sales/pay targets, develop the formula. You already know the answers: your three pay targets. Now work back to a formula that will produce those answers—or something close to them. You can use simple graphs and a calculator to work out the formula and to test variations, or use a computer to develop a formula that will fit your targets. A computer spreadsheet program makes an ideal tool for this kind of application. You can make any number of cut-and-try approaches until you arrive at a formula that fits the target pay amounts. You may find more than one formula that works. If so, choose the one that will be easiest for salespeople to understand.

Figures 5–7 and 5–8 show formula development for Acme Corp., using a simple graphic method. The company has been paying a base salary of $2,000 per month to each sales engineer. Figure 5–7 shows the following pay targets plotted against the criterion, gross profit:

	Gross Profit	Target Pay
High	$60,000	$5,000
Normal	40,000	3,500
Marginal	20,000	2,500

The graph in Figure 5–8 shows Pay Formula No. 1:
    Salary: $2,000
    Incentive pay:

- 2.5% of gross profit up to $20,000, plus
- 5.0% of gross profit from $20,000 to $40,000, plus
- 7.5% of gross profit over $40,000

FIGURE 5–7
Pay and Criterion Targets—Acme Corp.

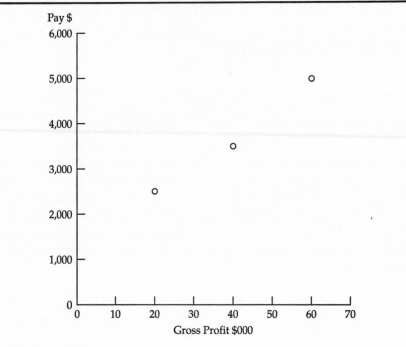

Here is how Pay Formula No. 1 was developed. First, the company decided to continue the $2,000 salary. That left $500 to be provided by incentive pay to reach the marginal pay target of $2,500 at $20,000 gross profit. The company made a policy decision to pay incentives on every dollar of gross profit, no minimum. Dividing $500 incentive pay by $20,000 gross profit gave the 2.5 percent incentive rate on the first $20,000 of gross profit. Combined with the base salary, that produced the target $2,500 total pay at a gross profit of $20,000.

The next step required reaching $3,500 total pay at the normal gross profit of $40,000. That meant adding $1,000 in incentive pay when gross profit increased by another $20,000 over the first

FIGURE 5–8
Targets and Formula No. 1—Acme Corp.

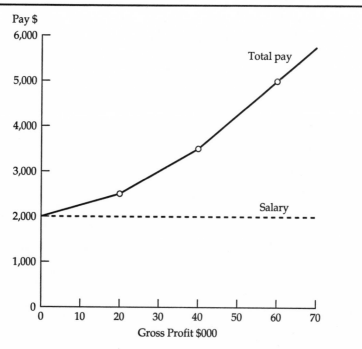

$20,000. Dividing $1,000 by $20,000 gave the 5.0 percent incentive rate that applies to gross profit from $20,000 to $40,000. It adds to the incentive pay earned on the first $20,000 of gross profit in the progressive-rate formula that is emerging.

To reach the high target of $5,000 total pay at $60,000 gross profit called for a further increase of $1,500 in incentive pay at the $20,000 increase in gross profit to the high target of $60,000. Dividing $1,500 by $20,000 gave the 7.5 percent incentive rate that applies to gross profit above $40,000. Thus, a progressive-rate formula has been developed that hits each of the three pay targets. However, Pay Formula No. 1 is not the only formula that could hit those targets.

FIGURE 5–9
Targets and Formula No. 2—Acme Corp.

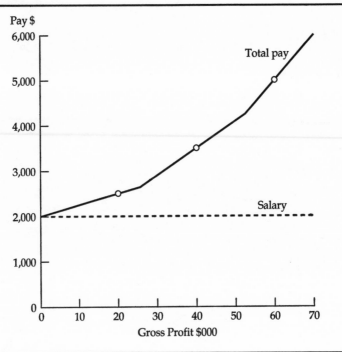

Alternative Formulas

Figure 5–9 shows another possible progressive-rate formula for Acme Corp.:

    Pay Formula No. 2
       Salary: $2,000
       Incentive pay:

- 2.5% of gross profit to $25,700, plus
- 6.0% of gross profit from $25,700 to $52,500, plus
- 10.0% of gross profit over $52,500

Pay Formula No. 2 provides a steeper rate for the highest sales category, 10 percent compared to 7.5 percent in Pay Formula No. 1. More exciting, but exposing the company to higher cost for gross profit above $60,000 in a month.

FIGURE 5–10
Targets and Formula No. 3—Acme Corp.

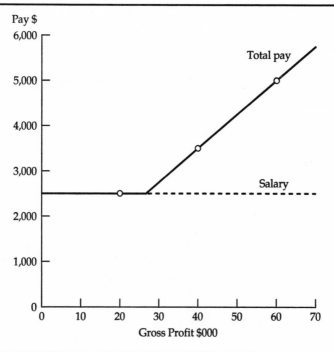

If the company would raise the base salary, Acme Corp. could use the set-aside formula illustrated in Figure 5–10:
    Pay Formula No. 3
      Salary: $2,500
      Incentive pay:

• 7.5% of gross profit in excess of $26,700

Pay Formula No. 3 may be simpler to understand, and the incentive rate matches the top rate of Pay Formula No. 1.

Each of those three formulas hits within a few dollars of Acme's target monthly pay at high, normal, and marginal gross profit for a month. However, the formulas differ in the total amounts they would pay during a year. Tables 5–2, 5–3, and 5–4 show projected earnings under each formula for three of Acme's sales engineers,

TABLE 5–2
Acme Corp. Sales Pay Examples at Low Gross Profit (Total pay
[salary + commission] under each of three pay formulas)

		Terry Timid, Sales Engineer		
Month	Gross Profit ($000)	Formula No. 1 (Pay $)	Formula No. 2 (Pay $)	Formula No. 3 (Pay $)
1	10	2,250	2,250	2,500
2	5	2,125	2,125	2,500
3	25	2,750	2,625	2,500
4	40	3,500	3,500	3,498
5	10	2,250	2,250	2,500
6	25	2,750	2,625	2,500
7	15	2,375	2,375	2,500
8	40	3,500	3,500	3,498
9	5	2,125	2,125	2,500
10	35	3,250	3,200	3,123
11	20	2,500	2,500	2,500
12	10	2,250	2,250	2,500
Total	240	31,625	31,325	32,619
Average	20	2,635	2,610	2,718

based on last year's sales records. Table 5–4 includes a summary of earnings.

The sales engineer who consistently produces very high gross profit would earn more under Pay Formula No. 2 than under Pay Formula No. 1 or No. 3 because Pay Formula No. 2 offers the highest top commission rate. On the other hand, the sales engineer with very low gross profit for the year would earn more under Pay Formula No. 3 than under either of the other two formulas, because Pay Formula No. 3 provides higher survival pay with its base salary of $2,500.

Additional formulas could be developed in which the incentive pay is calculated as a percent of salary or as a percent of the normal target pay. There are many ways to get to the answers that you want. Do not settle for the first formula that comes close to your

TABLE 5–3
Acme Corp. Sales Pay Examples at Normal Gross Profit (Total pay
[salary + commission] under each of three pay formulas)

		Robin Right, Sales Engineer		
Month	*Gross Profit ($000)*	*Formula No. 1 (Pay $)*	*Formula No. 2 (Pay $)*	*Formula No. 3 (Pay $)*
1	30	3,000	2,900	2,748
2	40	3,500	3,500	3,498
3	60	5,000	5,000	4,998
4	50	4,250	4,100	4,248
5	20	2,500	2,500	2,500
6	80	6,500	7,000	6,498
7	50	4,250	4,100	4,248
8	60	5,000	5,000	4,998
9	30	3,000	2,900	2,748
10	10	2,250	2,250	2,500
11	30	3,000	2,900	2,748
12	20	2,500	2,500	2,500
Total	480	44,750	44,650	44,232
Average	40	3,729	3,721	3,686

targets. Try other formulas. You might find one that better fits
your motivational aims or is easier to remember.

Changing Targets

As you develop the formula, you might want to change your
targets. Go ahead. Everything is tentative until the plan is final. Do
not feel locked into an early decision about the marginal pay target
or the high pay target. This is a cut-and-try process. Do not strive
for great precision. Suppose you had set normal target pay at
$3,000. To reach $3,000 at normal sales, you calculate a commission rate of 5.172 percent. A commission rate of 5 percent would
pay $2,900, $100 less than your target of $3,000. Settle for the
convenient, easy-to-remember 5 percent rate. Make up the additional $100 by adding it to base salary or to the target pay for
another incentive criterion.

TABLE 5–4
Acme Corp. Sales Pay Examples at High Gross Profit (Total pay [salary + commission] under each of three pay formulas)

		Willie Wonder, Sales Engineer		
Month	*Gross Profit ($000)*	*Formula No. 1 (Pay $)*	*Formula No. 2 (Pay $)*	*Formula No. 3 (Pay $)*
1	50	4,250	4,100	4,248
2	60	5,000	5,000	4,998
3	70	5,750	6,000	5,748
4	100	8,000	9,000	7,998
5	60	5,000	5,000	4,998
6	40	3,500	3,500	3,498
7	80	6,500	7,000	6,498
8	40	3,500	3,500	3,498
9	60	5,000	5,000	4.998
10	90	7,250	8,000	7,248
11	40	3,500	3,500	3,498
12	30	3,000	2,900	2,748
Total	720	60,250	62,500	59,976
Average	60	5,021	5,208	4,998

Summary of Averages

	Gross Profit ($000)	*Formula No. 1 (Pay $)*	*Formula No. 2 (Pay $)*	*Formula No. 3 (Pay $)*
Terry Timid	20.0	2,635	2,610	2,718
Robin Right	40.0	3,729	3,721	3,686
Willie Wonder	60.0	5,021	5,208	4,998

FORMULA TESTING

Finally, test the formula. Using your computer spreadsheet program, run the sales pay formula against a variety of sales patterns, month-by-month, as was done in the Acme Corp. example. Where possible, use sales data from your company's records. Use at least one year's data; three are better. Check the payouts and the cost of selling for several categories of sales results: median salesperson, high producer, superstar, marginal, poor. When you check earnings under the new formula, calculate earnings for 12 individual months. Do not assume that earnings for a typical month translate into total yearly earnings. Salaries, set-asides, progressive rates, and other variables affect monthly earnings differently. Take the time to calculate month-by-month sales and earnings, then sum the monthly figures to get the estimated annual earnings.

As a result of your testing, you might decide to fine-tune the formula or other features of the pay plan. You might even decide to discard the formula and start over. That is the purpose of testing. Chapter 6, "Pay Variance," gives you something else to look for in your testing.

Before you leave the computer, run one or two tests using sales results far beyond prior sales achievements of anyone in your sales force. Such a what-if may actually occur. This test gives you an opportunity to decide in advance how to deal with it. Chapter 10, "Windfall Sales," discusses this issue. Print out the various test runs to illustrate the new sales pay plan to other members of management and to the sales force.

NEGATIVE BALANCE

When designing a pay plan, you need to decide how you will deal with a negative incentive pay balance. Some companies treat all negative balances alike, others make a distinction between two types of negative incentive balance:

1. Positive sales volume, but less than the minimum in a set-aside formula.
2. Negative sales volume due to cancellation of previously credited sales.

In either case, the salesperson receives less sales credit than needed to earn incentive pay for that incentive period. The question is whether to consider that situation as simply a zero incentive period, or to treat the shortfall as a negative balance to be carried forward and charged against incentive earnings in later periods. That question has no one right answer for all companies. A review of the issues, however, might help you decide what best fits your company.

Zero-Balance

In a zero-balance pay plan, the company forgives negative balances. The salesperson gets a fresh start in the next incentive period. Under this approach, the salesperson who experiences very low sales months and high sales months receives greater total earnings than if the salesperson sold the same total volume in equal monthly amounts. It costs the company more and may overly reward the erratic producer. However, if sales fluctuate greatly in your company, a zero-balance plan may prove simpler to administer and less discouraging than a negative-balance plan. You can bring incentive pay earnings to your target amounts by planning for the kind of sales pattern of past sales records. If, however, salespeople in your business can manipulate the timing of sales orders or shipments, beware of creating an incentive to delay sales from a zero-incentive month into an incentive-earning month.

Carry-Forward

In a carry-forward pay plan the company charges any negative balance from one month to the following month or months. Under such an arrangement, the month-to-month pattern of sales has less effect on the salesperson's earnings. The carry-forward approach does require keeping records of balances and including them in the monthly incentive pay calculation. The satisfying reward for a good sales month may be dampened by the deduction of a negative balance from an earlier month. If the negative balance becomes large it might discourage the salesperson from continuing in the job.

You can minimize the negative motivation effects of negative balances with these two procedures:

1. Set quotas or minimums according to seasonal sales patterns. Do not allow an annual slow season to create a

motivational drag. Good results then means *good for this time of year*.

2. Use the rolling three-month average sales as the basis for monthly incentive pay. The three-month average may absorb enough month-to-month fluctuation in sales to eliminate negative balances as a practical issue. The rolling three-month average also minimizes the "magic day" issue that sometimes encourages delaying sales to build larger volume in the following month.

Whatever your decision about how to treat negative balances, state it clearly and illustrate it in the pay plan document. Both the salesperson and the manager should know exactly how a negative balance will be treated.

The incentive pay formula is a key element in the sales pay plan. By setting pay targets first, you can develop a formula that will produce the payout that you intend. Do not waste time experimenting with formulas until you decide what you want the formula to accomplish.

CHECKLIST FOR INCENTIVE FORMULAS

√ Consider the three most popular types of formulas: flat-rate, set-aside, and progressive.

√ Also consider less common types of formulas: step-up, step-rate, and declining-rate.

√ Select a formula type that fits the company's three pay/sales targets.

√ Develop the formula arithmetic by working back from the three pay/sales targets.

√ Test the formula on varied, realistic monthly sales records.

√ Test the formula on extreme sales results, and check management reaction.

√ Decide what to do about negative balances.

Chapter Six

Pay Variance

The secret to keeping excitement alive.

How much does the salesperson's pay vary from month to month? That fluctuation in income affects the salesperson's performance and satisfaction. The more that pay varies with sales results, the greater its motivational effect on the salesperson. High pay variance means that the salesperson experiences "the thrill of victory and the agony of defeat." A high sales month produces a large paycheck, and disappointing sales likewise reflect in an uncomfortably small paycheck.

Every sales manager knows that incentive criteria and the amount of pay are important elements of a sales pay plan, but many overlook another key element, **pay variance.** This chapter explains the importance of pay variance, how to measure it, and how to get the right amount.

THE FLAT BEER CASE

The Vice President of Marketing and Sales for a company selling ingredients to the brewing industry voiced his frustration. "We are losing market share and our salespeople act like zombies. Maybe they are too comfortable at the current commission rate." The salespeople received straight commission on total sales. No salary, no draw. Their income did exceed the industry median pay. The problem, however, was not too much pay but too little pay variance.

Orders flowed in steadily from established accounts. A typical salesperson experienced only 5 percent fluctuation in income from month to month. After a thorough study, the company adopted a new sales pay plan. It reduced the comfort level for business-as-usual. It also raised the reward for new accounts and for increased volume. Those changes increased the average salesperson's pay variance from the former 5 percent to 18 percent while maintaining the same average income. That meant less security, more risk, and about the same total pay! The salespeople complained long and loud. Gradually, those signs of anxiety faded. A new enthusiasm emerged as the salespeople rediscovered their selling skills and redirected their efforts. Company sales changed from flat to growing. In 18 months the company moved from fourth place in its industry to first place. Pay variance was the key.

WHAT PAY VARIANCE MEANS

Low pay variance gives the salesperson predictable, safe income month after month. Strong or weak sales produce little perceived effect on income. A month of good sales feels much like any other month, and a month of disappointing sales feels about the same. This robs the salesperson of a significant pay response corresponding to variations in sales results.

Steady pay helps satisfy the need for security, but it fails to satisfy the need for achievement. Most successful field salespeople have a strong need for achievement. Their interest declines when pay variance is too low. Some salespeople even refuse to consider a straight salary job because, consciously or unconsciously, they recognize their own need for achievement. They want pay to match accomplishment. Low pay variance produces a ho-hum motivational effect.

At the other extreme, high pay variance offers the salesperson volatile, risky income. Sales success and failure produce sharp swings of income. The salesperson experiences reward in proportion to perceived achievement. Interest and satisfaction remain strong for those with a strong need for achievement. The motivational effect becomes powerful.

When designing a sales pay plan, make sure that you provide strong motivational push. Keep it exciting but tolerable. In one company, a sales increase of 40 percent would be considered a fine achievement, hard to reach. In another company, 20 percent sales gain might be regarded as a notable accomplishment. The plan need not reward in direct proportion to absolute sales fluctuations. You may need to add **leverage** to the pay plan, or perhaps even dampen it. The reward should vary with what salespeople perceive as achievement in your company. To get the right amount of pay variance into your sales pay plan, you must first know how to measure it. Then you can tell when you have enough but not too much.

MEASURING PAY VARIANCE

Measure pay variance in four steps:

- Compile records
- Calculate total pay
- Calculate monthly variances
- Calculate mean variance

Compile Records

To measure pay variance, select for analysis the sales records of several typical salespeople. Choose ordinary producers, not the outstanding ones. You want to evaluate the pay variance expected for middle-of-the-pack salespeople. Later, you will also want to examine pay variance for high producers, marginal producers, and trainees. Include in your analysis at least 12 consecutive incentive periods. If you calculate incentive pay monthly, include at least 12 consecutive months. If you figure incentive pay quarterly, include at least 12 quarters. You may even use more than 12 incentive periods to increase the statistical reliability of your analysis. Recent data, however, generally give a more accurate forecast of the period-to-period sales pattern likely for next year. Study the records of several typical salespeople for the past one to three years. The simplified examples in this chapter show records of one salesperson for 12 months.

Calculate Total Pay

After compiling the records, determine the total pay received by the salesperson in each incentive period. When auditing an existing pay plan, record the actual pay received. When evaluating a proposed pay plan, apply the new pay formula to the old sales data and record the pay that would have been received. Study the total pay received, not the amount earned. Include all payments for salary, draw, commission, and bonus. Credit the amount of commission paid in excess of any draw or pay-back. Credit deferred compensation to the incentive period in which the salesperson receives the money. Count all pay received. Do not include automobile or other expense reimbursements. Such expenses should not be confused with the pay the salesperson receives.

The salesperson's 12-month record of sales and pay might look like the data in Table 6–1.

Calculate Variances

Now calculate the percent of change in total pay from period to period. Divide total pay for a period by total pay for the preceding period, and subtract one (1.00). The result is the variance for one period.

Pay Variance = (Month 2 Pay ÷ Month 1 Pay) − 1.00

Examples of pay variance calculation:

A. January total pay = $4,000
   February total pay = $4,400
   $4,400 ÷ $4,000   =   1.10
                           −1.00
                      _____
                      0.10 or 10% variance

B. February total pay = $4,400
   March total pay   = $3,500
   $3,500 ÷ $4,400   =   0.82
                           −1.00
                      _____
                      0.18 or 18% variance

TABLE 6–1
Sales and Pay Record Example (Sales in $ 000, pay in $. Commission 2.5% of sales)

Month	Sales	Draw	Commission Earned	Commission Balance	Commission Paid	Total Pay
			Ted Typical, Sales Rep			
1	$ 110	$2,000	$2,750	$ 750	$ 750	$ 2,750
2	120	2,000	3,000	1,000	1,000	3,000
3	70	2,000	1,750	(250)	0	2,000
4	120	2,000	3,000	1,000	750	2,750
5	120	2,000	3,000	1,000	1,000	3,000
6	140	2,000	3,500	1,500	1,500	3,500
7	130	2,000	3,250	1,250	1,250	3,250
8	150	2,000	3,750	1,750	1,750	3,750
9	90	2,000	2,250	250	250	2,250
10	130	2,000	3,250	1,250	1,250	3,250
11	130	2,000	3,250	1,250	1,250	3,250
12	140	2,000	3,500	1,500	1,500	3,500
Total	1,450					36,250
Average	120					3,020

Record the absolute variance percentage, omitting plus (+) and minus (−) signs. If total pay for a period is zero, record 999% as the variance for the zero pay period and for the following period.

Record the variances in a column added to the salesperson's work sheet, as shown in Table 6–2.

Calculate Mean Variance

The mean, or average, variance provides a convenient number for evaluating the pay variance of a sales pay plan. Add the variances for all periods under study and divide by the number of variances, as in Table 6–2. Twelve months of pay data provide 11 variances. The mean of those 11 variances shows the motivational impact that you can expect from the sales pay plan. The larger the mean variance, the greater the motivation value—within limits.

TABLE 6–2
Pay Variance Calculation Example (Sales in $ 000, pay in $. Commission 2.5% of sales)

			Ted Typical, Sales Rep				
			Commission			*Total Pay*	
Month	*Sales*	*Draw*	*Earned*	*Balance*	*Paid*		*Variance*
1	110	$2,000	$2,750	$ 750	$ 750	$ 2,750	
2	120	2,000	3,000	1,000	1,000	3,000	9%
3	70	2,000	1,750	(250)	0	2,000	33
4	120	2,000	3,000	1,000	750	2,750	38
5	120	2,000	3,000	1,000	1,000	3,000	9
6	140	2,000	3,500	1,500	1,500	3,500	17
7	130	2,000	3,250	1,250	1,250	3,250	7
8	150	2,000	3,750	1,750	1,750	3,750	15
9	90	2,000	2,250	250	250	2,250	40
10	130	2,000	3,250	1,250	1,250	3,250	44
11	130	2,000	3,250	1,250	1,250	3,250	0
12	140	2,000	3,500	1,500	1,500	3,500	8
Total	1,450					36,250	
Average	120					3,020	20

LOW LIMIT

How much pay variance is enough? What does it take to avoid a ho-hum condition? The author's consulting experience indicates that mean pay variance of 10 percent should be considered as the low limit. Below that amount of variance, excitement and satisfaction abruptly drop away. In company after company, 10 percent has proved to establish the "**threshold** of indifference" in pay variance. A commission plan with 8 percent mean pay variance provides a motivational effect no greater than that of a straight salary plan. You must have at least 10 percent mean pay variance to get real motivational push.

The Ted Typical example shown in Table 6–2 provided mean pay variance of 20 percent. Ted Typical experienced an exciting amount of pay variance as his sales rose and fell month by month

TABLE 6–3
Low Pay Variance Example (Sales in $ 000, pay in $. Commission 2.5% of sales)

			Ted Typical, Sales Rep				
				Commission		Total	
Month	Sales	Draw	Earned	Balance	Paid	Pay	Variance
1	110	$2,800	$2,750	$ (50)	$ 0	$ 2,800	
2	120	2,800	3,000	200	150	2,950	5%
3	70	2,800	1,750	(1,050)	0	2,800	5
4	120	2,800	3,000	200	0	2,800	0
5	120	2,800	3,000	200	0	2,800	0
6	140	2,800	3,500	700	50	2,850	2
7	130	2,800	3,250	450	450	3,250	14
8	150	2,800	3,750	950	950	3,750	15
9	90	2,800	2,250	(550)	0	2,800	25
10	130	2,800	3,250	450	0	2,800	0
11	130	2,800	3,250	450	350	3,150	13
12	140	2,800	3,500	700	700	3,500	11
Total	1,450					36,250	
Average	120					3,020	8

during the year. If the company were to raise Ted's draw from $2,000 to $2,800, as in Table 6–3, the mean variance would fall to a ho-hum 8 percent. This example illustrates how paying too much in draws or salary can kill the excitement of a pay plan, even though the total pay for the year remains the same. In the example shown in Table 6–3, Ted Typical experiences little change in monthly total pay. The differences in his monthly sales are largely blotted out of Ted's paycheck by the large draw.

HIGH LIMIT

Although low pay variance dampens enthusiasm, too much pay variance also produces negative results. Excessive pay variance can drive away satisfactory producers who lack the financial or emotional resources for large swings in income. Everyone likes upswings, but many cannot stand large downswings. Sometimes it is the spouse who prefers steady income, even if the total pay is lower. A two-income family, however, may find enough cushion in two paychecks to cover basic living expenses when the salesperson has a few low months.

Some managers argue that a good salesperson should not have low months. "That's his problem, not mine." Some managers even like the idea of letting low pay drive poor producers out of the sales force. In reality, however, many potentially satisfactory producers do suffer slack sales periods. Sales may sag for many reasons: seasonality, temporary business interruptions, a trainee learning to sell, vacation time, sickness, or the normal ebb and flow of sales orders. The sales manager should be concerned about how the salespeople react to their pay, and about keeping potentially satisfactory producers in the sales force. The decision to retain or terminate a salesperson remains a management responsibility. The pay plan, however, should supplement the manager's efforts to build a productive sales force by providing the right pay variance.

Just how much pay variance is too much? The answer to that question depends upon three factors:

- Amount of pay
- Incentive periods
- Personality

Amount of Pay

The author's experience shows that, more than any other factor, the amount of pay normally earned by the salesperson determines acceptable pay variance. The higher the pay, the greater the pay variance that salespeople will tolerate. Table 6–4 shows the maximum mean monthly pay variance that salespeople generally will tolerate at different pay levels.

In designing a pay plan for lower-paid sales jobs, you face a narrow range of suitable pay variance. For example, at $2,000 per month normal total pay (salary, draw, and commission), the pay plan should provide mean monthly pay variance of at least 10

TABLE 6–4
Maximum Acceptable Pay Variance, by Pay Level

Typical Monthly Total Pay	Tolerable Mean Variance
$ 2,000	15%
3,000	20
4,000	25
5,000	30
6,000	35
7,000	40
8,000	45
9,000	50
10,000	55

percent but not more than 15 percent. For salespeople whose earnings average $10,000 per month, however, the acceptable mean monthly pay variance may range up to 55 percent.

Table 6–5 shows sales pay variance for a sales representative named Rocky Rhodes. The variance exceeds the acceptable limit for most salespeople at the level of pay shown. The months at $2,000 income create hardship for sales rep Rhodes, who is accustomed to earning about $3,000. The discomfort may prompt Rhodes to make a job change, even though total pay for the year is acceptable.

Table 6–6 shows pay variance similar to that for Rocky Rhodes, but in this case H. V. Hitter has higher average earnings. The salesperson will accept the low months even though the mean pay variance is high. Sales rep Hitter finds satisfaction in the same mean pay variance that sales rep Rhodes found unacceptable. They differ only in the level of earnings. Higher average earnings allow the salesperson to tolerate greater variation in total pay from month to month.

TABLE 6–5
Excessive Pay Variance Example (Sales in $ 000, pay in $. Commission 2.5% of sales)

			Rocky Rhodes, Sales Rep				
			Commission			Total	
Month	Sales	Draw	Earned	Balance	Paid	Pay	Variance
1	70	$2,000	$1,750	$ (250)	$ 0	$ 2,000	
2	70	2,000	1,750	(250)	0	2,000	0%
3	120	2,000	3,000	1,000	500	2,500	25
4	160	2,000	4,000	2,000	2,000	4,000	60
5	140	2,000	3,500	1,500	1,500	3,500	13
6	180	2,000	4,500	2,500	2,500	4,500	29
7	120	2,000	3,000	1,000	1,000	3,000	33
8	150	2,000	3,750	1,750	1,750	3,750	25
9	120	2,000	3,000	1,000	1,000	3,000	20
10	80	2,000	2,000	0	0	2,000	33
11	70	2,000	1,750	(250)	0	2,000	0
12	160	2,000	4,000	2,000	1,750	3,750	88
Total	1,440					36,000	
Average	120					3,000	30

Incentive Periods

More frequent incentive periods increase tolerance for pay variance. Salespeople will accept up to one-third more pay variance in weekly than in monthly incentive periods. The shorter period means less at risk and a faster recovery time. If the incentive period is quarterly, those same salespeople will tolerate one-third less pay variance. These findings support the argument in favor of shorter incentive periods.

When the incentive period is daily or transaction-based, salespeople view their earnings in either weekly, monthly, or quarterly periods. To learn how they perceive the incentive pay period, listen to the salespeople. "This has been a slow month for me." "I really earned my pay this week." When in doubt, plan for one-month incentive periods. Table 6–7 shows the effect of the fre-

TABLE 6–6
High but Acceptable Pay Variance Example (Sales in $ 000, pay in $. Commission 2.5% of sales)

			H. V. Hitter, Sales Rep				
				Commission		Total	
Month	Sales	Draw	Earned	Balance	Paid	Pay	Variance
1	140	$2,000	$ 3,500	$1,500	$ 1,500	$ 3,500	
2	200	2,000	5,000	3,000	3,000	5,000	43%
3	220	2,000	5,500	3,500	3,500	5,500	10
4	300	2,000	7,500	5,500	5,500	7,500	36
5	280	2,000	7,000	5,000	5,000	7,000	7
6	400	2,000	10,000	8,000	8,000	10,000	43
7	240	2,000	6,000	4,000	4,000	6,000	40
8	300	2,000	7,500	5,500	5,500	7,500	25
9	250	2,000	6,250	4,250	4,250	6,250	17
10	160	2,000	4,000	2,000	2,000	4,000	36
11	150	2,000	3,750	1,750	1,750	3,750	6
12	250	2,000	6,250	4,250	4,250	6,250	67
Total	2,890					72,250	
Average	240					6,020	30

quency of incentive periods on the average pay variance that salespeople will tolerate.

Personality

Salespeople with a strong need for achievement find satisfaction in the very nature of high pay variance. They like having a tangible score (pay) based on their own sales results. However, salespeople have other motivational needs also. The opportunity to satisfy those other needs may reduce or increase an individual's tolerance for pay variance. For example, a person with a strong need for status may find enough satisfaction in representing a prestigious company to tolerate a large average pay variance. The personality of the individual combines with other satisfactions of the job to influence how much pay variance that person will accept.

TABLE 6-7
Maximum Acceptable Pay Variance, by Frequency

Typical Monthly Total Pay	Incentive Period		
	Weekly	Monthly	Quarterly
$ 2,000	20%	15%	10%
3,000	27	20	10
4,000	33	25	13
5,000	40	30	17
6,000	47	35	20
7,000	53	40	23
8,000	60	45	30
9,000	67	50	33
10,000	73	55	37

Unfortunately, no simple test can tell you how much pay variance each person will accept. You have to generalize about the degree of pay variance that will fit your sales force. You control two factors, amount of pay and incentive periods. The third factor, personality, reminds you that no general guideline applies in all cases.

INCENTIVE/SALARY RATIO

Pay variance depends partly on the ratio of incentive pay to base salary. If the normal incentive opportunity equals less than 20 percent of the base salary, it is unlikely that total pay variance will average above the 10 percent minimum mentioned earlier. However, you can determine whether the pay plan is motivationally strong only when you calculate the mean pay variance. In the Flat Beer Case cited earlier, the salespeople experienced extremely low pay variance even though the company paid on a straight commission plan with no draw or salary. Pay variance depends on sales patterns, pay plan components, and incentive pay formula in addition to the incentive/salary ratio. Changing the incentive/salary ratio is only one of several ways to control pay variance.

CONTROLLING PAY VARIANCE

Before making the pay plan final, bring pay variance within the limits of effectiveness (low limit) and acceptability (high limit). The higher the mean pay variance, the stronger will be the motivational power of your pay plan. However, if you find that pay variance is too great, reduce it with one or more of these changes:

1. Increase salary, reduce incentive pay.
2. Increase draws.
3. Lengthen the incentive period (consider a rolling three-month average).
4. Reduce or eliminate a set-aside and lower the commission rate.
5. Reduce or eliminate a progressive-pay formula.
6. Adopt a declining-rate pay formula.
7. Reduce or eliminate bonuses.
8. Increase the number of incentive pay criteria.

If you want to increase pay variance, make one or more of these changes:

1. Reduce salary, increase incentive pay.
2. Reduce or eliminate draws.
3. Shorten the incentive period.
4. Increase a set-aside and increase the incentive pay rate.
5. Make the incentive formula more progressive.
6. Offer larger bonuses.
7. Reduce the number of incentive pay criteria.

Follow a process of cut-and-try. A computer spreadsheet program is the ideal tool for trying out various pay arrangements. Decide how much pay variance you want, then modify the plan to get it. Make a change and test it on the sales records of typical salespeople (median producers). You will soon arrive at a plan that produces both target pay and suitable pay variance for typical salespeople. Then test it on the sales records of high producers and marginal producers. You may find additional opportunity to fine-tune the plan.

If you revise the plan, verify that the revised formula will produce the intended target pay amounts at normal, high, and marginal sales levels. Anything that changes pay variance also
changes the pay earned in high sales periods. Check for the effect
on the earnings of high producers. If their pay falls below the
amount that you intend, add to the pay plan a bonus or a special
incentive rate that applies only to consistently high sales results.
On the other hand, if the revised pay plan produces more pay than
you intended for high producers, reconsider your high pay target.
High pay for a few high producers costs only a small fraction of the
company's total selling expense. You will make a detailed cost
analysis later. For now, satisfy yourself that the pay plan comes
close to your pay targets and that it provides an exciting degree of
pay variance.

A HAZARD

Increasing the pay variance usually revitalizes a sales force.
However, it does not always work that way. Security-seekers may
find only anxiety in an achievement-oriented pay plan. The character of the sales force changes as achievement-seekers replace the
security-seekers who leave. If that turnover is abrupt and extensive, however, the company may suffer by losing continuity in
customer relations. The company may also lose sales momentum
as it replaces moderate producers with trainees. To avoid a dis-
turbing upheaval, increase pay variance gradually. Make pay plan
changes in steps over six months, or guarantee a minimum level of
earnings during several months of transition. A manufacturer of
industrial chemicals guaranteed no reduction in earnings for six
months after a new, higher-risk pay plan went into effect. That
brought a sigh of relief to those who had been worried about the
reduced salaries that accompanied increased incentive opportunity in the new pay plan. In less than four months they were all
selling well ahead of quota—and earning more than before.

Adequate pay variance is essential to a motivationally powerful
pay plan. Anyone would accept a low-risk, high-reward opportunity. Many will accept low risk, low reward. To produce top sales

results, however, you need those who will accept a high-risk, high-reward opportunity. Pay variance measures the degree of risk provided. Make it risky enough to be exciting—and satisfying to the achievement seekers.

You may be surprised to observe the metamorphosis of formerly security-oriented salespeople to achievement-seekers. This may occur as they experience the reality of opportunity pay and learn that they can perform well and prosper accordingly. From the Flat Beer Case through many others, the author has often witnessed such changes in salespeople. It is true that most people gravitate toward jobs and behaviors that conform to their established motivational pattern. Security seekers tend to find jobs that offer security. However, people can learn new sources of satisfaction. Before writing off any trained salesperson as nonresponsive, give that person a chance to try out the excitement and reward of a sales pay plan with plenty of pay variance.

CHECKLIST FOR PAY VARIANCE

√ Measure pay variance as the absolute percentage change in total pay (salary + commission + bonus) month to month.

√ Test for average monthly pay variance for ordinary salespeople.

√ Provide at least 10 percent average pay variance to keep interest alive.

√ Provide up to the maximum tolerable pay variance to get maximum motivation value.

√ Adjust the sales pay plan as needed to produce enough but not too much pay variance for ordinary salespeople.

√ Adjust the sales pay plan as needed to produce target pay amount and adequate pay variance for high producers also.

Chapter Seven

Salaries and Draws

Survival income: Enough, not too much.

Both salaries and draws serve the same purpose in sales compensation: survival income. That is, money to carry the salesperson over occasional low months. Recruiting and retaining a superior sales force usually requires that the company provide some form of survival income. Few full-time salespeople today will work for straight commission only.

Although they share the same purpose, salaries and draws function quite differently. Draws offer potential for mischief to sales force morale. Salaries, on the other hand, can provide a means to recognize individual qualifications and length of service—without the problem potential of draws. And salaries need cost no more.

This chapter explains the advantages and disadvantages of both salaries and draws. It includes guidelines for where and how to use each form of survival income.

Without survival income, some potentially satisfactory salespeople will leave the sales force. Low income will force them out during a slack sales period. Even well-trained, experienced salespeople encounter slow sales periods. The reasons vary, from business cycles to personal illness. Companies concerned about preserving their investment in salespeople usually offer a draw or a salary. Some companies find that they can recruit the salespeople they want only if they provide some such form of survival income.

DRAWS

A draw provides an advance payment against future commission income. A draw is a loan from the company to the salesperson, to be repaid out of the salesperson's commission earnings. If it is charged only against commission for the month in which the draw is granted, it is called a **guarantee** or a **nonrecoverable draw.** Most draws, however, are **recoverable** by the company out of commission earnings of later months. If the salesperson leaves the job, the company absorbs any negative balance as a loss. A draw, compared to straight commission, shifts some risk from the salesperson to the company. Table 7–1 illustrates pay calculations under a recoverable draw arrangement.

Management may negotiate draws on an individual basis. One company offers large draws to experienced sales applicants as a demonstration of confidence in the person's ability to earn that much eventually in commissions. A heavy equipment manufacturer negotiates draws only if and when requested by the salesperson. For example, a salesperson brings in a large order, but shipment and commission income will occur three months later. The salesperson may request the company to advance one-half the commission as a draw. In another company, a long-service salesperson's commissions have been low for three months. He needs a new set of tires for his car, so he asks for a draw. Some companies individually negotiate a regular monthly draw for each salesperson. They may base the draw on the amount requested and the salesperson's past or projected earnings.

Individually negotiated draws permit the manager to exercise discretionary control over the amount at risk for each salesperson. That control may seem attractive from the company's financial viewpoint, but it also brings a negative effect. It puts the salesperson into a dependent posture, pleading for kindly consideration from the manager. At least, that is the emotional effect on those salespeople with a strong need for achievement. They are the ones who love to control and hate to be controlled. Negotiating draws with salespeople tends to lower the manager's leadership stature, putting the manager into a reactive position instead of a strong,

TABLE 7–1

Recoverable Draw Example (Negative draw balances carried forward. Sales in $ 000, pay in $. Commission 2.5% of sales)

			Mildred Median, Sales Rep			
			Commission			Total
Month	Sales	Draw	Earned	Balance	Paid	Pay
1	110	$2,000	$2,750	$ 750	$ 750	$ 2,750
2	120	2,000	3,000	1,000	1,000	3,000
3	60	2,000	1,500	(500)	0	2,000
4	95	2,000	2,375	(125)	0	2,000
5	120	2,000	3,000	875	875	2,875
6	110	2,000	2,750	750	750	2,750
7	120	2,000	3,000	1,000	1,000	3,000
8	130	2,000	3,250	1,250	1,250	3,250
9	70	2,000	1,750	(250)	0	2,000
10	120	2,000	3,000	750	750	2,750
11	110	2,000	2,750	1,125	1,125	3,125
12	100	2,000	2,500	500	500	2,500
Total	1,265					32,000
Average	105					2,666

proactive role. Individually arranged draws can also lead to charges of favoritism or discrimination. The alternatives are either a regular formal draw policy or no draws.

Draw Amount

Companies with large sales forces usually avoid individual discretionary deal making about draws. Most establish a regular policy to govern draws. The draw policy may set a fixed dollar amount, such as $1,500 per month. Another method bases the draw on prior commission earnings, such as 50 percent of the salesperson's prior 12-month average commission.

If you set the draw too high, it may rob the salesperson of job satisfaction. When sales are low, the draw may fill the income valley too much. When sales are high, repayment of the draw cuts down the income peak. A large draw thus reduces the salesperson's opportunity to experience monthly rewards and penalties consistent with sales results. One month seems much like any other. Thus, the major—and often unrecognized—risk of a large draw is that it may reduce pay variance to the level of indifference. (See Chapter 6, "Pay Variance," for guidelines to the pay fluctuation needed to keep excitement alive.)

In extreme cases, draws not only reduce job satisfaction but they force turnover—the very thing the draws were intended to prevent. The salesperson may come to feel that three months of good sales would not be enough to wipe out accumulated indebtedness to the company. The salesperson then leaves the job for a fresh start elsewhere. The company absorbs the negative balance and spends additional money to recruit, train, and start over with yet another beginner. You can help avoid problems with draws by setting the draw at a low level of survival income. See Chapter 3, "Pay Targets," for a discussion of acceptable low survival income.

Accounting for Draws

Company accounting practices often hide the compensation cost of draws. The accountant may charge draws as loans, separate from sales compensation, because the salesperson has not yet "earned" that amount as commission on completed sales. By accounting for draws as loans, the company defers payroll taxes and overstates its current income. When the salesperson later sells enough, the earned commission repays the draw balance to the company. The salesperson is then obligated to pay taxes (income, social security, etc.) on the money received earlier as draws. In some cases, this leaves no money for the salesperson to take home. As earned commissions repay earlier draws, the company reduces the draw balance and charges the earned commission amount as compensation cost.

If the salesperson leaves the job owing a negative draw balance, the company may charge the amount as a bad debt. After all, it was never "earned" as commission. Such accounting practice may let the company avoid payment of payroll taxes. The same tax loophole also hides the draw as part of the sales compensation cost. To understand the actual cost of your company's sales compensation, record the forgiven and absorbed draws together with other compensation costs. Do this for internal analysis if not for tax reporting purposes.

Inside Straight

Never draw to an inside straight. That familiar advice for poker players recognizes two points. First, you have little chance of drawing the card you need. Second, even if you do catch the right card, another player probably will hold a better hand and you will lose anyway. Drawing to an inside straight is for losers. You can say the same for some sales pay draws. Consider the case of a company we will call Inside Straight, Inc. The company manufactures office machines. It sells directly to businesses of all types and sizes.

This company designed its sales pay plan on the philosophy of "pay what the company can afford." It was a commission-with-draw plan. Recruiting difficulties gradually pushed up the draw to $2,000 per month. However, few trainees could earn $2,000 per month in commissions during their early months on the job. The negative balance of their draw accounts sank them deeper and deeper into debt to the company. About every 12 to 18 months, complaints and turnover would rise to an alarming degree. Whenever that happened the company forgave the negative draw balances and gave everyone a fresh start. Those with large balances felt relieved. Those who had recently paid off their balances felt cheated.

The company later adopted a new draw repayment policy. It allowed the salesperson to keep at least half of the commission earned in a month, regardless of a negative draw balance. This feature helped morale somewhat. However, it added to the complexity of recordkeeping. Errors and confusion surrounded draw account records and the rate at which a salesperson could climb out of the hole was slowed. Salespeople saw the new policy as a mixed blessing, at best.

Turnover at Inside Straight, Inc. continued at the astounding rate of 12 percent per month! Most who quit did so owing the company from $4,000 to $6,000. The company discharged anyone whose draw balance threatened to exceed $6,000. The controller treated forgiven draws as bad debts, and did not include them in sales compensation cost reports. This hidden cost was buried among other bad debts.

Inside Straight, Inc. was a second-tier company, with limited brand name recognition, small market share, and a history of product quality problems. Those factors combined to make this a difficult selling job. It was especially difficult for the marginally qualified juniors the company hired. They could not survive on the company-affordable commission schedule. They were drawing to an inside straight. The pay plan did nothing to create a winning situation for either the salespeople or the company.

A horror story like this needs a happy ending, and there is one. A new president ordered an independent study of sales compensation. The compensation consultant found that the hidden cost of draws added four percentage points to the already worrisome cost of selling. The greater problem, however, was the cost of turnover. The company constantly fielded a rookie team. Too few stayed long enough to become satisfactory producers.

When he learned how the old philosophy of "affordable pay" was destroying the company, the president approved a new pay plan. The new plan pays an adequate base salary plus an attractive set-aside commission. Trainees are not permitted to earn commission until after graduating from an intensive one-month training program. The company pays no draws. Sales force turnover dropped to 1.8 percent per month from the former 12 percent, and sales rose dramatically. The company continues to build its share of market, with a healthy profit. The company might now be called Royal Flush, Inc.

Guarantee

If a company forgives any negative balance at each month end, that is called a guarantee or a nonrecoverable draw. The company

TABLE 7–2

Guarantee (Nonrecoverable Draw) Example (No carry forward of any negative draw balances. Sales in $ 000, pay in $. Commission 2.5% of sales)

		Norman Normal, Sales Rep		
Month	Sales	Guarantee	Commission	Total Pay
1	110	$2,000	$2,750	$2,750
2	120	2,000	3,000	3,000
3	60	2,000	1,500	2,000
4	95	2,000	2,375	2,375
5	120	2,000	3,000	3,000
6	110	2,000	2,750	2,750
7	120	2,000	3,000	3,000
8	130	2,000	3,250	3,250
9	70	2,000	1,750	2,000
10	120	2,000	3,000	3,000
11	110	2,000	2,750	2,750
12	100	2,000	2,500	2,500
Total	1,265			32,375
Average	105			2,697

promises that the salesperson will earn commissions equal to or above the guarantee amount. If not, the company makes up the difference. It does not carry forward any negative balance to following months. Table 7–2 illustrates pay calculations under a guarantee or nonrecoverable draw.

A flat-rate commission plan with a guarantee functions the same as a salary with a step-up commission formula. The guarantee ensures survival income. The company calculates commission on all sales from the first dollar, provided that sales exceed the volume needed to earn the guarantee.

Companies often provide a guarantee during a training period. When training is completed, the company may replace the guarantee with a regular draw or no draw. This arrangement avoids discouragement during the training period. It lets the new salesperson experience the thrill of victory without the agony of defeat.

Solving Draw Problems

Draw arrangements with the fewest problems usually provide two features. First, they hold draws to a low level of survival pay. Second, they offer enough earning opportunity to permit almost all salespeople to repay their draws within two months. Draws that are large in relation to commission earnings invite trouble. Complex or inaccurate recordkeeping, with frequent questions about the correct balance, also invite trouble. Confidence deteriorates when salespeople sour on the way draws are managed. If you have difficulties with draws in your sales pay plan, consider one of the following three solutions.

Guarantee. Cancel negative draw balances at the end of each month. This is less likely to seem unfair to the high producers. It is almost the same as paying a salary.

Automatic forgiveness. Cancel all negative draw balances every 3, 6, or 12 months. This may seem unfair to salespeople who have repaid their draws, but it gives a fresh start to those who are in debt to the company. Such a modified guarantee may reduce sales force turnover.

Eliminate draws. Change the pay plan to provide built-in survival pay. Provide a commission schedule that ensures adequate income for the salesperson whose performance is marginal or better. The alternative most likely to help in recruiting and retention is to offer survival pay in the form of a salary.

SALARIES

A salary is the simplest method to build survival income into your sales pay plan. A salary means regular base pay, paid monthly, semimonthly, biweekly, or weekly—without regard to sales results. You can include salary as part of any sales pay plan, regardless of the type of incentive pay arrangement. Salary provides survival income to satisfy the need for security while incentive pay provides variable income to satisfy the need for achievement, that is, security pay and opportunity pay. Base your decision about including salary on considerations of motivation, not on cost. The decision to provide a salary need not affect the pay plan's total cost.

Sales salaries usually are administered under one of four methods:

- Single rate
- Territory rate
- Performance rate
- Experience rate

Single Rate

Companies that pay salespeople under a salary-plus-incentive plan usually administer the salary portion separately from the company's regular salary program. The fact that salespeople receive a substantial part of their total pay in the variable form of incentive pay makes direct comparison to other salaried jobs difficult, impossible, or irrelevant. Job evaluation and the traditional classification of jobs into grades and salary ranges usually does not fit comfortably into the incentive-oriented thinking of sales managers and salespeople. The company may set the salary for all salespeople at a single figure, such as $2,000 per month. By increasing the salary from time to time, the company can keep total pay (salary plus incentive) at competitive levels. This is the most common sales salary arrangement—simple if not elegant.

Territory Rate

Another method fits each salesperson's salary to the specific sales territory. The company pays larger salaries in high-volume territories to reflect the added work of servicing many accounts. Or, the company may pay larger salaries in thin territories to recognize the lower incentive pay opportunity and the greater effort needed in missionary work. Territory-based salaries are not widely used, but this technique does fit the needs of some companies with widely differing territory potentials.

Performance Rate

Some companies use a performance-based salary program. The salary depends upon the salesperson's sales record. At the end of the year, management evaluates each salesperson's results. Top performers receive large salary increases, others get ordinary increases, and poor performers get no increase. In other arrangements, the company may grant salary increases by management discretion, by traditional performance appraisal rating, or by a formula defined at the start of the year.

Experience Rate

Another sales salary method that fits the aims of many companies bases each salesperson's salary on length of service and related experience. A schedule of starting salaries and subsequent increases guides individual salary actions. A standard schedule of salaries helps to ensure fairness throughout the sales force at hiring and it helps to control costs. Table 7–3 shows one company's sales salary schedule.

The company represented in Table 7–3 places value on experience. Each year of experience increases the monthly salary by $100, or about 5 percent. Experience beyond six years, however, has no added value in this company. The company finds no difference in productivity or stability between salespeople with 7 years of experience and those who have been selling for 10 to 20 years. The salary schedule reflects the company's evaluation of experience and of the competitive labor market.

The company reviews its salary schedule each year to keep total pay (salary plus incentive) at the competitive target level. When surveys show that competitive pay has increased by 4 percent or more, the company adjusts its salary schedule. They also adjust the salaries of all the salespeople. Thus, in one year a salesperson might receive an experience-based increase to the next salary level plus a schedule-adjustment increase. The aim is to keep total pay competitive while also reflecting the value of added experience.

TABLE 7–3
Sales Representative Salary Schedule Example

Years of Related Sales Experience	Monthly Salary
0–1	$ 2,000*
1–2	2,100*
2–3	2,200*
3–4	2,300*
4–5	2,400*
5–6	2,500†
6+	2,600†

* Increases must be based on added length of experience plus satisfactory sales performance.
† Not a hiring rate; promotion only. Requires superior sales performance for increase to this salary.

An experience-based salary schedule can help in hiring and in retaining salespeople. It provides a consistent guide to salary determination for field managers throughout the company. The step increases recognize the value of added years of experience and give the salesperson another reason for staying. Many salespeople accept a published salary schedule more readily than they accept discretionary control of their salaries.

Even with an experience-based salary schedule, the manager is involved. The hiring procedure calls for the manager to evaluate prior sales experience. Some companies provide guidelines to assist the manager, such as the example shown in Table 7–4.

A large company can establish experience-equivalent guidelines from statistical analysis of sales successes and failures among the company's sales force. A company with a small sales force, however, may lack a sufficient statistical base for analysis. In that case, the company must rely on the judgment of the manager.

TABLE 7–4
Sales Experience Guidelines Example

Sales Experience	Length of Service Equivalency
Field selling in our company	1 year = 1 year
Field selling other packaging machines	1 year = 0.8 year
Field selling other large industrial machines	1 year = 0.6 year
Field selling any industrial product	1 year = 0.4 year
Field selling any product or service	1 year = 0.3 year
Inside selling industrial/mechanical products	1 year = 0.2 year

If you use an experience-based salary schedule, you may also consider relating quotas to salary. Do you expect the more experienced salespeople to bring in greater sales volume than their less experienced colleagues? If so, you can build that into the quotas or the incentive formula. Reexamine the expected sales amounts for various levels of experience. Revise the quotas or formulas to produce the pay you want at the sales you expect for each level of experience.

CAUTION

Whatever method you use to set salaries or draws, do not base the starting salary or draw on the new salesperson's past earnings in another company. That practice could land your company in expensive litigation charging illegal discrimination. It did so in the case of *KOUBA and EEOC v. Allstate Insurance Company*, 27 FEP Cases 938 (1982). The theory is that a salary based on past earnings may perpetuate past pay discrimination. Female and minority applicants can sue. To avoid that kind of legal hassle, establish simple, uniform guidelines for salaries and draws. Do not leave it to each manager's notion of what is fair. Offer salaries or draws that recognize the value of the job in your company and the value of the individual's training or experience. Decide upon your pay plan, then find the best people you can get for the pay you offer.

Pay them fairly. That will not only keep your company out of court, it will help your company prosper.

Straight commission without salary or draw may be sufficient if substantial sales momentum assures your salespeople of regularly earning commissions at or above a minimum survival income. Much industrial and wholesale selling, however, requires a salary or draw to attract suitable people to the job and to provide survival income over low periods. If you use salary or draw, keep it at an uncomfortable survival level. Let incentive pay provide the swing that keeps total pay variance exciting and rewarding.

CHECKLIST FOR SALARIES AND DRAWS

√ Use salary or draw to provide survival income for low sales periods.

√ A draw is a loan or advance, to be repaid from future commission earnings.

√ A large negative draw balance may discourage the salesperson.

√ A guarantee is a draw with no negative balance carried forward.

√ A salary provides regular base pay, with no offset against commission earnings.

√ A salary need cost no more than a draw, if the pay plan is properly designed.

√ Keep salaries and draws low enough to avoid dampening pay variance below the level of exciting motivation.

Chapter Eight

Bonuses, Contests, and Awards

Special achievement = special reward.

When your marketing strategy or tactics call for a special achievement, consider offering a special award. You may use a cash bonus plan or a contest with substantial prizes or a simple award program providing a plaque or lapel pin. These powerful tools of sales management remain neglected by too many companies.

This chapter explains how and where such special motivators work best. Knowing why bonuses and contests work may help the sales manager get more motivational mileage out of the regular sales pay plan elements. The guidelines for bonuses, contests, and awards also point out pitfalls to avoid.

Universal Optical Products Company pays $500 whenever a sales representative opens a new account. That is a bonus. And, for this year, the company will also provide a European trip for two to the sales representative who sells the largest volume of a new line of eyeglass frames. That is an award or a prize. Bonuses, contests, and awards overlap in concept and in the principles that can make them powerful add-ons to most sales pay plans.

Bonuses and awards differ from regular commissions. Companies pay commissions on a regular basis, such as once a month. Companies pay bonuses and awards infrequently, such as once a year or upon a special accomplishment. Commissions generally reward near-term sales results, whether measured in dollar volume, units, gross profit, or some other measure. Bonuses and awards reward something other than the regular, day-to-day sales function. Many of the principles of incentive pay planning presented in earlier chapters apply also to bonuses and awards.

Some managers overlook the potential of bonuses and awards. They fail to recognize the special value of giving an extra push toward certain goals. Surveys report that fewer than one-half of all companies use bonuses or awards in their sales compensation programs.[1] One manager feels that the regular salary and commission should be enough. To that manager, bonuses and awards seem to be gimmicks that are not worth the added cost. Another manager rejects these special incentives because of a disappointing early experience. Yet another manager has never looked into the possible application of bonuses and awards.

Certainly bonuses and awards do not suit every company. However, 9 out of 10 companies would benefit from a well-designed bonus or award plan. You can decide whether your company has sales goals that would fit a bonus or award program. You can then design the program for those goals.

BONUSES

Bonus Criteria

You can use a bonus as a reward for sustained high-level performance over a long period or for a special achievement. The following are some examples of bonus criteria from various companies.

High sales volume. "The company will pay a bonus of $1,000 to any sales representative whose sales exceed 10,000 cases in any quarter. The bonus will be paid in addition to the regular commission."

---

[1] See, for example, *1991/92 Sales and Marketing Personnel Report* (Fort Lee, N.J.: Executive Compensation Service, Inc., 1991), p. 40.

High gross profit. "The company will pay a bonus at year-end, based on territory gross profit percentage (GP). The bonus will equal the sales engineer's base salary multiplied by 5 times the territory GP over 30 percent. Thus, if the GP is 33 percent, the bonus will be 15 percent of salary."

New accounts. "For every new account over three, the sales representative will earn a bonus of $200 each quarter. A new account is one that has not bought over $500 in the past 12 months and orders $1,500 or more in one quarter."

Full-line sales. "The company will pay a bonus of $1,000 to each sales representative who sells 20 percent or more of his/her total quarterly sales volume in each of the A, B, and C product categories. A sales representative will earn no bonus if any category is less than 20 percent of total sales."

New product sales. "You will earn an extra 10 percent commission at the end of June this year on all sales of Model 1038 during this three-month introductory period. In addition, you will be paid a bonus of $50 for each in-store special promotion exhibit you set up before the end of July this year. (Submit photo of exhibit and store manager agreement.)"

Expense control. "If your travel and entertainment expenses (measured as a percentage of sales) for this year are less than last year's percentage, you will earn a bonus of $500."

Collections. "The company shall pay a bonus of $200 to each sales representative whose accounts receivable average less than 40 days during a quarter."

Special activity. "Any sales engineer who staffs a booth at one of the regular trade shows will earn a bonus of $200 for each day spent on working the show."

Bonus Timing

Schedule bonuses according to the bonus criteria. For recurring measures such as high sales volume, make the bonus periods quarterly or semiannual. Some companies pay bonuses when a certain transaction occurs, such as any sale of $50,000 or more. Some pay a bonus when a salesperson reaches a certain goal, such as establishing the 10th new account. Occasional or irregular bonuses are useful where the criterion is a special event or is short-lived, such as launching a new product or clearing old inventory.

Do not be concerned that providing an occasional bonus might set a precedent that you must follow for every future similar event, such as a new product introduction. Just make sure that you explain the bonus plan to the salespeople, and make clear that it is a one-time bonus opportunity. However, if you repeat such bonuses frequently, your actions will establish expectations regardless of what you say. Keep your practice consistent with your statements. If it is to be an ongoing bonus opportunity, design it that way. If it is to apply only to a single event, do not repeat it frequently. You do not want to create a temptation for salespeople to postpone sales in anticipation of the next bonus opportunity.

Bonus Size

Make the bonus opportunity big enough to capture the attention and interest of your salespeople. Small bonuses produce small effort. Ideally, the bonus should provide a realistic opportunity to earn at least 10 percent over normal total pay (salary plus commissions) for the bonus period. However, in some low-risk/low-opportunity jobs, bonuses as small as 5 percent have stimulated extra effort.

A longer bonus period lets you talk about larger dollar amounts for bonuses. However, salespeople react on a percentage-of-pay basis, even if they do not consciously recognize that concept. A $2,500 bonus opportunity each quarter will stimulate more motivation than a $10,000 bonus opportunity for the year. The same principle of frequency applies here as with regular commission or incentive pay. (See Chapter 6, "Pay Variance.")

To limit the cost while providing bonuses of adequate size, you can (1) reduce the number of bonus offers, (2) raise the bonus criteria, or (3) otherwise reduce the number of potential winners. Better yet, budget enough money to make attractive bonuses available to many. For strong motivation value, design the bonus program so that about 30 percent of the salespeople are likely to earn bonuses.

Risk

Provide enough risk to keep it interesting. Avoid predictable bonuses. If most of your salespeople can plan on receiving a 15 percent bonus at the end of every year, the bonus is no longer an effective motivator. Adjust the bonus criteria to provide an opportunity to earn a special reward for special achievement. Otherwise, the salespeople will regard the bonus as deferred salary or an entitlement. Use a set-aside formula with a high minimum or use a highly progressive bonus formula. Do not make it too easy to win—nor too difficult. Provide a real chance to win big, to win small, and to win not at all. Use the same kind of analysis of expected results that was discussed in Chapter 3, "Pay Targets."

Document

If the bonus is not part of the regular sales pay plan, draft a separate bonus plan document. As with the salary and commission parts of your sales compensation program, put the bonus plan in writing. Give each salesperson a copy of the signed and dated bonus plan that includes:

- Eligibility—Who is in, who is out, effect of employment termination
- Criteria—What results will earn a bonus
- Size—How large is the bonus
- Timing—When the bonus period begins and ends

Discretionary Bonus

Avoid discretionary bonuses. Chapter 2, "Pay Plan Types," discusses the psychological reasons that discretionary bonuses lack strong motivational value. Congratulate effort, but pay for results.

The salesperson must know in advance how to earn the bonus. Even if you base the bonus on a subjective evaluation of performance, the salesperson needs to know in advance what elements you will evaluate. Make those criteria as specific as possible.

For example, one company pays a bonus to each salesperson whose presentation at a trade show is rated satisfactory or better by the sales manager. This compensates the salespeople for the time they take to prepare and to attend the trade show. It encourages them to rehearse for first-rate presentations. They know they will be judged on the quality of visual aids, clarity of key points, and audience reaction.

Discretionary bonuses primarily satisfy the person granting the award. However, because the bonus is decided after the fact, it does nothing to steer effort. Do not waste money on discretionary bonuses. Instead, invest in a bonus plan that rewards for clear, defined goals.

AWARDS

The Million Dollar Roundtable, the President's Club, Top Salesperson of the Year . . . those are recognition awards that companies offer to encourage sustained effort. Companies usually grant such recognition awards for a full year's sales results or cumulative achievement over a longer time. Some grant them for short-term objectives, such as Most New Accounts in July. Awards offer the most flexible sales compensation element you can use.

A few companies grant awards with large dollar value, such as an all-expenses paid cruise for two to exotic ports. Many companies offer merchandise awards by assigning points to certain sales accomplishments. The salesperson exchanges points for merchandise from a catalog. Opinions differ about the motivational potential of high-value awards versus purely symbolic awards. You can hear wonderful stories from vendors of prizes about the stimulus gained by adding a few thousand dollars in prizes. Yet, many companies operate effective awards programs at little cost. They provide recognition with certificates, plaques, and pins. Decide how much to invest in prizes based on your knowledge of the salespeople and the company's culture.

What makes an award program effective? Recognition is the key factor for success—all else is secondary. Awards appeal to the widespread motivational need for recognition—to be somebody, to stand out. Smart sales managers long ago spotted the opportunity to use recognition as a positive motivational tool. Few managers outside of sales have yet learned the power of recognition in managing people. Some executives even dismiss the notion that people work for more than just money. Those same executives, however, may insist upon their own recognition symbols: a reserved parking space, large office, beautiful furniture, and certificates hanging on the wall. The need for recognition is indeed widespread. The field salesperson spends most working hours away from the people whose recognition means the most—the boss and fellow workers. An award program provides a means to help fill that void with an opportunity to satisfy the need for recognition.

Publicize Awards

Let every salesperson know how to win an award. Dramatize the program with advance publicity and continuing progress reports. Make the award ceremony something special and memorable for the winners. (That probably rules out the company cafeteria as the site for the ceremony.) In no case should you just mail out the awards. The aim is not prizes, but recognition. And that means that every employee should know about the awards.

Perhaps the idea of arranging and conducting an enthusiastic awards ceremony does not fit your own personality. Perhaps it seems childish to you. If so, get someone else to do it. Select someone who is alert to the motivational needs of people. Perhaps the organization culture of your company would not be consistent with balloons and a Dixieland jazz band at the awards ceremony. If so, you might find some ideas in the Nobel Prize ceremonies— the same room is available for rent in Stockholm. If Sweden seems too far away in miles and cost, you might consider a dining yacht or dinner at a fine restaurant. Borrow a page from the entertainment industry with their Oscar and Emmy award ceremonies for the Hollywood stars. (How they thrive on that recognition!)

Provide a permanent physical symbol of the award—your own Oscar, a plaque, a pin, a trophy, a framed certificate, a necktie or scarf with the company logo woven in. Yes, salespeople *do* hang those plaques in their homes and offices. They *do* wear the pins and tie clasps that they win. Recognition value can survive for a long time, if you plan for it.

As you plan the awards program, make sure the publicity reaches into the home. Involve the salespeople's spouses or companions by inviting them to the awards ceremony. Extend recognition for their support of the salespeople. Acknowledge their tolerance of the long hours and travel. Recognize the spouses'/companions' contributions through encouragement and interest in the salespeople's careers. It costs little to involve them, but the payoff can be big when you get two people working for the same goal.

Prizes, Prizes

Scale your contest awards to the level of achievement. Offer several prizes in a contest. Many salespeople simply will not try for a single prize. "The guy in Chicago has a hot territory—he's bound to win." Although many salespeople seem competitive by nature, few will strive for prizes that seem out of reach. Do offer awards in different categories or for different levels of achievement: bronze, silver, and gold. Here are some prize categories that companies have used to get wide interest: top sales territory in each region, most sales in first year, greatest improvement, most new accounts, most orders over $1,000, largest single order. With multiple prizes, most of your sales force will see the contest as an interesting opportunity—one worth working for.

If you decide to offer valuable awards, do not ignore the recognition element. Include recognition with the valuable prizes to multiply their motivational worth. Make sure that the prizes are luxury items, products of deluxe quality. Even with a limited budget, you can meet this standard. It is better to award a $100 gold pen and pencil set than to award a $100 12-inch television set. They cost the same, but only one is deluxe. Fit the prizes to the interests of your salespeople. Not everyone wants a set of golf clubs. A young couple with small children may not be able to enjoy a cruise to exotic ports. Consider alternative-choice awards—the trip *or* a video entertainment center. The catalog prize services fit this need by letting the winner choose the prize at the designated point value. Do not miss the opportunity to engrave the award information on the prize itself. In any case, give a plaque or framed certificate with the prize. No matter how much the prize may be worth, the major value of an awards program is in the recognition that you provide with it.

Bonuses and awards can add another dimension to your sales motivation objectives, and at a reasonable cost. Include them in your sales compensation budget and planning.

CHECKLIST FOR BONUSES, CONTESTS, AND AWARDS

√ Add a bonus, contest, or award plan to provide special reward for special results.

√ Make the bonus or contest period short enough to keep interest alive.

√ Provide a bonus worth working for—10 percent of salary or more.

√ Include enough leverage to make the bonus risky—not too easy, not too difficult to win.

√ Put the plan in writing to avoid misunderstandings.

√ Avoid discretionary bonuses.

√ Provide plenty of recognition in any contest or award program.

√ Give only luxury prizes, if any.

√ Give multiple prizes, many chances to win.

Chapter Nine

Territories and Quotas

How to set them, when to change them.

This chapter is for the 80 percent of companies in which territories and/or quotas matter—or should matter. Here is advice on how to determine whether a company should consider one or both of these elements in sales pay plan design. Guidelines for setting territories include advice on when and how to change them.

A quota-based pay plan can give the company flexibility in changing territories and quotas can help control costs and excessive compensation. Setting quotas, however, provides the most frequent source of morale-busting complaint in sales organizations. This chapter explains how to earn respect for your decisions about territories and quotas.

A **territory** is the geographic area and/or accounts assigned to a salesperson. The salesperson is expected to sell in that territory, and the salesperson will get credit for sales from the assigned territory. A **quota** is the amount of sales expected of the salesperson. Territories and quotas often go hand-in-hand in the process of designing the sales pay plan.

Some companies use neither territories nor quotas. They reward any sale from anywhere. Salespeople may overlap, even compete with each other. This condition characterizes such industries as insurance, real estate, securities, and many other types of consumer-direct selling. In every industry, however, some companies decide not to follow the crowd. Instead, they do what makes sense for them.

Many companies assign salespeople to territories but do not use quotas. The company assigns the salesperson to a geographic area but specifies no expected level of sales results. Management does not tell the salesperson what sales results are expected, and the company uses no quota in determining pay. Flat-rate commission plans usually operate without reference to quotas, even though the salespeople may be assigned to territories. The territory assignments separate the salespeople, preventing overlap, and ensure coverage of the market. Almost all industrial and wholesale organizations assign sales territories, even if they do not use quotas. Thus, territories and quotas are separate but related topics.

TERRITORIES

Use of Territories

For most companies, sales territories serve important purposes. The company manages its market coverage by assigning each salesperson to a sales territory. The territory may include (1) a specific geographic area such as a city, state, or several states; (2) a certain category of accounts such as independent department stores, national store chains, or government agencies; or (3) accounts designated by name. Sometimes the territory combines a geographic area and assigned accounts.

Territory layout should provide effective and efficient sales coverage of the market. The company wants a certain level of sales presence in the areas most likely to produce sales—or perhaps in all areas. In some companies, however, sales compensation becomes the major reason for arranging sales territories. "When a salesperson starts to earn too much, the company reduces the territory." That charge, often made by salespeople, rarely proves valid. More often, when a company allows compensation objectives to intrude into territory layout, it is for the opposite reason. "We should add another rep in California for the additional coverage. However, if we reduce Bob's California territory, he will earn less. We do not want to lose Bob." The company passes up the opportunity for increased sales coverage in California to keep

Bob's earnings up. Forcing territory to follow compensation is seldom desirable and never necessary. Most successful companies design territories strictly for sales coverage. They then design the pay plan to fit the expected pattern of sales results.

Planning for an intended level of sales presence helps both the company and the salesperson. The company establishes a clear level of expectation. Both parties then know how well results measure up to those expectations. Both know where the salesperson should invest time to avoid costly wandering and overlapping.

Setting Territories

Territory layout means more than drawing lines on a map to separate salespeople. Territory layout usually considers sales potential and efficiency of serving the area. You might estimate sales potential for an area from one or more statistics, such as:

1. Sales forecasts by company salespeople
2. Company's past sales
3. Total industry sales
4. Number of prospects
5. Economic capacity to buy (e.g., see *Sales & Marketing Management* magazine's annual "Survey of Buying Power")
6. Sales correlates (e.g., housing starts predict sales of plywood, roofing felt, furniture, carpeting, appliances, landscape plants, and telephones)

Sales potential, if used alone, may fail to establish territories that the salespeople will regard as fair and reasonable. Consider also the ease of access: How difficult and time-consuming will it be for salespeople to reach the prospective customers? A "rich" territory offers many good prospects concentrated in easy-to-reach locations. A "thin" territory might have the same total sales potential, but the prospects are spread over a large area. Sales in a thin territory come more slowly and require more effort. Not only territory size but competition may influence the evaluation of a territory as thin or rich.

While every salesperson would like to have a rich territory, management may regard the rich territory as understaffed. Management sees sales being missed due to insufficient contacts and follow-up. Management may also regard the salesperson in the rich territory as getting a free ride, working only the best leads, and leaving too many sales to competitors. The salesperson is too comfortable and could do more.

In contrast, management may view coverage in a thin territory as ideal. The company seems to be getting almost all the sales it could get from the area, and the salesperson must travel and work hard for those results. The ratio of compensation to sales results may seem ideal in a thin territory. However, it pays to examine the total cost of selling in relation to sales results for the total sales force. In analyzing sales force productivity, you probably will find that neither extremely thin nor extremely rich territories produce an ideal ratio of sales volume to cost-of-selling. The optimum territory usually stands somewhere between rich and thin, leaning somewhat to the thin side.

Changing Territories

Analyze territories at least annually to spot opportunities to improve sales force productivity (sales divided by cost-of-selling). Look for places to improve sales coverage or to lower cost by adding or reducing salespeople or realigning territories. Changing territories, however, may disturb established customer relationships. "Just when I get used to working with a representative from your company, you bring in someone new." If that sort of customer complaint concerns you, use caution in making territory changes.

Salespeople as well as customers may become upset by territory changes. A territory change can seem like having to start over. The salesperson must build new customer relationships, break ties with former customers, and work harder. The change could mean expanded opportunity and increased earnings. However, when you announce a territory change, the common reaction is likely to reflect anxiety. Few companies do a good job of explaining to their salespeople the rational analysis behind territory changes. Techniques described later in this chapter can help you change territories without creating a major anxiety attack in the sales force.

A few companies use territory assignment as a promotion opportunity. When a rich territory becomes available, the company offers it to the salesperson with the strongest sales record. If that person does not want the territory, the company offers it to the person with the next best record, and so on. Most companies, however, do not offer an open territory as a reward to other salespeople. Companies generally follow one of two practices to fill an open territory: (1) appoint the salesperson who seems best suited to the territory or (2) hire a new salesperson for the open territory. Transferring an established salesperson into a vacant territory fills one opening but creates another—with twice the number of customers subjected to a change of relationships. The company concerned about ongoing customer relationships should be reluctant to move a salesperson who is producing satisfactory sales results.

When future territory changes seem likely, such as in a rapidly expanding sales organization, try to make those changes in small steps. Frequent changes establish the expectation of change, and small changes are easier to accept than large changes. This practice helps destroy the notion that the salesperson owns the territory. It may also avoid a painful reduction from overly high earnings.

Moving a salesperson to a richer territory seldom poses a problem. However, if you are asking a salesperson to surrender part or all of an established territory for a thinner territory, consider a phase-out/phase-in arrangement. A distributor of semiconductor chips uses the policy shown in Table 9–1 when changing territory assignments.

QUOTAS

Using a quota-based incentive pay formula reduces any economic reason for a salesperson to fear a change of territory. A quota-based pay plan provides rewards for sales results in relation to the sales potential of the territory. A rich territory with a high quota

TABLE 9–1
Phase-Out/Phase-In Policy

If an account is transferred from one sales engineer to another, the company will divide credit for sales from that account between the sales engineer losing the account and the one gaining the account as follows:

	Sales Credit	
Month	Losing Sales Engineer	Gaining Sales Engineer
1*	100%	0%
2	80	20
3	60	40
4	40	60
5	20	80
6	0	100

* Through the first full month following account transfer. Example: Transfer March 10, credit losing sales engineer 100% through April, 80% through May, etc.

may equal the income potential of a thin territory with a lower quota. The company pays for results measured against the potential of the territory. Thus, the quota balances the earnings potentials of otherwise unequal territories. However, the prospect of dislodging established, comfortable customer relationships may still present something of a hurdle. (See Chapter 4 for discussion of absolute and relative incentive criteria and Chapter 5 for discussion of incentive pay formulas.)

Setting Quotas

What does *quota* mean to you? In some companies it means 100 percent of expected sales. In other companies *quota* means a lower or higher amount. Companies A, B, and C anticipate sales of $100,000 per month from a territory. Company A sets its "realistic" quota at $100,000, a sound basis for planning and for evaluating results. Company B sets a "minimum" quota at $80,000, the lowest acceptable level of sales, not the full sales volume expected. Company C, in contrast, sets a "stretch" quota of $120,000. The salesperson could reach that stretch quota, but $100,000 is expected. The sales manager in Company C believes that salespeople strive to reach quota—as long as it seems accessible. Therefore, that company uses a stretch quota for its sales pay plan.

Which quota definition is correct? Take your pick. While neither the realistic, minimum, or stretch quota is right or wrong, each is clearly different. Make sure that those concerned with pay planning and budgeting in your company understand your definition of quota and how it relates to sales forecasting. This book uses quota to mean 100 percent of expected sales volume. The realistic quota fits into any type of sales pay plan, and it facilitates tracking actual sales against expected results. Regardless of which quota definition you use for sales compensation, the financial executive will use the realistic quota amount (actual sales forecast) to plan cash flow and financing for the year ahead.

Whether you intend to use a realistic, minimum, or stretch quota for sales management, you need a procedure for setting the quota for each salesperson. Companies use a variety of quota-setting procedures, such as the following.

Arbitrary. The president of one distributing company meets with his banker and accountant. They decide what income the company will need to service its debt and to produce the desired return to the stockholders. The president uses that figure to set the company's total sales goal for the year. He then divides the total sales goal among the sales territories as quotas. Not surprisingly, the salespeople regard their quotas as arbitrary, unrelated to market conditions. The company lacks sales force buy-in for the quotas, and the motivational effect is negative.

Territory trend. The most common method of setting quotas is simply to project each territory's sales from prior years. This may be simple, but consider what it does to the best salespeople. The person's own sales record establishes a higher quota that may unfairly penalize the salesperson for past sales success. One way around this issue is to apply to each territory the same company-wide sales trend. For example, the company expects a 15 percent total sales increase, and that amount is applied to each territory. Under that arrangement, the salesperson who has been growing a territory by 20 percent per year continues to benefit from that past performance instead of being hobbled by it.

Multiple inputs. Sales projections by salespeople often suffer from optimism, "sandbagging," and other impediments to accuracy. Sometimes the person is just too close to the trees to see the forest. Recent events, perceived threats from competitors, or shaky relations with a key customer can color the salesperson's projections. To balance the field view of potential sales, the company may use multiple inputs to the quota-setting process.

One manufacturer bases quotas on a company-wide sales forecast developed from three sources. First, the company develops a mathematical trend analysis of company and industry sales over five years. (Such sales trend analyses usually produce more accurate forecasts when calculated on a percentage or logarithm basis instead of a dollar or unit basis.) Second, the company compiles territory projections by individual salespeople. Third, the marketing and sales executives give their opinion of market outlook. The president reviews all three inputs and decides upon a sales forecast. He explains the analysis and conclusions to the sales force. The president then allocates the sales forecast among the territories, applying similar multiple inputs for each territory. The salespeople in this company recognize that the forecasting process is thoughtful and analytical. Although no system is perfect, the salespeople accept the quotas as reasonable. The salespeople have been involved in the process, and they know how carefully the president has planned.

Correlation analysis. Sales trends and correlation analysis can provide powerful statistical tools for quota setting. A manufacturer of specialty food products found that a logarithmic trend line from past sales provided a highly accurate forecast of future total sales. It was more accurate than the combined projections of individual salespeople and the regional sales managers. The national sales manager then allocated the trend-line total sales forecast among territories according to the Buying Power Index from *Sales & Marketing Management* magazine. This produced quotas that the salespeople accepted as fair and reasonable.

Statistics alone can trap the unwary sales manager. A manufacturer of outboard motors found that sales in the Midwest generally correlated with the acres of open water in a territory. The more acres of water, the more outboard motors sold. The sales manager extended the formula to other parts of the country. However, acres of open water in New York Harbor and San Francisco Bay produced few sales for small outboard motors. The company lost some good salespeople through quota frustration before the sales manager abandoned the magic of computer-generated quotas. Complete mathematical objectivity can be a mixed blessing in quota setting. Management judgment should continue to provide an important part of the process.

BUYING POWER

The most widely used statistical basis for territory analysis and for setting quotas is the annual Survey of Buying Power published by *Sales & Marketing Management* magazine. Primarily directed toward consumer sales, the same statistical base has applications also in wholesale and industrial sales. The survey compiles data by state, city, county, and metropolitan area. It covers three major categories of data:

- Demographic
- Economic
- Distribution

Demographic

The demographic information includes population- or household-based data by categories of sex, age, and so on. You might reasonably expect to sell more where there are more people of the age and sex who buy your products—if other factors are equal.

However, other factors are *never* equal, so you need to know about other factors.

Economic

People in some areas have more money to spend than do those in other areas. Income levels are important, but so are taxes; the difference is disposable income. Those people with greater disposable income present the potential for buying more than others. The survey shows disposable income levels for every area.

Distribution

The third factor describes store sales by types of stores in each area. From drugstores to automobile distributors, you can learn the sales volumes in each area. Such distribution data can help you determine where your products should be moving.

The survey provides store sales volumes with three categories of demographic, economic, and distribution data for each state, county, city, and metropolitan area, and for the total United States. From that information, you can calculate the percentage of your company's total sales to be expected from each geographic area and each demographic category. That can be a key to establishing reasonable, realistic territories and quotas.

The annual survey report published by *Sales & Marketing Management* magazine includes detailed instructions about how to use the data to set quotas and evaluate territories. It may seem complicated at first reading, but work out some examples for yourself to see its value. If you do not like to deal with so many numbers, consider having a consultant assist in the analysis. The annual Survey of Buying Power provides a valuable source of basic market data. It is available at modest cost from:

Sales & Marketing Management
Bill Communications
633 Third Avenue
New York, NY 10017
(212) 986-4800

APPEAL PROCESS

Even with the best of management intentions, any territory or quota assignment might seem unfair to some salesperson. Should you negotiate with the salesperson and risk loss of leadership stature—or should you stick to your decision and risk seeming arbitrary and dictatorial? The most capable managers choose a middle course. First, they tell the salespeople how they set the territories and quotas. They explain the statistical analyses and the judgmental considerations in their efforts to provide fair and reasonable sales expectations. They then offer an appeals process. Any salesperson who believes that an error has been made in fact or in judgment may submit a written appeal. If management review finds the appeal to be valid, the manager makes the change if possible. In any case, senior management replies promptly, explaining why the appeal was or was not approved.

A simple appeal procedure, presented in writing and followed faithfully, can demonstrate management's concern for fairness. It does so without implying that complainers get favored treatment or that management fears questions about its decisions. Requiring that the appeal be submitted in writing places the burden on the salesperson to think through the complaint and assemble a credible argument.

If yours is one of the 80 percent of companies in which territories and/or quotas matter for compensation purposes, give those important elements the careful attention they deserve.

CHECKLIST FOR TERRITORIES AND QUOTAS

✓ Plan sales territories for efficient sales coverage, not primarily for compensation purposes.

✓ Revise territories reluctantly and, if possible, in small increments.

✓ Use quota-based pay to reward in relation to territory potential.

✓ Explain how quotas are set, to obtain acceptance of the quotas as reasonable.

√ Use multiple inputs to quota setting, including salespeople, sales managers, statistical correlations, and trend analysis. Add a full measure of management judgment.

√ Include an appeal process to resolve possible unfairness in quotas.

Chapter Ten

Windfall Sales

A problem or what?

A huge sale or a sudden surge in sales volume—what would that mean for the salesperson and for the company? Too many companies fail to consider the possibility of windfall sales when designing the sales pay plan. Dealing with the matter later may seriously harm management credibility and sales force morale.

Three possible responses to the question of windfall sales lead to two possible courses to follow in sales pay plan design. If windfalls can happen and the company is concerned about the potential payout, this chapter tells what to do. It includes advice on how to minimize the negative effects of windfalls without discouraging selling effort.

After a heavy wind, one can gather many apples from the ground with little effort. Hence the term **windfall** means an unexpected large increase in sales. A large order that the salesperson did little or nothing to produce is called a windfall. It comes as an unexpected gain. Some companies call it a **bluebird,** the symbol of happiness. A windfall sale, however, does not always spell happiness.

VIEWS DIFFER

Chapter 1 included the story of a company president who was unwilling to see a salesperson earn more than the president for a few months—even with a huge order and high profit. Telling this incident to sales managers from different companies brings out three kinds of responses. No one response is right for every company, so consider your own situation.

Some say, "That could never happen in our company. The nature of our selling makes a windfall sale impossible." If that is your situation, you may want to omit the balance of this chapter.

Those giving the second kind of response say, "That was a lucky break, and lucky breaks are part of the attraction of selling. The company made a nice profit. There's nothing to worry about." If your company does not mind paying big when a salesperson gets lucky, then you may want to move ahead to the next chapter.

Managers giving the third kind of response say, "That sale might have been pure luck. No sales rep deserves that much pay, even if the salesperson performed some work to get the order. Advertising, pricing, and the product all contribute to the sale. We have an obligation to the stockholders to control costs and not throw away their money. We do not have to pay that much to keep a good sales force. The company should have some control." If this viewpoint seems reasonable to you, read on. The balance of this chapter can help in planning for windfall sales.

How you plan for windfall sales will depend on the chance of such sales occurring in your company and your philosophy about the amount of reward that is appropriate. Because there is no one right answer to the question of what to do about windfalls, you should consider the alternative methods of control.

CONTROL METHODS

Companies use four methods to control the compensation connected with windfall sales:

- Negotiated commission
- Commission limit

- Carry-forward
- Declining-rate

Negotiated Commission

A negotiated commission may arise without planning. An unusually large order comes in. It may be a surprise even to the salesperson. It may be at a special price. For whatever reason, management regards it as a windfall sale. Normal commission would provide unjust enrichment for the salesperson—at least in the manager's view. The manager decides to impose a reduced commission on that order.

If the manager acts unilaterally after the company accepts the order, the salesperson will feel robbed. State labor commissions keep busy with just such cases of after-the-fact decisions to withhold earned sales commissions. The salespeople who take such claims to the state labor commission or to court almost always win. Instead of trying to force a unilateral decision, the manager can negotiate with the salesperson. The manager may succeed in convincing the salesperson that a reduced commission is reasonable and in the best interest of all parties. If so, the negotiated commission arrangement may be acceptable. (The manager should be commended for superior skills of persuasion.)

More often, an awkward attempt to negotiate a reduced commission frustrates both parties. The salesperson gives up a significant amount of money and may lose respect for the manager. The salesperson may even feel coerced, inferring in the manager's remarks a threat to terminate the salesperson's employment or to kill future chances for advancement. The manager risks losing the negotiation and losing the salesperson's continued loyalty. Such a lose-lose situation results from lack of planning for the possibility of a windfall sale.

Few companies plan for negotiated commissions. However, a policy on negotiated commission can offer the greatest flexibility.

A stated policy alerts the salesperson that it can happen. In case of a legal challenge, a formal policy statement can help the company defend its position, especially if you complete the negotiation before accepting the customer's order. Here is one such policy statement:

> The National Sales Manager may designate any order as a windfall sale before the order is accepted by the company. The National Sales Manager will negotiate with the Sales Representative to arrive at a reduced commission for the windfall sale. Consideration will be given to the work by the Sales Representative in getting the order and the company's gross profit on the order. A reduced commission must be agreed upon before the company accepts the order or the regular commission will apply.

Commission Limit

Some companies put a cap on the commissions that a salesperson can earn in a month, quarter, or year. Here is an example:

> In no event may a Sales Engineer's commissions in any month exceed three times base salary for that month.

Many salespeople and managers react in horror to the idea of limiting the earnings of a salesperson. The very idea of a cap on earnings may seem to violate the traditional slogan of unlimited earnings potential. Many believe that the slogan of unlimited earnings contributes to a pay plan's motivating power. However, studies of sales force turnover indicate that salespeople seek more than a slogan. Experience shows that companies that cap commissions do not suffer from that limitation on earnings—if the maximum commission amount is rarely reached. If less than 2 percent of the salesperson-months reach the limit, the company probably will experience no major morale problem in having such a cap on commissions.

Table 10–1 illustrates the effect of a commission limit on windfall sales. In that example, the large sales volume of month 6 results in the limited commission of $10,000, instead of the $19,000 that the regular commission would otherwise produce.

TABLE 10–1
Commission Limit Example
(Commission = 5.0% of sales up
to $200,000, $10,000 maximum
commission for any month)

Month	Sales ($000)	Regular Commission	Limited Commission
1	$ 80	$ 4,000	$ 4,000
2	90	4,500	4,500
3	100	5,000	5,000
4	120	6,000	6,000
5	100	5,000	5,000
6	380	19,000	10,000
7	100	5,000	5,000
8	80	4,000	4,000
9	120	6,000	6,000
10	100	5,000	5,000
11	140	7,000	7,000
12	80	4,000	4,000
Year	1,490	74,500	65,500
		Difference:	(9,000)

Commission limits can pose some potentially serious problems. A limit on single orders may steer the salespeople away from customers likely to place such orders, especially if large orders require substantial effort to obtain or much additional work after the order is placed. The message to the salespeople may seem to be that the company does not welcome large orders. If the limit is for a short period, such as a month, the salesperson may try to divide or delay orders to stay below the limit. Such manipulation of orders by salespeople may risk losing customer good will. If the limit is for a long period, it may discourage further sales effort after the salesperson reaches the limit. Because of such potential problems and because commission limits seem to run counter to the whole idea of incentive pay, most companies prefer other methods of control.

Carry-Forward

One control method carries forward to the next month any excess credit for windfall sales. Here is one company's policy statement:

> If a Sales Rep's sales volume exceeds $400,000 in any month, the excess will carry forward and be credited in the following month. The carry-forward may roll into successive months.

This method is generally acceptable, especially if the windfall figure is set high enough. Under a flat-rate commission formula, it does not reduce the salesperson's eventual earnings. However, under a progressive-rate formula or set-aside formula, a carry-forward policy would be likely to reduce earnings. The main function of such a policy is to cap the amount payable in one month while still giving full sales credit over time. Table 10–2 illustrates a windfall carry-forward in a flat-rate commission plan. In that example, the excess sales volume from month 6 spreads into months 7 and 8.

If you use this kind of policy, be sure to include a statement in your plan document explaining whether and when carry-forward sales credit will be paid to a terminated salesperson. Many companies dislike the idea of paying anything to a person no longer employed by the company—perhaps even working for a competitor. A step-up or set-aside pay formula can help you avoid paying for such residual sales credits after termination. (See Chapter 5, "Incentive Formulas.") Whatever your policy, spell it out in the sales pay plan to avoid having a judge decide the policy for you.

Declining-Rate

The most effective policy for controlling payments in the event of windfall sales assigns a reduced incentive pay rate to the windfall excess. Here is an example:

> A windfall excess is that sale amount larger than twice the territory's average order for the prior 12 months. One-third of the regular commission rate will apply to the windfall excess.

TABLE 10–2

Carry-Forward Example (Commission = 5.0% of sales up to $200,000, amount over $200,000 credited to following months)

Month	Sales ($000)	Regular Commission	Sales Credit	Carry-Forward Commission
1	$ 80	$ 4,000	$ 80	$ 4,000
2	90	4,500	90	4,500
3	100	5,000	100	5,000
4	120	6,000	120	6,000
5	100	5,000	100	5,000
6	380	19,000	200	10,000
7	100	5,000	200	10,000
8	80	4,000	160	8,000
9	120	6,000	120	6,000
10	100	5,000	100	5,000
11	140	7,000	140	7,000
12	80	4,000	80	4,000
Year	1,490	74,500		74,500
		Difference:		0

Salespeople generally accept this kind of policy without resentment if the windfall definition is set high enough. The salesperson continues to earn something for the added sales volume, even though at a lower rate. The company reduces its cost exposure, with less risk of inviting order delays. You can apply such a declining-rate provision to any incentive pay formula, even a progressive-rate formula. Table 10–3 illustrates payments under a declining-rate provision attached to a flat-rate commission formula. In that example, the large sales volume of month 6 produces the regular commission on the first $200,000 of sales ($10,000), plus a reduced commission on the $180,000 excess sales ($2,600), for a total commission of $13,600. Although it is less than the regular commission would be ($19,000), the declining-rate commission still provides an attractive reward for a large sale or added sales and it is paid in the month of that special accomplishment.

TABLE 10–3
Declining-Rate Example
(Commission = 5.0% of sales up to
$200,000 + 2.0% of sales over $200,000)

Month	Sales ($000)	Regular Commission	Declining Commission
1	$ 80	$ 4,000	$ 4,000
2	90	4,500	4,500
3	100	5,000	5,000
4	120	6,000	6,000
5	100	5,000	5,000
6	380	19,000	13,600
7	100	5,000	5,000
8	80	4,000	4,000
9	120	6,000	6,000
10	100	5,000	5,000
11	140	7,000	7,000
12	80	4,000	4,000
Year	1,490	74,500	69,100
		Difference:	(5,400)

Have you decided that you want to include in your sales pay plan a provision to cover windfall sales? If so, draft a policy statement that covers these points:

Definition

- Single large order or large total sales in a month, quarter, or rolling three-month average?
- "Large" means fixed dollar size or multiple of prior year's average size?
- Applies to any such order or only an order from a company not called on in prior 12 months?
- Set the definition so that less than 2 percent of total salesperson-months in a year will likely reach the windfall category.

Pay Method

- Negotiated
- Limit
- Carry-forward
- Declining-rate

The time to develop a windfall policy is *before* the big event occurs. Make sure that the policy is well communicated as part of the sales compensation program so that there will be no surprise for the salesperson or manager.

CHECKLIST FOR WINDFALL SALES

√ Decide in advance whether windfall sales can occur and whether the company would be concerned about a large commission payment.

√ Define a windfall policy as part of the sales pay plan, if it could become an issue for the company.

√ Specify the definition of a windfall.

√ Specify the special controls on pay that will apply to windfalls.

Chapter Eleven

Costing and Auditing the Plan

Measuring total sales force productivity.

How is the sales pay plan working? How will it work? Whether evaluating an existing sales pay plan or a proposed new one, cost remains an important consideration—the second most important consideration after motivation. Too much emphasis on cost too early in the evaluation can lead to faulty conclusions. Motivation should take precedence in the planning process, but cost cannot be ignored.

This chapter explains how to test the cost-of-selling, territory-by-territory and for the total sales force—even before the new plan is launched. When considering the cost of a pay plan, primary attention should be directed to total cost and total sales results, that is, total sales force productivity. **Productivity** equals sales volume, gross profit, or some other measure of sales results —divided by the cost-of-selling. Productivity means what the company gets for what it spends on selling.

Productivity should not be confused with profitability. Some companies with high cost-of-selling nevertheless produce the highest profits. However, if the cost analysis shows an unacceptable cost-of-selling, the sales pay designer must modify the plan. If cost-of-selling proves too high only in certain territories, other changes may be needed. Here is how to analyze the cost of an old or new sales pay plan.

COSTING

Cost Analysis

Concentrate first on total sales force production (however measured) and total cost-of-selling. Avoid being distracted by the earnings of a single salesperson or the cost of a single sale. Start with last year's sales records. Calculate what each salesperson actually earned and what the earnings would have been each month if the new plan had been in effect last year. If your sales force is large, you can reduce the work of analysis by basing calculations on a representative sample of salespeople. Include at least 20 salespeople in the sample for statistical reliability. Do not select them randomly, but sample at various levels of sales performance. You might pick two from the top 10 percent, two from the next 10 percent, and so on. This will give you a representative cross section of data for cost comparison—what statisticians call a stratified sample.

Old and new. Calculate total cost-of-selling under the new plan and the old plan. Include salaries, draws, commissions, and bonuses. Include travel and entertainment expenses if you are changing those arrangements with the new pay plan. Include the cost of benefits such as paid vacation time, medical insurance, retirement plan, and so on—even if only an estimate—because they are part of the total cost-of-selling. Add in the cost of advertising, promotions, and sales expense. If you limit the cost analysis to cash compensation only, the results will exaggerate the relative cost of any proposed change. Include an allowance for payroll taxes also, but keep the percentage tax allowance the same for both sides of your comparisons. Do not let a change in tax laws confuse the cost analysis.

Be sure to include comparable costs for both the old plan and the new plan. Compare the actual total cost for last year under the old plan and the projected total cost of selling under the new plan. New versus old is the first comparison most executives want to see. In addition to the dollar cost comparison, provide other ways to compare the total cost. Show cost as a percent of sales, and—if at all possible—as a percent of gross profit. Such cost ratios provide useful perspective for anyone considering a proposed change in the sales pay plan. An example of a cost comparison, including measures that give perspective to the dollar figures, is shown in Table 11–1.

Other comparisons. Cost analysis serves as a selling tool to convince others (and yourself) that the new plan makes sense for your company—if in fact it does. In addition to comparing new versus old costs, you might include industry cost data and sales pay survey data, as in Table 11–2. When using survey data, take care to compare similar items. Some surveys do not include the cost of benefits and taxes.

Cost-of-selling includes the total direct selling expenses of all sales representatives—including salaries, commissions, bonuses, and benefit costs, plus travel, meals, lodging, entertainment expenses, and other sales-related expenses. Cost-of-selling usually is expressed as a percentage of the company's total sales, even though companies differ in the percentage of total sales made through the sales force. Therefore, industry-wide statistics should be considered as a rough indicator at best.

The median cost of selling was about 2.2 percent for manufacturing companies in 1991, but one in four companies reported 1.0 percent or less, and one in four reported 3.8 percent or more.[1] Clearly, individual companies differ more within an industry category than one industry average differs from another. A smaller, custom survey may focus more sharply on companies in your particular industry segment. Even so, your own company's historical cost pattern might prove a more useful guide to improvement than the costs of other companies that may operate differently and report costs differently.

Extend your analysis beyond last year's sales and pay data. Show projected future costs at low, normal, high, and very high sales. Remember to calculate costs monthly on realistic sales pat-

---

[1] *1991/92 Sales and Marketing Personnel Report* (Fort Lee, N.J.: Executive Compensation Service, Inc., 1991), p. 38.

TABLE 11–1
Cost Comparison, New versus Old Sales Pay Plans

Example			Old Plan Cost	New Plan Cost	Difference
A. Last year actual					
		Cost Amt.	$4,000,000	$4,000,000	$0
Sales	*$40,000,000*	Cost/Sales	10.0%	10.0%	0.0%
GP 25%	*$10,000,000*	Cost/GP	40.0%	40.0%	0.0%
B. Same sales, higher GP%					
		Cost Amt.	$4,000,000	$4,640,000	$640,000
Sales	*$40,000,000*	Cost/Sales	10.0%	11.6%	1.6%
GP 33%	*$13,200,000*	Cost/GP	30.3%	35.2%	4.8%
C. Higher sales, higher GP%					
		Cost Amt.	$4,250,000	$5,300,000	$1,050,000
Sales	*$50,000,000*	Cost/Sales	8.5%	10.6%	2.1%
GP 33%	*$16,500,000*	Cost/GP	25.8%	32.1%	6.4%
D. Very high sales, very high GP%					
		Cost Amt.	$4,500,000	$6,800,000	$2,300,000
Sales	*$60,000,000*	Cost/Sales	7.5%	11.3%	3.8%
GP 40%	*$24,000,000*	Cost/GP	18.8%	28.3%	9.6%
E. Lower sales, lower GP%					
		Cost Amt.	$3,750,000	$3,020,000	($730,000)
Sales	*$30,000,000*	Cost/Sales	12.5%	10.1%	−2.4%
GP 17%	*5,100,000*	Cost/GP	73.5%	59.2%	−14.3%
F. Lower sales, higher GP%					
		Cost Amt.	$3,750,000	$3,980,000	$230,000
Sales	*$30,000,000*	Cost/Sales	12.5%	13.3%	0.8%
GP 33%	*$ 9,900,000*	Cost/GP	37.9%	40.2%	2.3%

Cost includes salary, commission, bonus, benefits, and payroll taxes.

terns and add them for a year total. Do not assume that an estimated average monthly sales figure will produce a realistic annual
figure when multiplied by 12. Take the time to work out the data
for each salesperson each month. Computer spreadsheets make
this a fast, easy exercise. Give perspective to the dollar costs by
including percent of sales and percent of gross profit, as in the
earlier examples.

TABLE 11-2
Cost Comparison, New Plan versus Industry Survey*

	New Plan			Industry		
	Low	*Norm*	*High*	*20%ile*	*Median*	*80%ile*
Sales	900	1,400	2,000	840	1,200	1,750
Compensation	40.0	55.0	65.0	38.0	45.0	56.0
Comp/Sales	4.4%	3.9%	3.3%	4.5%	3.8%	3.2%

* Private survey of 18 companies in our industry.
Compensation: salary, commission, and bonus per sales rep.
Cost shown in dollars and as % of sales.
Amounts in $ 000, except percents.

Special Analysis

A special problem may require special cost analysis. One company had experienced high turnover among its salespeople. Cost analysis showed that lower turnover would automatically increase profits more than enough to pay for the new sales pay plan. Another company learned through cost analysis that its expansion program would virtually guarantee three years of losses. The expansion program was changed.

Use cost analysis to search for improvement opportunities. Analyze cost as a percentage of sales or gross profit for such categories as special account representatives, trainees, territories, product lines, and customer categories. The conclusions from such analyses may go beyond sales pay planning and open questions about marketing and sales strategy. A company providing office management services to independent health care professionals, such as physicians and dentists, learned that it could not afford to support a field sales representative in the intermountain territory of Idaho, Montana, and Wyoming. A realistic cost analysis showed that, when travel expenses were added to sales compensation, projected revenues would not warrant the cost of a salesperson in the field. Top management found it difficult to decide to stop field selling in an area where the company enjoyed an excellent reputation and held a major share of the market. However, the cost analysis convinced the chief executive and others that losses would continue, even under the best of projections. The company removed its field representative from the territory and invested part of the cost savings in increased advertising and telemarketing in the territory. After a drop in sales volume for the first four months, the volume gradually grew beyond the former level. The major difference, however, was that the territory now produced a profit—even when sales were low.

Cost analysis might convince you to hire fewer rookies and more experienced salespeople, or you might find that certain customer categories deserve more sales attention than they have received. The power of cost analysis extends beyond pay planning and into marketing strategy. However, your initial concern will be whether the company can afford the proposed new pay plan.

Cost Too High

Perhaps your cost analysis leads to the conclusion that the proposed new pay plan's total cost seems excessive. What can you do? Before considering methods for reducing costs, reexamine whether you really want to reduce the cost. A low sales compensation cost, measured as a percentage of sales, does not necessarily mean high profit. Analyzing cost as a percentage of gross profit may present a different conclusion, as shown in Table 11–1. In that example, the cost of sales compensation, as a percentage of gross profit, proved acceptable although cost as a percentage of sales exceeded the original goal.

Even the total cost of selling—which includes advertising, promotion, and sales expenses as well as sales compensation—may not disclose the whole story about profit and growth. In some industries the most profitable and fastest growing companies report above-average cost-of-selling. Industry leaders often carry a relatively high cost-of-selling. When market conditions tighten, such companies may increase their cost-of-selling to hold or broaden market share. On the other hand, a high cost-of-selling certainly does not guarantee profit and growth. Extremely high costs occur largely in two categories of companies: those struggling to establish a place in the market and those sinking from sight. Any expenditure for advertising or for salespeople in such companies may figure large in relation to their weak sales volume and small capital base.

You might decide that the advantages of the proposed new pay plan are worth the cost. Reduced turnover, improved quality of sales force, higher standards of performance . . . such objectives might well justify the cost. In that case, you can proceed to draft the new pay plan document. However, if your cost analysis dictates that you must lower the cost of the new pay plan, follow the steps below.

Sales targets. First, reconsider the sales targets upon which you built the new pay plan. Can you realistically set higher sales targets? Would they be reachable with a stronger, well-motivated sales force? Would new products, advertising, or price changes help? If your first sales targets were optimistic, you have no room left for cost improvement by resetting sales targets.

High pay target. After reviewing the sales targets, next consider the pay targets on which the plan is based. You have established the pay targets by careful analysis of competitive pay data and your own company's past pay levels. Do you want to reduce those pay targets? Probably not, but that is one option to consider. You have three pay targets. Start with the high one. Reduce it as much as you dare, while keeping in mind your aim of good pay for high performance. Review the guidelines in Chapter 3, "Pay Targets." Readjust the incentive pay formula and test it on your total sales force cost analysis. Perhaps that change will be enough to lower the total cost to an acceptable level. Check again for the pay variance in your plan. Reducing pay for high performance usually reduces pay variance in general. You may have to make other changes to restore adequate pay variance without increasing total cost. See Chapter 6, "Pay Variance," for tips on how to adjust pay variance to keep it exciting.

Low pay target.   After exploring for a cost reduction opportunity in the high pay target, look next at the low pay target. Perhaps the marginal producers can tolerate less survival income than you had estimated. If so, reduce the target pay for marginal sales results to the minimum survival level. Again, adjust your incentive pay formula to fit the new pay targets and test it. You probably will not have to make any change to preserve adequate pay variance, but check it anyway.

Normal pay target.   Perhaps you will find that trimming high pay for high performance and reducing survival pay for marginal performance still gives less cost reduction than you need. The last place to cut cost should be a reduction of target pay for normal sales results. That is, after all, the core of your sales force. If necessary, revise the incentive pay formula for the new pay targets. Test the cost, and check the pay variance.

Other avenues.   Cost still too high? If your company cannot afford to provide competitive pay at the expected levels of sales, the company may need more than a new pay plan. An underpaid sales force is not likely to produce optimum profit and growth. Reexamine your basic marketing and sales strategy. Perhaps more advertising would increase sales force productivity to an affordable level. You might consider reducing the sales force and giving each salesperson a larger or more productive territory.

Perhaps you could use alternative selling methods for some or all of the areas now covered by field salespeople. Telemarketing, catalog, direct mail, independent representatives, and other distribution channels may deserve attention. Perhaps your company could benefit from more or fewer special account representatives, pull-through selling, enhanced sales support, expanded training for staff and distributors. . . . Such issues of marketing and sales strategy are beyond the scope of this book; however, the process of analyzing pay plan costs will help you think constructively about other opportunities for improving profit and growth.

AUDITING

Beyond the initial cost analysis, you will also want to evaluate operational aspects of the new sales pay plan after it is in place. If you prepare for such auditing before introducing the new plan, not only will you then be ready but you may identify opportunities for improvement in reporting and recordkeeping. Audit regularly (such as quarterly or semi-annually) all of the data categories that you used in developing the sales pay plan. That list probably starts with records of sales activity.

Sales

Tracking sales activity is not new. You reviewed sales reports before the new sales pay plan was developed. Now, however, you may become a more critical and demanding user of sales data. Sales records for accounting purposes seldom fill all the needs for sales force management—including appraisal of the salespeople and the pay plan. You will continue to be interested in total sales, regional sales, and especially individual sales. Beyond gross sales dollars or units, you will want to track individual results on incentive criteria such as gross profit, new accounts, multi-line orders, and so on.

Do not settle for thick computer printouts of all the data. Such printouts are hard to read and typically fail to provide real analysis or guidance. What you need may be buried somewhere in the mass of microscopic type, but you need information, not raw data. To understand the sales story, you need trends and analysis. Tell your management information specialist what trends you want to watch. Ask for simple graphs that show what happens month-by-month. Add a rolling three-month average to the graph. Even if not used as part of the pay plan, the rolling average can provide a clearer picture of trends than do the monthly data alone or year-to-date data.

Figure 11–1 is an example of a graphic monthly sales track for an individual salesperson. If the size of your sales force does not

FIGURE 11-1
Sales Track, Ted Typical (*Black & Smith Iron Specialties, Inc.*)

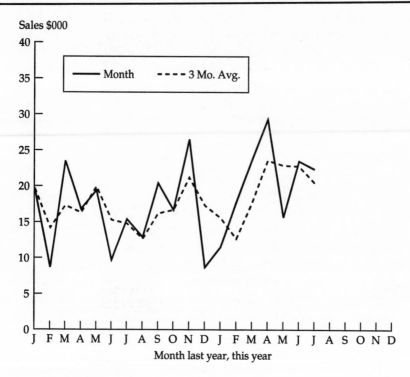

permit you to review each salesperson's results individually, make sure that the immediate supervisor is doing so. Copies of your tables and graphs can help the supervisor in this function. They become an especially effective attention-getter when sales supervisors and salespeople learn that senior management takes an interest in such analyses of sales records.

Cost

Reexamine the cost of selling periodically, just as you did when designing the sales pay plan. At least every six months, check the cost of selling as a percentage of sales and, if possible, as a percentage of gross profit. Make the analysis for each territory and for other analytical categories such as product line and customer type.

Such analyses go beyond sales compensation and may involve decisions about sales force staffing and deployment, methods of selling, and marketing strategy. Consider nothing as a given or fixed element of the sales program; review every opportunity for improving profitability.

Quality

Auditing the sales compensation program need not be limited to studying numbers. Look beyond sales volume, gross profit, and cost data. Consider qualitative aspects of the sales operation from the customer's side. How do customers regard your salespeople? Is their image consistent with the company's marketing objectives? Are customers getting the attention and service that will keep them buying from the company? Are customers paying promptly, or do they silently protest by delaying payment?

To get a current reading on customer responses, talk with the customers—many of them. The company's top executives certainly should talk with key account executives at least every six months. If that is too large a task for the company's senior executives, they should delegate some contacts to the next lower executive level. After all, you do not want the salesperson to own the customer. The company might even use nonsales executives for this function. If the company does not have key accounts, or perhaps repeat customers cannot be identified, apply sampling techniques. Let the manager chat with every 20th customer—in person or by telephone.

Salespeople

Talk to the salespeople. Wait until the new pay plan has been operating for six months or more. Then inquire about their reactions to the pay arrangements. Talk to each salesperson, if possible. Otherwise, talk to a selected cross section of salespeople, not just one or two superstars. Avoid direct, yes/no questions such as, "Do you like the new pay plan?" Instead, ask a more casual, open-ended question, such as, "How are the new pay arrangements working out for you?" Then follow up with additional questions about any issue raised by the salesperson. Your response should not be defensive, but inquiring. Explain details or reasons only if the salesperson presses for such explanation. This is an exploratory conversation, not a sales pitch. You might conclude with this final question, "What suggestions would you make for the next time we review the sales pay plan?" This indicates that you are interested in identifying improvement opportunities, but you are not eager to make any major change at this time.

When you talk to the salespeople about their pay, do not expect to find them in a state of euphoria. Neither delirious joy nor placid contentment marks a winning sales force. Highly productive salespeople may never be satisfied with their pay, just as star athletes are never content with past records. What is called a "hungry" sales force means one striving for more. It does not mean undernourished. So, expect to hear some healthy griping while you search for any serious opportunities for improvement.

Some salesperson may tell you that another company pays more, and some may say that they were better off under the former pay plan. Rather than debating such assertions, move on to ask, "How can you earn more money for yourself under this plan?" You want to learn how well they understand the incentive criteria and their responsibility for making something happen. Also ask if they are getting their checks on time and if the pay calculations are accurate.

If someone reports a serious problem, tell the person that you will look into it. Do so, and let the person know what you found. Deal immediately with errors, especially any that delay or distort the salesperson's rewards. Make note of other issues, but remember the first commandment of employee relations: **Thou shalt make no promises.**

The purpose of auditing is to identify opportunities for improvement. Those opportunities may include problems that need immediate correction. Most, however, will be items to be considered when a future audit signals that the time has arrived for an overhaul of the sales pay plan.

CHECKLIST FOR COSTING AND AUDITING THE PLAN

✓ Analyze total sales force production and total cost of selling.

✓ Compare new-plan to old-plan costs, and project future costs at various sales levels.

✓ Compare the ratios of cost to sales and cost to gross profit, as well as dollar costs.

✓ Use cost analysis to identify special profit improvement opportunities, in addition to evaluating the sales compensation plan.

✓ Adjust pay plan cost, if necessary, in the following order:
1. Sales targets
2. High pay target
3. Low pay target
4. Normal pay target

✓ Audit the sales pay plan's operation by tracking sales results, cost, and quality of operations.

Chapter Twelve

Pay Plan Document

Avoiding legal and morale problems.

All the big decisions have been made regarding such features as pay targets, criteria, salary, and incentive formula. Pay variance and projected cost meet the company's standards. You have a sales pay plan—almost. At this point the pay plan must be converted from penciled notes to a formal document.

Properly drafted, the pay plan document anticipates and answers virtually all questions that could arise. It reduces the risk of misunderstanding. It provides a strong shield for the company in the event of future legal action regarding terms of the salesperson's employment and compensation.

A checklist of topics and multiple examples of plan provisions in this chapter show how to write a sales pay plan document that covers all essential points. Included are guidelines for making the document user-friendly while legally correct. Three examples of complete sales pay plan documents appear in Appendixes A, B, and C.

THE NEED

Every company that employs salespeople should have an adequate sales pay plan document, but most do not. About 5 percent of companies operate with nothing more than a spoken agreement and past practice to guide sales compensation. Somewhat better than that are the 75 percent of companies with plan documents that fall short of being fully adequate. Such companies may provide a one-page outline or a brief letter of understanding that summarizes a few key features of the sales pay arrangement. Such minimum documentation may seem sufficient—as long as no problems arise. However, problems eventually *do* arise from termination of employment, an unusual order, price changes, new products, or new management.

The president of a communications systems manufacturing company phoned a consultant and asked, "Could you be available as an expert witness to testify about common industry practice in sales compensation?"

The consultant replied, "I do serve as an expert witness from time to time. What is this case about?"

The president explained that a discharged sales representative was suing the company for commission on an order booked two days before his termination. The company traditionally paid commissions after receiving payment from the customer. This order required three months of engineering and much consultation and customer hand-holding before the project was completed and paid for. Other sales representatives and engineers had to fill in for the terminated sales representative. The company refused to pay the full commission demanded by the former sales representative for a sale finally consummated long after his termination.

The consultant asked, "What does your sales pay plan say about orders booked before termination?"

After a long silence, the president quietly said, "I'm afraid our sales pay plan doesn't cover that."

The consultant replied, "I advise you to spend no more money on lawyers and experts to fight this case. Negotiate the best settlement you can get. Then, let us prepare a plan document that properly protects your company for the future."

No company wants to spend the management time and legal fees that can result from pay disputes. A properly drafted sales pay plan document avoids legal hassles. Company and employee understand in advance what is to be paid to whom and when. This makes it unnecessary for attorneys and a judge to decide what they think your pay policy should have been. Beyond that, a well-written document helps keep the salespeople satisfied. They know that they are treated fairly and consistently—no favoritism, no haggling with the boss.

WRITING

Although most companies lack documentation for their sales pay plans, about 10 percent go to the other extreme with legalistic overkill. The sales pay plan reads like a 20-year lease for a downtown office building. Written in "legalese" instead of plain English, the plan is difficult to understand and conveys an adversarial tone. It seems to set the company against the salesperson. While trying to protect the company's interests, someone lost sight of human relations in dealing with the sales force. Only about 10 percent of companies have sales pay plan documents that adequately cover all essential points in clear, easy-to-read language.

These tips can help make your sales pay plan document user-friendly.

1. Write it yourself or have it written by someone skilled in communicating with ordinary people—someone in human resources, public relations, advertising, or consulting.

2. Write in the direct-address style, second person—the way you talk to an employee. "You will earn one day of paid vacation. . . ." This style has a friendly tone that draws the reader along and it avoids the awkward "his/her." Never use only "he," "him," or "his"—which might suggest less than equal opportunity for all women and men.

3. Use active voice where possible. Tell who will do what, when. "The company will pay you an incentive award

each month. . . ." Although the word *shall* is the imperative form for second- and third-person statements, you can use *will* or *must*, which sound more conversational. "You must turn in your weekly expense report by 9 A.M. Tuesday to receive reimbursement."

4. Use short sentences, no more than 25 words. One thought, one sentence.

5. Use plain, everyday words. Avoid jargon, legalese, abbreviations, and code words. Spell it out for the benefit of the new employee. "Sales to original equipment manufacturers (OEMs) will be credited when booked."

6. Include examples to illustrate numerical calculations and other complexities.

7. Add plenty of side heads to guide the reader through the document.

8. Test readability with RightWriter™, Grammatik™, or a similar computer software program.

9. When the plan document is complete and clear, ask an employment law specialist to check it for any possible legal pitfalls. Not every lawyer is expert on the laws and cases pertaining to employment. However, do not let the lawyer destroy your clear, plain writing.

As you draft the plan, number each topic and paragraph. For example:

5. *New Account Premium*

5.1 *The company will give you double sales credit from each new account that you open.*

5.2 *That premium will continue for one year after the account's first order of $500 or more.*

The numbering makes for easy reference during the initial drafting and rewriting. Yes, rewriting. No matter how well and thoroughly you write, you and others will find opportunities for improvement before the document is completed. Sales, human resources, accounting, and legal specialists can contribute. The sales pay plan document is too important to be composed by only one person. Expect to make three to five or more revisions before the document is finally ready for the chief executive's signature.

TOPICS

The first step in drafting a sales pay plan document is to identify the topics to include. The following list shows topics most often covered. If a topic clearly does not apply to your sales pay plan, omit it. When in doubt, include the topic in the first draft and note it for further consideration. You may combine short or related topics under one major topic heading.

Topics to include, as they may apply to your company:

1. **Eligibility:** who, when
2. **Salary:** amount, criteria for increases, review time
3. **Draw or guarantee:** amount, limits, payback provision
4. **Quota:** basis, reviews, appeals
5. **Commission or incentive pay:** definition of sales, when credited, formula, basis
6. **Bonus:** formula, basis
7. **Territory:** area or account assignments, basis
8. **Split sales:** how to share credit, who decides
9. **House accounts:** how identified, no credit, part credit
10. **Windfall:** definition, how treated
11. **Special duties:** what is expected, special pay
12. **Benefits:** vacation, holidays, sick leave, insurance
13. **Expenses:** what is covered, how paid
14. **Termination:** final pay, amount, timing, orders in process
15. **Changes:** authority to change plan, protection
16. **Rights and limitations:** legal details
17. **Transition:** ending the old plan, starting the new one, credit for orders in process

SUMMARY

Covering all or most of those topics will require several pages of typed text—and that may seem intimidating. So, add another page—one that provides a brief summary of the plan's main features. Put that summary page at the front of the plan document so the new salesperson can quickly grasp the general picture of the pay plan. The rest of the document then supplies the necessary details. Table 12–1 shows an example of a plan summary. Other examples are shown in Appendixes A, B, and C.

Note that the summary page in Table 12–1 is clearly labeled as "highlights," with the further explanation, "This brief summary is not part of the plan." That treatment is to avoid possible conflict of interpretation. The summary page contains few words, perhaps not even complete sentences. Yet, the sideheads and capsule statements give the reader a general picture of the plan. The presence of a summary page and examples at the back make the plan document less intimidating and easier to understand.

Take one topic at a time, and write what you intend as policy and procedure. Following are some points to consider under each topic, with examples. The examples here and in Appendixes A, B, and C illustrate what some companies have said in their pay plans, but are not intended as recommendations. You should write your own document to fit your own company.

ELIGIBILITY

You can omit eligibility as a topic if there is no risk of confusion about who is included in the plan and when. However, if you want to clearly separate inside from outside salespeople or managers from representatives, this is the place to do so. Here are three examples.

- Your name on the last page of this plan indicates that you have been employed as a sales representative (rep) of Acme Services, Inc. (the company). You will be covered by this plan as long as you continue as a rep for the company, or until the plan is changed.
- You are eligible under this plan if you are a regional sales manager (RSM) employed by Advanced Products Company (the company) to manage sales to the commercial market.
- This plan applies to each sales engineer and senior sales consultant. It does not apply to trainees, inside sales

TABLE 12-1
Example of Sales Pay Plan Summary Page

Sales Pay Plan Highlights

This brief summary is not part of the plan. Pleas read the plan for details.

Salary Class	Experience	Salary
1	0–12 months	$2,000 month
2	12–24	2,100
3	24–36	2,200
4	36–+	2,300

GM Commission
- Based on monthly gross margin (GM) from your sales
- 50% of GM over $1,000 minimum per month

Fee Commission
- Based on monthly service fees for 12 months
- 33% of fees over $1,000 minimum per month
- Lower monthly minimum for less than 12 months experience

Quota Bonus
- 5% of total GM if over quota quarterly and yearly
- Quota based on length of experience

Expenses
- Company reimburses expenses
- Auto at current IRS rate

Examples
- At end of Plan

---

representatives, or independent representatives. You are covered by this plan after you have completed training and have been assigned to a territory.

Note: Do not use *probation* or *permanent* when writing or talking about the status of an employee. Some courts interpret those words to mean that the company is promising lifetime employment.

SALARY

If the company pays no salary—only commission and draws—you can omit this section. However, if a regular salary is part of the sales pay plan, you should explain it in this section of the plan document. The explanation should include how the starting salary will be established and when and how salary increases will be determined. The person with authority to set salaries should be identified. It may be sufficient to say that sales salaries will be administered in line with the company's regular salary management program. Most companies, however, manage sales salaries apart from other salaries, with different guidelines and different authority.

Do not list only an annual salary amount. Some court might decide that was a promise to pay the full amount even for less than a full year's service. You may show the salary schedule as a separate exhibit, making it easy to revise each year. Otherwise, issue a memo updating the salary schedule. Here are two examples.

- The company will pay you a salary within the range for your position. A separate memo shows salary ranges for the year. Your classification and salary will be based on your qualifications—as evaluated by the vice president of sales and marketing. The evaluation will include the following considerations: your education, training, and related sales experience.

- The company will pay you a regular salary, paid semimonthly. Your salary will be based on your related sales experience, according to the schedule in effect. The following schedule is for 1992. The company intends to review the salary schedule yearly and adjust it as necessary to keep your total earnings opportunity in line with competitive pay generally.
  The sales manager will evaluate your sales experience to determine your salary classification. Direct sales experience with another industrial supply firm will receive one-half credit. That is, 12 months there will equal six months with our company. Other types of sales experience may receive less credit, depending on the quality of that experience and how closely it relates to selling for our company. In no case

EXHIBIT 1
1992 Salary Schedule

		Salary	
Class	Experience	Semimonthly Rate	Yearly Rate
1	0–12 months	$550	$13,200
2	12–24	600	14,400
3	24–36	650	15,600
4	36–48	700	16,800
5	48+	750	18,000

will outside experience be credited beyond 36 months.

Example: A person with six years (72 months) or more industrial supply sales experience would start in Class 4 with 36 months' credit. One year later that person would move to Class 5, providing his or her sales results are satisfactory or better.

If your sales results are less than satisfactory, the sales manager will notify you. Your reclassification may be postponed for up to three months. At the end of that time, you will be reclassified or your employment will be terminated.

DRAW OR GUARANTEE

If draws are to be a regular part of the sales pay plan, explain the policy and procedure in detail. Will draws be set by formula or at the discretion of a manager? Is there a limit on the negative draw balance that may be owed to the company? How will the draw balance be paid back? Is there a dollar or percentage limit on the amount repaid each month? Calculation examples can illustrate how draws and paybacks may influence earnings received by the salesperson. Much like a draw, a guarantee may be included as in the last of the six examples below.

- The company will pay *no* draws or advances against future earnings.
- The company discourages draws against future earnings, but in some circumstances the vice president of sales and marketing may approve a draw.
- The company will pay you a draw of $2,000 per month. The draw will be deducted from your commission earnings. The deduction will not exceed 50 percent of your commission earnings in any month. Your draw balance may not exceed $6,000. If your balance reaches that amount, the company will pay you no further draws until you repay at least $2,000 from your commission earnings.
- You may obtain a draw for one month or regularly each month. The draw may not exceed one-half of your prior 3-month average commission.
- The company will pay each sales representative a draw of $2,000 per month. The company will deduct any negative draw balance (draws in excess of commissions earned) before paying any additional commissions to the sales representative.
- The company guarantees that your total earnings (salary plus incentive pay) will equal at least $2,500 per month during each of your first three months on the job as a rep. If your actual gross earnings (before payroll deductions) are less than $2,500 for a month, the company will pay you the difference. No negative balance will be carried forward. The company may renew this guarantee for another three months if warranted. For example, this could happen if a rep were making good progress in opening a new, difficult territory.

QUOTA

Quota means different things to different people. You might consider using terms such as *target* or *minimum*. Whatever the term, explain it if it affects sales pay. If you use a quota for inspiration or evaluation but not for pay, there is no need to explain it in the sales pay plan. Here are two examples.

- The vice president of sales and marketing will approve the sales target for each region at the beginning of the year, based on a least-squares trend analysis of past sales in the region—plus consideration of new products, competition, pricing, and other factors affecting sales. Normally, the sales target will not be changed during the year. However, the vice president of sales and marketing may change the target at any time if there is a major, unforeseen change in factors affecting sales.
- *Quarter quota:* Your quota for a quarter will be based on your salary classification at the start of the quarter.

Class	Quota
1	$5,000 GM
2	6,000
3	7,000
4	8,000

COMMISSION OR INCENTIVE PAY

The word *commission* means a percent of sales—at least to many people. Therefore, a company changing to a different basis for sales pay may choose to emphasize the change by using the term *incentive pay* or *incentive award*. For more than one criterion, write separate sections, such as Sales Award and New Accounts Award. Define terms as you come to them. If the definition is long, enclose it in parentheses or put it in a footnote. Remember that you are writing for the new employee who knows nothing of your jargon and past practice. Define sale, gross margin, new account, and so on. Specify when the company will give credit for a sale: at booking, billing, or receipt of payment. Define any reductions the company may make for slow pay accounts, returns, and so on— and when those may be recovered.

Use examples to illustrate unusual or complex calculations, such as a set-aside formula that pays only for results above a

minimum. Include an example of any plan feature that the salesperson may view as a limitation or a negative feature. It is better to
be open about such matters, than to have surprises and complaints later. Here are two examples.

- The company will pay you a sales incentive award
  semimonthly. The award will be based on the dollar
  volume of sales in your region as a percentage of your
  annual sales target. Sales will be credited when shipped.
- The company will pay you a monthly commission on the
  gross margin (GM) credited to you for that month.
- *Gross margin:* The company will issue to you a confidential
  price list including GM. The GM is an assigned value, not
  necessarily the actual gross margin. You are authorized to
  sell within the prices listed. At full price (column 1) the GM
  credit normally will be 50 percent of list price. The company
  may assign a larger or smaller GM for certain items or
  quantities. Your confidential price list will show the
  assigned GM. If you sell below full price, the amount of
  price reduction will be deducted from the full price GM.
  Every dollar of price reduction reduces your GM credit by
  one dollar.

Example

	Price	GM
List price	$100.00	$50.00
Discount	−20.00	−20.00
Selling price	$80.00	$30.00

Commission: Your GM commission will be 15 percent of
your GM credit over a monthly minimum. The monthly
minimum will be based on your salary level:

Level	GM Minimum
1	$3,000
2	3,300

3	3,600
4	3,800
5	4,000

If your GM for a month is below your minimum, you will receive no GM commission for that month. For every $1 of GM credited to you above your minimum, the company will pay you a GM commission of 15 cents.

Example

Month sales	$50,000
Month GM	20,000
Minimum	4,000
GM com base	$16,000 × 15% = $2,400 GM commission

BONUS

The word *bonus* usually means an occasional or infrequent payment as reward for sustained or special achievement. The terms *incentive pay* and *incentive award* may be used here also. Follow the same writing suggestions as for commissions. Here are two examples.

- *Quarter bonus:* If your GM credit for a quarter is at or above your quota, the company will pay you a quota bonus equal to 5 percent of your total GM for the quarter. This will be in addition to your regular monthly GM commissions.

    Example

Quarter quota	$6,000
Quarter GM	8,000
5% × $8,000	= $ 400 quota bonus for quarter

Year bonus: If your GM credit for a year is at or above your year quota, the company will pay you a quota bonus equal to 5 percent of your total GM for the year. This will be in addition to your quarterly bonuses and regular monthly GM commissions.

Example

Year quota $24,000
Year GM   35,000
5% × $35,000 = $ 1,750 quota bonus for year

• You will be eligible to earn a management award every six
  months. The management award will be based on your
  territory management results compared to goals established
  for the six-month period. Normally, the vice president of
  sales and marketing will establish three to six goals for each
  six-month period, before the year begins. Each goal will be
  given a percentage weight according to its importance. The
  weights must total 100 percent. At the end of the six-month
  period, the vice president of sales and marketing will rate
  your results on each goal. The individual goal ratings will
  be as follows:

Results	*Rating*
Superior: accomplishment much greater than expected	200%
Above expected: accomplishment clearly above goal	150
As expected: accomplishment about as expected	100
Marginal: accomplishment marginally below goal, even if a good effort was made	50
Poor: accomplishment clearly below goal or a major failure to meet expectations	0

The individual goal ratings will be combined into a rating of
overall performance. Your overall performance rating (P)
will be the sum of goal ratings multiplied by the goal
weight. Your management award will be your overall
performance rating (P) times 25 percent of your salary for
the six-month period.

Example

Performance (P) × 25% × Salary = Award
135% × 25% × $20,000 = $6,750 Award

TERRITORY

If the company does not assign sales territories, you can omit this section. Most companies, however, assign each field salesperson to a designated geographic area and/or certain accounts. Many companies prefer to identify sales territories in a memorandum separate from the sales pay plan. To smooth changes of area or accounts, you can provide for phase-in/phase-out credits as shown in some of the examples below. Such gradual adjustment avoids discontent when the salesperson believes a big order was ready to fall at the time of the change. Here are two examples.

- The national sales manager will assign you to a sales territory of a certain geographic area and/or designated accounts. Your territory may be changed at any time. If there is a change in territory, the GM credit from a changed account will be phased out for the losing rep and phased in for the gaining rep as follows:

	Losing Rep	Gaining Rep
Month 1*	100 %	0%
Month 2	50%	50
Month 3	0%	100

* Includes the month in which the change occurs plus the first full calendar month after the date of change.

- If an account is transferred from one sales engineer to another, the vice president of sales and marketing may designate credit for bookings from that account to be divided between the sales engineer losing the account and the one gaining the account, through the months following the transfer, as follows:

Month	Losing Sales Engineer	Gaining Sales Engineer
1*	100%	0%
2	80	20
3	60	40
4	40	60
5	20	80
6	0	100

* Through the first full month following account transfer. *Example:* Transfer March 10, credit losing sales engineer 100% through April, 80% through May, etc.

SPLIT SALES

If more than one salesperson may be involved in a sale, include a section on split sales. Some companies establish a fixed formula for split sales credit, such as 70 percent to the territory booking the order and 30 percent to the territory where delivered. Most companies, however, follow a more flexible policy. This section of the plan should clearly state who is responsible for determining split sales credit. If split sales do not occur in the company, omit this section. Here are three examples.

- The sales manager may divide GM credit for a sale if more than one rep is involved in developing and completing the sale. Normally, GM credit will not be divided or reduced because the sales manager or another member of management assists in the sale.

- If more than one sales engineer is involved in obtaining and servicing an order, the vice president of sales and marketing will divide the booking credit among those involved, with consideration of the time, effort, and importance of each sales engineer's contribution to the order. Any sales engineer may request split sales credit by submitting a written note to the vice president of sales and marketing specifying the sales engineer's activity in connection with the order.

- The national sales manager may designate any order for split credit among two or more reps who may contribute to making a sale or to providing subsequent local support to a sale from another region. Normally, split sales credits will total 100 percent of the regular GM value of the sale. However, in some cases, the split sales credits may total more than 100 percent. In no case will split sales credits total less than 100 percent unless the sale is to a house account.

HOUSE ACCOUNTS

Explain how house accounts, if any, will be identified. Avoid the frustration of retroactive decisions about house accounts by committing the company to identify them in advance. Explain what house account means, for the benefit of the inexperienced salesperson. Here are two examples.

- House accounts will be designated in writing by the vice president of sales and marketing, and will not be included in your region.
- The national sales manager will designate in writing any accounts that will be considered as house accounts. You will not be expected to call on house accounts, and you will receive no GM credit for sales to house accounts unless the national sales manager specifically assigns a split-sales partial credit to you for helping to make or support a house account sale.

WINDFALL SALES

Does the company intend to give special treatment to exceptionally large or unexpected sales? What is a windfall sale? Who decides? When? What commission rate applies? Explain it all in this section to avoid disputes later. Here are two examples.

- If the orders from one account total more than $500,000 in any three consecutive months, that is a windfall. The regular 10 percent commission applies up to the first $500,000. The commission will be 5 percent for the amount over $500,000.
- The national sales manager may declare a sale to be a windfall sale if (1) the sales representative's call reports show no call on the account within the prior 12 months and (2) the sale is more than three times the territory's average sale for the prior 12 months. One-half of the windfall sale amount will be credited for commission. The company will pay no commission for the other half.

SPECIAL DUTIES

Does the company expect the salesperson to perform any nonselling duties that may take time away from selling? Will the company pay for those duties? Define what pay, if any, will be provided. Here are three examples.

- From time to time you may be assigned to perform special marketing duties. These might include such tasks as collecting market research data, placing point-of-sale displays, or serving in a booth at a trade show. Such duties are a normal part of your job, for which the company pays you a salary. The company provides no additional pay for performing such duties.
- The company occasionally assigns special duties to sales representatives. If such nonselling duties take more than 12 hours in any month, the company will pay you for the time over 12 hours. The company will pay at the hourly rate of your prior month's commissions divided by 173.
- If the regional manager assigns a sales representative to conduct a training class for customers or others, the company will pay the sales representative $50 for each hour of class time.

BENEFITS

Explain in this section whether the salesperson will get the same benefits as other employees. Are there special pay arrangements for holidays and vacations? How much of the salesperson's total pay will the company credit for pay-related benefits such as a pension or profit-sharing plan, life insurance, and disability insurance? Here are two examples.

- You will be eligible to participate in company employee benefit programs under the same conditions as other employees, with your total earnings treated as "salary" for purposes of the savings and investment account and the pension plan.
- You will be eligible to participate in the company employee benefit programs under the same conditions as other employees, except as noted here. You will receive paid vacation time according to the company's vacation policy for other employees. Your vacation pay rate will be 140 percent of your base salary as of the last working day before you start your vacation time. For paid holidays, you will receive your regular base salary.

EXPENSES

What expenses does the company pay for? What evidence is required? Are there any limits? Explain the policy on expenses here or in a separate memorandum. Here are two examples.

- The company will reimburse you for all reasonable and necessary expenses connected with travel and customer entertainment. Submit your expense voucher each Monday. Include receipts for any items over $20. Use your company credit card for gasoline and auto expenses.
- The company will pay you a per diem allowance of $80 for each night away from home. The company will also reimburse for air fare, auto rental, and cab fare.

TERMINATION

How will the company handle final pay arrangements? How much? When paid? Are orders-in-process a possible issue? Define these matters here, and avoid problems later. Use the phrase "employment terminates." Some courts hold that "is terminated" applies only to a discharge, not to a quit. Some authorities further clarify the point by adding "whether voluntary or involuntary."

Having different policies for different types of termination can become confusing and a source of dispute. Treat all terminations alike to avoid arguments and discrimination charges. Here are three examples.

- If employment terminates for any reason, whether voluntary or involuntary, the company will pay you as follows:

    1. The company will prorate your salary through the date of termination. The company will pay the amount due promptly at time of termination.

    2. The company will pay commission on orders booked through date of termination. The company will pay the amount due within 60 days after termination, after allowance for any charge backs.

- If your employment terminates for any reason, the company will pay the regular commission on orders that you booked, less any draws or other amounts you may owe to the company. You will be paid when the company receives payment from the customer.

- If your employment terminates for any reason, whether voluntary or involuntary, you will be paid as follows:

    1. Your salary will be prorated through date of termination, and will be paid promptly upon termination.

    2. Any sales incentive that you have earned on sales shipped and billed through date of termination will be paid within 30 days after termination.

    3. A management award earned for the six-month period prior to termination, if not already paid, will be paid within 30 days after termination. There will be no proration or adjustment of a management award for a period less than a full six months, regardless of goal achievements.

CHANGES

Conditions may change; therefore, it is well to state that the company may change the pay plan. To reassure the salesperson, provide some protection in case of a change in the pay plan. State that the company will not take away anything already earned. Here are two examples.

- The company may change territories, quotas, commissions, or any other part of this plan at any time with 30 days prior written notice to the sales rep. Any change of this plan will not reduce the commission value of any order booked before the effective date of such change.

- The company may change or terminate this plan upon one month's written notice to you. The notice may be delivered in person or sent by mail to your last known address. Any change or termination of this plan may not reduce your earnings properly credited prior to the change or termination. If the company changes or terminates this plan, your earnings will be prorated as in the case of employment termination.

RIGHTS AND LIMITATIONS

This is the odds-and-ends section. You might even name it "Miscellaneous" or "Other Provisions." Put the legal details in this section and minor items that you expect to use rarely, if ever. This could include some items discussed in sections above, such as benefits, expenses, and changes. Some companies prefer to omit legalistic items, but your employment law specialist probably will recommend including some items such as the following seven examples.

- *Only agreement:* This plan is the only agreement governing compensation matters between the company and you. This plan supersedes any prior agreement or understanding regarding compensation.

- *Only pay:* Nothing in this plan may be construed to give any person any right to be paid any amount other than under the terms of this plan, or ensure employment to any person for any period of time.

- *Employment at will:* Your employment by the company is at will. This means that either the company or you may terminate the employment at any time for any reason or for no reason.

- *Employment limitations:* While employed by the company, you may not engage in any business that competes with the

company. You may not do so either directly or indirectly.
You may not serve as an employee, employer, consultant,
agent, officer, or representative for any organization,
product, or service that competes. While employed, you
may not accept employment with any other employer
without prior approval from the sales manager or the
president. If you have any question about a proposed
situation, please consult with the sales manager or the
president.

- *Secrets:* As an employee, you will learn company trade
  secrets. These secrets include such things as: identification
  of customers and prospects; prices; features and design of
  systems, products, and services; selling methods; and
  details of conducting the business. The law recognizes
  these things as the property of the company. Even though
  you learn about these secrets or help in developing them,
  they belong only to the company. You may never use or
  disclose these secrets outside the company. This restriction
  applies while you are an employee of the company and
  even after you leave the company. To avoid the
  embarrassment and cost of possible legal action against
  you, always treat information that you learn in the
  company as confidential.

- *Arbitration:* Any controversy or claim arising out of or
  relating to this plan, or the breach thereof, will be settled
  by arbitration in accordance with the Commercial
  Arbitration Rules of the American Arbitration Association.
  Judgment upon the award rendered by the arbitrator(s)
  may be entered in any court having jurisdiction. The law of
  the State of California will apply.

- *Effective:* This plan will be in effect from the date signed
  until the plan is changed or terminated.

TRANSITION

You may need some administrative details to cover the ending of
the old pay plan and the starting of the new one. A change from
credit-on-booking to credit-on-shipping can leave the salesperson
with an interim period of low income. If the new plan seems
riskier, the company may provide some security pay arrangement

to reassure the salespeople and to bridge their income from old to new. Include such details as a final section of the pay plan document or in a separate memorandum. People hired after the new plan is in effect will have no need for such transition information. Therefore, you can eliminate the transition section later. Here are four examples.

- The company will pay under this new plan for any orders booked on or after the effective date. The company will pay under the old commission schedule for any orders booked before the effective date, with payment made when the order is shipped and billed.
- The company will pay you under the former Sales Compensation Plan for sales billed before the effective date shown below. The company will pay you under this plan for sales billed on or after the effective date of this plan.
- The company will pay each current sales representative a special draw against commissions for the first three months under this new plan. The draw will equal 75 percent of the sales representative's average commissions for the last three months under the prior pay plan.
- For the first four months under the new Sales Pay Plan, the company guarantees that your earnings will equal at least 90 percent of your average monthly earnings during the year before. If your earnings are less than that amount for any month the company will pay you the difference at month end. There will be no negative balance carried forward.

SIGNATURE

The final, official sales pay plan document should be signed by a company officer and dated. Some managers question whether the salesperson should be required to sign also, feeling that this seems legalistic, authoritarian, and distrustful. However, experience proves the value of getting a signature from the salesperson.

A former sales representative for a data services company sued for extra commissions that he claimed the company owed for sales outside his regular territory and at a special rate orally promised

TABLE 12–2
Signature Form

I have received, read, understand, and agree to serve as a Regional Sales Manager under the terms of the Company's Sales Manager Pay Plan.

Level _____ Experience Credit _____ Salary $_____ semimonthly

Signature _____ Date _____

Print Name _____

Address _____

City _____ State _____ Zip _____

Telephone (___) _____

Witness _____ Date _____

For the Company _____ Date _____

                        ABC Company
                        123 Fourth Street
                        Anycity, State 98765
                        (415) 555-4321

---

years earlier. The lawyers for both sides took lengthy depositions. The case was coming down to the word of the poor, abused former employee against the word of powerful corporate executives. Not hard to guess how a jury would decide on that! Finally, one more search of company files turned up a copy of the sales pay plan, signed by the employee, stating that it was the only pay agreement. Case dismissed! That company, like many others, obtains a signature from each salesperson on each update of the sales pay plan.

A few companies also require the salesperson to initial and date each page of the plan document. Some companies file only a signed receipt for the plan document rather than a signed copy of the document itself. You may also consider whether to require a witness signature. Ask your employment law specialist for advice on what is best for your company.

TABLE 12–3
Sales Pay Examples

				John Doe, Sales Rep			
Month	Month Sales	3-Mo Avg.	Award Base	Sales Award*	Mgt. Bonus	Salary	Total Pay
1	110	110	10	$ 500		$ 2,000	$ 2,500
2	150	130	30	1,500		2,000	3,500
3	160	140	40	2,000	600	2,000	4,600
4	80	130	30	1,500		2,000	3,500
5	90	110	10	500		2,000	2,500
6	100	90	0	0	300	2,000	2,300
7	140	110	10	500		2,000	2,500
8	210	150	50	2,500		2,000	4,500
9	220	190	90	4,500	900	2,000	7,400
10	200	210	110	5,500		2,000	7,500
11	120	180	80	4,000		2,000	6,000
12	100	140	40	2,000	600	2,000	4,600
Year	1,680			25,000	2,400	24,000	51,400

* Sales Award = 5% of 3-month average sales over 100
Sales amounts in $000s.

The example shown in Table 12–2 could appear on the last page in the plan document or as a separate receipt.

EXAMPLES

You may have included calculation examples in the body of the sales pay plan document. However, it is desirable to add a few comprehensive examples at the back of the document. These examples show the salesperson how pay will be calculated under various conditions. Include at least three examples illustrating the probable range of earnings for marginal, normal, and high sales results. Avoid fantasy examples. Use realistic sales data, as you did in the planning process. Use round numbers so the salesperson can easily check the calculations. Show a full year, and include some low months and high months. Use the examples to show how a set-aside formula may produce zero incentive pay in some months and how a windfall provision operates. Examples such as the one shown in Table 12–3 help to avoid surprises later. Appendixes A, B, and C provide examples of complete sales pay plan documents.

CHECKLIST FOR THE PAY PLAN DOCUMENT

√ Draft a complete, detailed document explaining every aspect of the sales compensation arrangement.

√ Use plain language.

√ Cover every topic that might apply.

√ Include a brief summary of key points.

√ Include examples.

√ Have it checked by an employment law specialist.

√ Get the salesperson to sign.

Chapter Thirteen

Launching the New Plan

Putting the pieces together and selling it.

Here is how to make the transition from an old to a new sales pay plan. Suggestions and examples cover such changes as between credit-on-shipment and credit-on-booking, between commission-with-draw and salary-plus-incentive, and between incentive-on-all-sales and incentive-on-sales-over-a-minimum. Included are techniques for easing into a more risky plan and for bridging from old to new with added security for the salespeople.

The sales force awaits disclosure of the new pay plan in a state of high anxiety. From experience elsewhere or from the folklore of the sales world, they expect the worst. Management faces the task of presenting the new plan to that suspicious audience. This chapter offers guidelines for management's presentation of the plan— from scheduling meetings to using visual aids and responding to the unexpected question. Pleasant news makes an easy sell, and anyone can handle it. However, managers need guidance for dealing with difficult situations, such as a major reduction in base salary or even lowered total earnings opportunity. The advice in this chapter may help.

TRANSITION

Your planning for the new sales pay plan should include consideration of the transition from old to new plans. You may have no problems; however, consider whether any of the following issues need to be covered in a special transition arrangement.

Change Commission from Booking to Billing

If the average time from booking to billing is more than two weeks, you will want to protect your salespeople from an earnings blackout. In the past they were paid upon bookings, now they must wait until the orders are billed—perhaps months later. After the new plan is operating for several months, the flow of earnings will be reestablished. Until then, however, the salesperson faces a period of no commission income while awaiting billing of orders booked after the new plan goes into effect.

You can bridge the blackout period with a temporary salary, guarantee, or draw. (See Chapter 7 for suggestions about using draws.) Limit the transition period to the time required for commissions to resume flowing from orders booked after the start of the new plan. Limit the rate of draw repayment to smooth the transition, and avoid transferring the earnings blackout two or three months into the future. Paying a salary during the transition period avoids the problems of a draw, but could cost more. A monthly guarantee for three to six months provides the best approach in many such situations—and at a lower fixed cost than a salary. For example, your policy statement might read, "If your earnings in any of the first three months under the new plan are less than your average earnings for the last six months under the old plan, the company will pay you the difference."

If you change from commission on billing to commission on booking, there is no need for bridge compensation because commission payments will now come sooner than under the old plan. Explain, however, that the company will continue to pay on billing for those orders booked under the old plan.

Reduction of Salary

Changing from a plan with a high base salary to a plan with lower salary and increased incentive pay may create some anxiety among the salespeople. The prospect stirs feelings of insecurity, even among some who are eager for added opportunity pay. To counter that anxiety, offer an earnings guarantee for three to six months. You can extend the period if the salespeople are adapting to the opportunity more slowly than expected. It should never be necessary to extend a guarantee beyond six months as a temporary transition. The sales force must learn to work according to the terms of the new plan—without a safety net. They must be given the opportunity to experience the thrill of victory and the agony of defeat.

Change of Incentive Formula

Perhaps you believe that the salespeople will be skeptical about their earnings opportunity under the new incentive formula. As in the case of a salary reduction, you could provide a guarantee for a few months. Another and especially interesting technique when changing the incentive formula is to offer a choice of timing for starting under the new plan. "You may choose to start under the new sales pay plan as of the first of any month up to six months from now." That gives the individual some sense of control, small as it is. It also permits the person to verify earnings under the old and new plans before leaping into the uncertainty of the new plan. This technique sparks great interest and a more open-minded analysis of the new plan. After all, delay could cause the person to miss out on some good months. The negative aspect of this technique is the administrative complexity of operating two pay plans and keeping track of when each person switches plans. You should set a deadline by which all salespeople will come under the new plan. Otherwise, the company would not get the values designed into the plan.

Reduction of Total Earnings

Probably the most difficult adjustment to present to salespeople is a reduction in their earnings. Even if the salespeople have become grossly overpaid and the company can no longer afford the excessive cost, lowered earnings may seem to be a slap in the face. The salesperson sees the reduction as an attack on the individual's concept of self-worth. You can provide a gradual transition to the new, lower pay level to ease the adjustment. Scale back the salary and/or incentive formula in steps over several months. For example:

Month 1	10.0% commission rate
2	9.5%
3	9.0%
4	8.5%
5+	8.0%

Someone may propose continuing the current salespeople at their existing salary and/or commission rates and applying the reduced earnings plan to new salespeople only. Such "grandfathering" results in a two-tier pay program. After a year or two, the pay inequities will likely become a source of widespread discontent among salespeople hired under the new plan. The newer salespeople, especially the high performers, see no rational basis for the pay difference.

Instead of letting hire date determine pay difference, you might consider the transition arrangement adopted by a distributor of industrial chemicals. They set up a salary schedule for sales engineers based on years of service. Those with 15 years or more service received the maximum salary. This company calculated incentive pay as a percentage of base salary, so a higher salary also meant a higher total earnings potential. When the new plan was established with recognition of service up to 15 years, the company also announced that the maximum credited service would be reduced by one year during each of the following five years. At the end of that time, salaries would rise only to the 10-year level. With annual adjustments to the salary schedule, this arrangement, in effect, froze the salaries of long-service sales engineers and provided a gradual transition over five years to a lower salary schedule. All sales engineers received the same fair treatment in a well-rationalized plan that did, in fact, lower the company's cost of selling. (See Chapter 16 for a discussion of excessive pay.)

ADMINISTRATION

Before presenting the new plan to the sales force, make sure that all necessary administrative procedures are in place and working. Do you have a supply of new price lists and order forms? Has the computer been programmed for the new salaries, the new commission formula, the new bonus? Is the accounting department ready to generate needed earnings reports to salespeople and to management on a timely basis?

Up to this point, the administrative convenience of the new sales pay plan has largely been ignored. You concentrated first on sales goals and motivation. You then considered the plan's cost. Now is the time to check out the recordkeeping and reporting. Generally, a capable accounting manager can adapt procedures and computers to accomplish what management wants in a sales pay plan. The sooner you alert the accounting manager to the prospect of a changed sales pay plan, the better. Include the accounting manager in your planning sessions, but do not allow appeals for easier administration to divert you from your motivational aims. However, if the accounting department needs more time to get the administrative support functioning effectively, you may have to postpone introducing the new plan.

If, in the extreme case, administration would be too difficult or too expensive, you may have to modify the sales pay plan. You want to ensure that administrative errors and delays do not defeat the motivational aims of your sales pay plan. Sales reports must be correct and paychecks must be accurate and on time. Anything less would damage management's credibility with the salespeople and work against the company's sales goals.

PRESENTATION

Management would like the sales force to accept the new pay plan calmly, quietly, and perhaps even gratefully. After all, much work went into developing a sales pay plan that would motivate the salespeople and would be affordable for the company. However, most of the salespeople are likely to approach the new plan with caution, suspicion, and even distrust. The extent and intensity of those feelings will depend largely upon the openness and fairness of the company's past dealing with its sales force. For this review, let us assume that past dealings by earlier managers have left a residue of skepticism in the sales force. Even if past dealings have, in fact, built trust and confidence in management, assume at least some doubt. It is better to plan for it than to be surprised by it.

Assume further that the new plan contains elements that the salespeople will dislike. How can you best launch a new, not-so-attractive pay plan to an already skeptical sales force? Even if you know that the new plan is an attractive improvement, make those negative assumptions while preparing for the presentation. Then you will treat the task as the selling job it is.

Plan for an in-person presentation by senior executives—at least by senior sales executives, perhaps backed by the presence of the Chief Executive Officer or the Chief Operating Officer. If a consultant assisted in designing the new plan, have the consultant present. Make sure, however, that everyone understands that it is the XYZ Company's sales pay plan, not the consultant's plan. The consultant should recede into a supporting role as a technical resource, while top management asserts ownership of the plan.

If gathering the entire sales force together for one presentation is not practical, schedule several simultaneous presentations or conduct them in quick succession. The company grapevine will carry its own version of the plan immediately after the first meeting. Avoid premature leaks, and schedule your presentation(s) to beat the rumor process so that every salesperson receives the same, accurate information.

Videotape Presentation

You could mail out videotapes as the method of presentation, but that would be little better than sending a memo. It lacks personal contact and the opportunity for feedback and questions. For a large sales force, however, you might use a videotape presentation of the plan as the central part of a local meeting conducted by the most senior executive available.

Video Conferencing

Consider using a video conference, if that's the best you can do. Although the technology and convenience of video conferencing may appeal to senior executives, it still feels remote and impersonal to many salespeople. Would you want your physician to use this method to tell you that you need a serious operation? Most people still prefer in-person contact for major communications—especially about something affecting one's livelihood.

The Meeting

You have taken great care not to leak the new sales pay plan prematurely. The sales force is assembled. False jocularity and gallows humor fill the room. Anxiety builds. You step to the front and welcome everyone. You think of telling the joke you heard yesterday, then you remember how the situation seems to the salespeople. You can almost hear their thoughts screaming, "Get on with it!"

You briefly explain that the company has been reviewing its sales compensation arrangements. You mention who worked on the project and what the objectives were. Now, here are the highlights of the new sales pay plan as approved by the CEO for the coming year. (That was a good idea to mention that it is already approved. You are here to explain the plan, not to negotiate about it.)

Visual Aids

You turn on the overhead projector—which you checked out when you arrived an hour earlier. The projector was dirty then. Aren't they always? You had time to clean it with a damp towel, and you checked for a spare bulb. You moved the big screen to a location where everyone in the room could see it. You focused the projector before the audience arrived. Now you are ready to display the transparencies as you talk. You had thought of putting your material on 35mm slides, but that requires a darkened room and gives less flexibility. With the overhead projector, they can see you and you can see them as you talk. After all, you called this meeting for a face-to-face presentation.

Transparencies

Your overhead transparencies are few and simple. They do not tell the whole story. That's what you are going to do. Each transparency contains only a few key words on a few lines—like advertising copy. The type is large, 18 point (one-quarter inch) or larger. Even the people in the rear of the room can read it easily. The transparencies provide memory hooks to help the audience organize and remember the key points of your message. The transparencies also help you keep your presentation concise and on track. Do not read the transparencies to the audience. They can do that for themselves. Instead, talk about and explain each of the key points.

Transparencies for the overhead projector can be prepared quickly and inexpensively on an ordinary office copier. For a few dollars each, you can get colored transparencies from the neighborhood copy center. Or, for pennies, you can add color to a black and white transparency by underlining with colored markers designed for use on transparencies.

Handouts

It is going well, just as you had rehearsed it several times at home. Finally, you get to the examples. Too much data for easy-to-read overhead transparencies. Now is the time to hand out copies of the plan with examples in the back.

You explain the calculations, showing how much the hypothetical salesperson would earn at normal, high, and marginal sales results. You do not pull any punches, you do not exaggerate. You then review the advantages and disadvantages of the new plan from the viewpoint of the salespeople, referring to each plan section involved. You do not want them to think that you tried to slip something past them.

Questions

When you ask if anyone has a question, an awkward pause follows. Finally someone asks for clarification of a point that you covered thoroughly in your presentation. However, it was not thorough enough—or the person was still thinking about an earlier point. You recognize that it is your responsibility to explain—and explain again if necessary—until the salesperson understands. That person's spoken question may represent similar unspoken questions in the minds of others. There is a reasonable limit, however. If the others show signs of restlessness, you can ask the questioner to stay after the meeting for further discussion.

Some questions may seem skeptical, challenging, or even outright hostile. Being an experienced presenter, however, you will not be drawn into an argument or take a defensive position. Instead, you acknowledge the speaker's feelings and go ahead with the explanation. You might say, "Sandra, I recognize that you have doubts about part of the new plan. Let's go on with the example to make sure that we all understand the rest of the commission calculations. Then we will come back to any questions remaining."

Surprise

From the back of the room comes an unexpected question. It raises an issue you have not considered. Even with all the time and effort put into designing the sales pay plan, this matter has not come up before. Although unprepared for it, you are tempted to give an answer right now. However, you know the chances are less than 50/50 that it will be the best answer. So, you tell the group that you will check into the matter and respond in a day or two. After analyzing it, you cover the new topic in a memorandum or even an amendment to the plan. Fortunately, you did not get trapped into making a snap decision that you might have regretted after more careful study.

MONITOR

Closely observe the new plan's operation for the first three months. How well are the salespeople managing the new forms and procedures? How well are the main office administrative tasks being handled? Do not permit delays in data processing or payroll to offset the positive values that you designed into the plan. If necessary, authorize overtime in the accounting department to ensure that orders are processed promptly and sales paychecks are issued on time. Follow up any questions or complaints from the salespeople. Make corrections as necessary in administrative details, but resist any change in the fundamentals of your plan design.

Positive sales results from the new plan may occur in the first month, especially if the new plan contains only small changes from the old plan. A new sales pay plan may require more time to show its effect. It may take three months or more before you begin to see results. The salespeople need to adjust to a plan that is much different from that to which they were accustomed. They need time to make it part of their thinking on the job. By six months, you should see clearly measurable progress toward your sales goals, providing only that the economy and your competitors cooperate by holding steady all other variables.

Regular monthly reports, including three-month moving averages, will enable you to track sales, gross margins, sales force turnover, and other indicators. At 6 months and at 12 months prepare a special analysis of progress. Include any information that you obtain from supervisors or salespeople about their reactions to the sales pay plan. In evaluating those reactions from the salespeople, remember that the goal is not to create a state of euphoric delight, but to motivate salespeople to work hard and to direct their efforts toward the company's sales goals.

One company changed its sales pay plan to a reduced salary schedule but added a six-month bonus for sales above quota. The day after the plan was presented to the sales force, one long-service salesperson called the president to express his displeasure. "I thought about quitting," he said, "but instead I'm going to stay and show you what a mistake you made. With that new bonus, I'm really going to get into your pocket."

He did. At the end of six months the president was delighted to sign a large bonus check for the salesperson. Remembering the earlier telephone call, the president cut a pocket from an old pair of trousers and enclosed the check in the pocket (inside a large envelope) with a note: "Congratulations, Bob, you really got into my pocket."

Six months later, Bob scored again, as did several others. The president soon exhausted his supply of old trousers to cut up. Now, the company buys a supply of new pockets from a local sewing center to carry the president's same message to every salesperson who earns the bonus.

CHECKLIST FOR LAUNCHING THE NEW PLAN

√ Prepare for the transition from old to new plans.
√ Provide a security bridge, if necessary.
√ Check for effective and timely administrative support.
√ Present the new plan in person to all salespeople at one time—or as close to that as possible.
√ Monitor the new plan's effectiveness, and correct any problems promptly.

Chapter Fourteen

Trainee Pay

Investing today for success tomorrow.

The particular issues in paying sales trainees may require special provisions in the pay plan or even a separate pay plan for trainees. The company wants to get the new person trained and productive as quickly as possible. During this period, the trainee needs survival income—and more. The trainee needs the opportunity to experience success. The same motivation principles that guide regular sales pay planning apply also to planning trainee pay. However, trainee performance standards should be based on expectations realistic to the person's level of experience. This chapter explains how to fit trainee pay to trainee results.

COST OF TRAINEES

Even if trainees receive only modest earnings, they remain the most expensive people in the sales force. Their pay is too high for what they sell. Training and extra supervision add to the cost of trainees. Their limited product knowledge and sales skills lose sales and customers. Industrial companies may spend $15,000 to $30,000 or more to recruit and train a salesperson before that person produces significant sales volume. A company selling big-ticket consumer products reported that a new salesperson typically misses $180,000 in sales that an experienced salesperson would have closed—and those customers do not return.

Add up the costs in your own company for (1) recruiting, (2) selection interviews and reference checking, (3) payroll processing, (4) training, (5) extra supervision, (6) samples, (7) auto and other expenses, (8) salary or draw, (9) incentive pay, and (10) missed sales opportunities, lost customers, and burned territories. If the accounting department cannot provide accurate costs, make an estimate. Calculate the cost-per-trainee for each month up to 12 months. Compare the cost to the gross margin on sales by the average trainee for each month on the job. You will then see that hiring a trainee constitutes a major act of faith in the future. If done without care, the hiring becomes a high-risk gamble with company funds. If hiring and training are done well, however, they provide a planned investment in success for both company and trainee.

TWO APPROACHES

Reacting to the expense of trainees, companies incline toward either of two approaches. One may be called the "minimum-investment" approach, the other the "return-on-investment" approach. Under the minimum-investment approach, the company hires almost anyone willing to accept the job, perhaps at little or no salary or draw. The employee accepts almost all the risk, the company accepts none. Recruiting and selection receive scant attention from management. Sales training is rudimentary or nonexistent—beyond how to write an order. Under the minimum-investment approach, sales force turnover runs higher than the all-industry average of about 15 percent per year. Some companies regularly accept 30 percent to 50 percent turnover as "normal." Sales force productivity stays low because of high turnover and because low producers are permitted to stay as long as they wish. A few trainees survive to become satisfactory producers or even superstars—and management wishes more young people were as capable and ambitious as those successful few. The pay may be straight commission, with little or no draw and no concession to the trainee's limited ability to produce sales. Minimum investment for the company means sink or swim for the trainee, and it may mean a large but hidden cost to the company.

In spite of obvious disadvantages, the limited-investment approach has proved satisfactory—or at least adequate—for some companies. Those are companies that worry little about lost sales or company reputation. Any sale is welcome, and potential customers far exceed the company's ability to reach them all. In that situation, the minimum-investment approach may be strategically sound. Much consumer-direct selling fits that pattern. However, some of the most profitable retailers and other companies follow a different approach.

The second approach, return-on-investment, fits most industrial and wholesale selling situations. Here the emphasis shifts from the cost of the trainee to the value received by the company. The company wants high sales force productivity through experienced salespersons and continuing customer relationships. They hire only candidates with a high probability of job stability and sales success. Sales managers are evaluated in part on their ability to pick winners and to keep them on the team. Accordingly, recruiting and selection receive careful attention from management. The company also strives to ensure success for those hired. Early, intensive training characterizes companies using the return-on-investment approach. Ongoing training and regular supervisory support help maintain high sales productivity as the salesperson advances from rookie to veteran.

TRAINEE PAY OBJECTIVES

Trainee pay can be a key factor in achieving the objectives of the return-on-investment approach. Both the method and the amount of compensation interact with all other factors to bring trainees with high potential into the company and to get their sales results up to standard. Pay arrangements for trainees should be designed to fit their needs. That may mean special trainee provisions in the regular sales pay plan or a completely separate plan for trainees. Top return-on-investment companies typically design their trainee pay arrangements to help accomplish the following six objectives.

Attract Enough Applicants

The more applicants, the greater the probability of hiring winners—those with a high likelihood of success on the job. That is a mathematical function known as the selection ratio. The selection ratio contributes importantly because hiring is not a random process. Even managers untrained in selection techniques achieve better than random chance results in picking people to hire. Those with selection training can do quite well in recognizing winners. However, any manager, trained or untrained, will automatically achieve a larger percentage of successful hires by seeing more applicants.

Pick one out of 50 applicants and you have a better chance of getting a winner than if you pick one out of five. That is why an attractive pay plan, openly presented in advertising and other recruiting, can help to build a strong sales team. If you provide a salary, incentive pay, benefits, and a car—say so in your recruiting communications. Tell what your average salesperson earns. Such details draw more applicants than the vague, mysterious advertisements seen in many newspapers and trade journals. Carefully processing a large number of applicants may seem to be a nuisance, but it is a profitable nuisance.

Attract Quality Applicants

When most of the applicants have the potential to fit the selling job offered, you have a greater likelihood of picking a winner. The percentage of potentially successful people in the total applicant group is called the quality ratio. In the selection process, the effect of a strong quality ratio may offset a weak selection ratio, and vice versa. If you attract mostly high-quality applicants, you could get by with seeing fewer of them before making a hiring decision. However, the ideal situation provides strength in both ratios, permitting you to select the very best from among many applicants who generally suit your employment standards. The selection ratio and the quality ratio then multiply together to help you build the best possible sales team.

To draw large numbers of well-qualified applicants, advertise details of a superior pay arrangement and other job features. Include the company name, the product line, the geographic area. The more you disclose, the more suitable applicants you will get.

Those not interested in the kind of job offered will not apply, saving you the time and trouble of screening them out. Those who do apply know something about the job opportunity. They are interested and probably are qualified. The process of natural preselection works for you when you provide enough accurate information in your advertisements and in your contacts with schools, employment agencies, and other applicant referral sources.

Encourage Complete Training

The pay plan can encourage the person to master the tools of success: product knowledge (company and competitors) and sales skills (time and territory management, prospecting, presenting, closing, follow-up). To accomplish that, the pay plan should encourage completion of the formal classroom and field training before the trainee is unleashed on customers. Forcing a half-trained person to rely on commission income works against full-line selling, customer service, and your company's image in the market. It also reduces the survival rate among potentially satisfactory salespeople, adding to the cost burden of sales force turnover.

Encourage Rapid Progress

When the trainee completes basic training, the pay plan should stimulate rapid growth up the learning curve to acceptable sales volume. When the trainee reaches that point, the company begins to gain a profit return on its investment in the trainee. The salesperson gains the satisfaction of rewards for solid achievement against standards appropriate to the person's level of experience.

Sustain Satisfactory Trainees

Early months can be difficult and discouraging for the trainee. Even the potentially successful salesperson can feel overwhelmed by all that must be learned and by slow progress in winning customer acceptance. The trainee needs emotional and financial support over low periods and setbacks. What the trainee does not need is a punitive compensation arrangement that puts the person in debt to the company. The company can view the small added cost of sustaining good people as insurance for the large investment already made in hiring.

Some managers would like the pay plan to automatically force out the unsuccessful person. That would relieve the manager of a distasteful management duty. Top companies, however, keep the initiative with management. They do not depend upon low earnings to weed out failures. The sales manager terminates the trainee's employment when less-than-satisfactory progress becomes clear and is not readily corrected. The sales manager does not wait for the salesperson to ride the job down to total disaster, with all that implies about lost sales and lost customers. A failing trainee usually represents a selection error by the manager. Having made the wrong investment choice, the manager's best course is to cut the loss for both company and trainee. Let the person move on to more suitable employment elsewhere, before the experience devastates the person's sense of self-worth.

Keep Costs Reasonable

The company treats the cost of trainee pay as part of the total cost of selling. Therefore, the productivity of other salespeople must absorb the initial cost burden of trainees—until the trainees produce enough to pay for themselves. If you hire trainees, you must accept the cost of training. Careful selection and monitoring the trainee's progress can help keep the cost reasonable and convert the cost to a profit-producing investment.

Enough applicants, quality applicants, complete training, rapid progress, support for the satisfactory, and keeping costs reasonable—these six objectives most often figure in planning trainee pay for top return-on-investment. "Lighting a fire under the trainee" is not one of those objectives. If you hire the wrong people, no pay plan will turn them into solid producers. However, if you hire people with a high probability of success, they will come to the job with eagerness to learn and to perform well. Their initial anxious tension stems from the desire to become familiar with the job and to get comfortable in their new duties and inter-personal relationships. The desire to survive drives them.

During the early weeks and months, trainees will work hard and long to get established. You can take advantage of that early drive—and satisfy the trainees at the same time—by giving them intensive training and plenty to study at night. Both management and trainees should think of this period as boot camp. It is not gradual growth on the job, it is concentrated learning, with no free time until graduation. Trainees enter with so much built-in motivation that you do not need to light a fire under them. You *do* need to encourage and sustain them.

TRAINEE PAY FEATURES

Sales trainees today often hold values different from those of trainees of several years ago. Few today will gamble on straight commission or will sacrifice greatly to get started in a promising career, and few will hang on for long if the going is rough. Companies that get and keep the best producers today generally provide trainee pay with four features.

Salary during Training

A straight salary during basic training enables the trainee to get started, and it keeps the person in training until graduation. No incentive pay is available until the trainee acquires the basic product knowledge and sales skills needed for a reasonable representation of the company to its customers. For most industrial selling, that usually takes one to two months. For wholesale selling of familiar products, the time may be two to four weeks. About 10 percent of manufacturing companies make the mistake of holding the new salesperson in the trainee status for too long—even up to a full year or more. Overly long trainee status tends to frustrate the people with the strongest achievement drive, and it may send the wrong message about the company's standards of performance. Keep the training wheels on the bicycle only until the person is no longer a danger to self or the company.

Adjusted Incentive Pay

The incentive portion of total pay gradually increases in line with the normal learning curve for the company. Some companies provide a gradually reducing guarantee. Some apply graduated commission rates or an increasing minimum in a set-aside incentive formula. The objective of such methods is to gear trainee rewards to sales results expected of trainees. A trainee with prior sales experience may be expected to advance more rapidly up the learning curve. Therefore, the experienced person may be granted less income protection in accordance with the higher expectations for that level of experience.

No Debt

To avoid discouraging the new salesperson, any draw balance may be forgiven at the end of each month, making it a guarantee, or at the end of 6 or 12 months. The company absorbs that cost to enable the salesperson to advance without a burden of debt. The simpler course is to pay a salary and totally avoid the issue of draws and indebtedness.

Graduation

Successful completion of basic training is celebrated with a certificate, perhaps awarded at a dinner with spouses invited. Graduation signals the end of special consideration as a trainee and passage to the regular sales pay plan. Only those who are well trained and selling at a reasonable level graduate.

COMPETITIVE TRAINEE PAY

Designing the trainee pay plan requires information about competitive pay and about the sales results that you can reasonably expect from trainees. The advice in Chapter 3 about obtaining and using sales pay survey data applies equally to trainees and other sales classifications. If you can obtain comparative data only for sales representatives and senior sales representatives, you can estimate median trainee total pay (salary plus incentive) at about 70 to 75 percent of the median total pay for sales representatives with three years' experience in the same industry, or about 55 to 60 percent of median total pay for senior sales representatives. However, obtaining actual industry pay survey data is clearly preferable to using such rough estimates.

LEARNING CURVE

The **learning curve** shows what may be expected from salespeople at various levels of experience. Here is how to determine the learning curve for your sales force.

Monthly Sales Records

First, compile sales records by months-on-the-job for every salesperson hired during the past three years. The examples here use dollar sales volume. However, you should use unit sales, gross margin, or whatever measure best fits your marketing strategy and sales goals, as explained in Chapter 4. Sort the data from low to high sales by months-on-the-job. Consider Month 1 to be the time from the salesperson's date of hire to the end of the first full calendar month after that. Thus, a person hired on May 10 receives credit for all sales from May 10 through June 30 as Month 1. If necessary, adjust the sales amounts to reflect any major price changes in the past three years. You want data that realistically represent the current selling environment. The reason for reaching back three years in this analysis is to get a data sample large enough to be statistically reliable.

Your data might look like the example in Table 14–1. The first column shows the Month 1 sales volumes for every salesperson who worked at least one full month during the past three years. The second column shows sales data for Month 2, and so on. Some of those people are no longer employed by the company, but their sales data are part of the record that you want to examine. Table 14–1 shows only a few months for illustrative purposes. You should compile data to Month 12 or beyond.

TABLE 14–1
Sales By Months-on-the-Job (Sales in $ 000.)

Number of Reps	Months-on-the-Job				
	1	2	3	4	5
1	0.0	0.0	0.0	0.0	5.7
2	0.0	1.8	0.0	3.5	5.9
3	2.0	2.0	4.2	6.5	8.4
4	2.3	2.0	6.8	6.9	14.6
5	2.3	2.9	8.9	8.6	22.5
6	2.8	3.4	11.3	9.1	24.8
7	2.9	4.5	12.4	12.5	25.8
8	3.5	5.6	13.6	12.8	27.2
9	3.8	6.2	14.0	15.0	33.3
10	4.6	7.0	15.0	25.8	38.4
11	5.4	7.4	17.8	28.2	48.9
12	5.5	7.5	21.0	29.1	54.1
13	5.6	7.9	21.1	34.1	58.9
14	6.0	9.0	22.7	39.8	75.5
15	6.9	10.2	34.1	51.1	78.1
16	7.8	16.2	35.2	52.3	
17	8.6	18.5	41.3	69.3	
18	8.6	20.4	51.8		
19	10.8	24.2			
20	12.5	30.4			
21	15.0				
Number	21	20	18	17	15
Median	**5.4**	**7.2**	**14.5**	**15.0**	**27.2**

Median Sales by Month

The second step is to determine the median sales volume for each month-on-the-job. Do not use the average, which can be distorted by extreme values. Use the median—the middle value in the sorted array for each month. In Table 14–1 there are 21 values for Month 1. Therefore the median value is the 11th entry on the list. That is $5,400. Half the people hired in the past three years sold

$5,400 or more in their first month, and half sold $5,400 or less. For Month 2, there are 20 values, meaning that the median value is between the 10th and 11th value, or $7,200. Month 3 shows 18 values, so the median is between the 9th and 10th values, or $14,500.

Continue that process of finding median sales values for each of 12 or more months-on-the-job. Your list of median sales values might look like Table 14–2.

Graph

Now plot those median sales values on a graph like the one in Figure 14–1, with months-on-the-job on the horizontal scale and sales on the vertical scale. Can you see the pattern of the learning curve? Sketch in a smooth curve showing that pattern. Do not try to connect every point, but let the curve flow through the general pattern of points. A useful tool for this purpose is a drafter's flexible curve. You might consider using a mathematically fitted curve, especially if your organization includes many engineers or scientists. However, a curve drawn by visual inspection meets all practical needs. That curve represents the general pattern of sales development for trainees in your company. It shows the median sales to be expected at each level of experience. You can read those sales values from the graph with sufficient accuracy for this purpose. The example learning curve is shown in Figure 14–2.

Learning Curve Analysis

The sales learning curve can provide valuable diagnostic insight as you seek opportunities to improve sales force productivity and plan for changes. A company with a sales learning curve much like the one shown in Figure 14–2 found that a typical salesperson reached the minimum acceptable sales volume of $50,000 per month in about eight months. However, rapid expansion and high turnover had left the company with a sales force averaging only seven months on the job. (Those with over one year were counted as 12-month employees in this analysis because the learning curve

TABLE 14–2
Median Sales by Months-on-the-Job
(Sales in $ 000.)

Months-on-the-Job	Median Sales
1	5.4
2	7.2
3	14.5
4	15.0
5	27.2
6	34.0
7	37.5
8	52.8
9	67.2
10	73.3
11	78.5
12	80.0
13	78.5
14	76.2

showed no further growth in median sales beyond 12 months-on-the-job.)

When management became aware of the cost implication of adding more trainees and thereby lowering the average months-on-the-job even further, they put their expansion plans on hold. In that case, the learning curve told the whole story. Low average months-on-the-job equaled low average sales, and that meant low total sales force productivity.

Because new salespeople took too long to reach an acceptable (break-even) sales level, the company adopted a new program for trainees. The program coupled intensive initial training with a new pay plan. The resulting new learning curve is shown in Figure 14–3. Under the revised program, no sales were credited to a salesperson until after graduation from the intensive one-month formal training. Coaching in the field continued. The new program increased the company's initial cost burden with lower sales

FIGURE 14–1
Median Sales/Months-on-the-Job

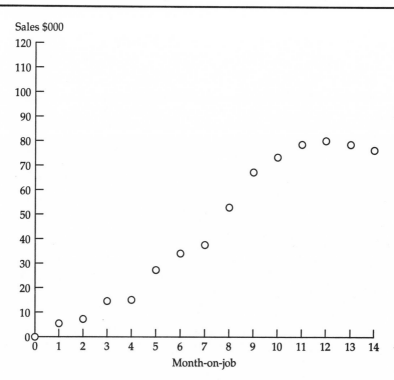

Sales $000

Month-on-job

through the early months and a heavy investment in the training school. However, median sales reached the acceptable level of $50,000 at five months, instead of eight months, and the curve rose to new heights as the company attracted and retained stronger performers. The company's investment in training and early survival pay was soon repaid many times over.

A sales learning curve may decline after reaching its peak. In such a case, the decline is usually due to a loss of high producers from the sales force while other salespersons continue to sell at their former (lower) level. Promotions and resignations take away the high producers from the sales force. That leaves the lower median sales volumes among the survivors at longer service

FIGURE 14–2
Learning Curve

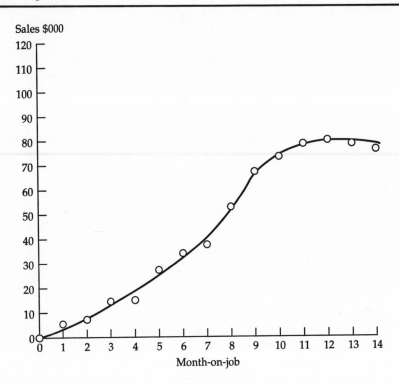

months. Studying the sales learning curve may help identify such opportunities for improvement in your company.

TRAINEE PAY FORMULA

The concern here is with planning the pay for trainees in relation to the sales results expected of them. The learning curve shows what is reasonable to expect. About one-half of the trainees will sell at or above the learning curve value for each particular month-on-the-job. The learning curve value may be less than the company wants, but the record shows that is what you should expect as the norm for now.

FIGURE 14–3
New and Old Learning Curves

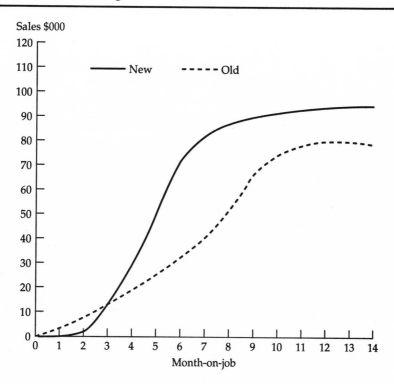

In addition to the median learning curve, you can develop a high curve representing the top 20 percent of sales values for each month-on-the-job and a low curve for the lowest 20 percent. Figure 14–4 shows high, normal, and low curves. Using high, normal, and low sales values from those curves, you can set corresponding pay targets. Then design a pay formula that will produce the intended pay amounts in the expected range of sales values. Follow the same process described in Chapter 5. The difference for trainee pay—and a complicating factor—is that the expected sales values change each month. The trainee pay plan may have to adjust for each month-on-the-job to produce the intended total pay amounts.

FIGURE 14–4
High, Normal, and Low Learning Curves

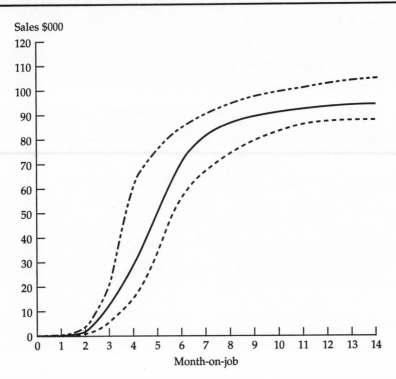

Sales $000

When fitting pay to expected sales results, you can adjust salary, quota, minimum, or incentive rate. However, you should not seek high-precision fitting to the trainee pay targets if that would result in an overly complicated plan. The key is whether trainees can understand and remember how they are being paid. Progressively raising the minimum may provide enough adjustment for the trainee's growing experience. Or try a gradual reduction of salary or draw. As with other sales pay planning, the cut-and-try method should be tested with realistic sales data on computer spreadsheets before any formula is put into effect.

LIMITATIONS

Trainee sales performance may prove difficult to measure where there is substantial sales momentum. The continuing flow of repeat orders masks for a time the struggles of a new salesperson in the field. The trainee's performance or lack thereof may be hidden from management and from the trainee by the ongoing flow of business. In such a situation of high sales momentum, the sales manager must get into the field frequently to check the pulse of activity. Call reports and customer comments may be as close as one can get to an objective measure of job performance by the trainee. Long sales cycle situations also prove difficult to measure, even if there is no sales momentum. In either situation, a learning curve for trainees would prove meaningless since no clear measure of the trainee's performance exists month by month.

One-shot selling (that is, little or no repeat sales volume) with a short sales cycle provides the ideal situation in which to measure a trainee's results. With no sales carried over from a predecessor and a short-to-moderate time between initial call and an order, you can see clearly how well the trainee performs each month. Examples in this chapter are based on such data. Perhaps your situation provides less than the ideal measurement of trainee results. If so, you may wish to apply these concepts in a general way, even though lacking detailed analysis.

When designing the trainee pay plan, do not worry too much about the cost. The cost of trainees will always be high. Consider it as an investment. Your return on that investment will be great when the pay plan helps build a strong, stable, and highly productive sales force.

CHECKLIST FOR TRAINEE PAY

√ Accept the fact that trainees are expensive, and make that expense into an investment.

√ Design trainee pay for six objectives: enough applicants, quality applicants, complete training, rapid progress, sustain the satisfactory, keeping costs reasonable.

✓ Provide four features: salary, adjusted incentive pay, no debt, graduation.

✓ Study the trainee learning curve as the basis for pay plan design.

✓ Provide a pay formula that rewards trainees according to trainee results.

Chapter Fifteen

Manager Pay

Building a team: Coach or competitor?

The person assigned to supervise salespeople finds, perhaps for the first time, that the job requires more than one's own product knowledge and selling skills. Some fail to make the transition from salesperson to sales manager. They remain senior salespersons in outlook and function. The company, however, can compensate sales managers for success in managing—and thereby increase the chances for success in sales management.

This chapter provides guidance in how to compensate the sales manager. It reviews pay methods that tie the manager's interest to the success of the sales team—from traditional override plans to plans targeted for multiple objectives. It also includes advice for avoiding common mistakes in paying for the manager's own sales.

Whether a supervisor of four sales representatives or national sales manager over a sales force of hundreds, a sales manager's primary responsibility is to build sales, or to build profitable sales, through the subordinate sales force. To fulfill that responsibility, the sales manager must select, train, organize, and direct the salespeople. If senior executives have not prepared the salesperson for the responsibilities of sales management, the new manager may be overwhelmed by the reality of those obligations.

A new dimension has been introduced to the person's life, and the new manager may not like it. Success as a salesperson came from hard work, long hours, close customer relationships, thorough product knowledge, skill in selling. . . . Now, however, the new manager finds that those talents are not enough. The manager no longer controls results through direct, personal effort and skill. The manager is cast into a role of partial dependency—not something that comes easily to the self-sufficient, independent-minded star salesperson.

The manager must depend upon subordinates to get the job done. The manager cannot force results from those other people. They determine sales results, not the manager alone. Some of those other people clearly lack the ambition and know-how of star performers. Most, in fact, are quite ordinary people. The manager's future success is in their hands—and in the hands of senior executives who will evaluate the manager's performance. This new role feels uncomfortably different from the independent, self-sufficient success the person enjoyed before. Considering the emotional hazard of moving from the position of star salesperson to the other-controlled position of sales manager, it is not surprising that some find it difficult to make the transition into management.

MANAGER PAY AIMS

The sales manager's compensation arrangement may help or hinder the management function. Too much reward opportunity for the manager in making personal sales may steer the manager toward functioning as a senior sales representative or key account representative. Too much security pay or corporate-executive incentive arrangements may lead to swivel-chair sales management. The sales manager then remains in the office, reading reports, writing memos, attending endless meetings, and planning the annual golf outing.

A quarterback can contribute little to the team while sitting on the bench, even less if seated in the owner's upholstered viewing box. The football team needs the quarterback on the field and the sales team needs their sales manager where the action is. Therefore, the company should provide a pay plan that involves the sales manager in the success of the subordinate sales force. The sales manager can then personally feel the "thrill of victory and the agony of defeat" of the total sales team. In that way, the manager quickly learns and never forgets that the job of managing is to make things happen through other people. Beyond a reward for the team's sales results, the manager's pay should also recognize the added managerial responsibilities beyond sales.

SALARY

Sales managers generally receive an important part of their pay in the form of salary. Often, the salary is too large and the incentive too small to permit sufficient pay variance. (See Chapter 6 for a discussion of pay variance.) The sales manager should not be deprived of the opportunity to experience major swings in total pay as total sales results rise and fall. That means keeping the salary low enough to permit a substantial amount of total pay to come from incentives for results in sales and in management.

The first-line sales supervisor may receive a base salary 20 percent above the base salary of a senior sales representative. Similar differentials of about 20 percent may apply also to the salaries of district manager and regional manager. The salary difference for different levels of responsibility in sales management should not be less than 10 percent.

Most companies have a formal salary management system including job evaluation, grades, and salary ranges for nonsales positions. Commonly, sales positions are excluded from such salary programs because of the large part of total pay at risk in the form of incentive pay. However, you may want to review the company's formal structure of salary ranges for some guidance in the planning of salaries for sales managers. Plan the base salary for sales managers from total pay objectives as explained in Chapter 3.

In planning salaries, it is well to remember that sales managers should receive at least 20 percent of total pay in the form of incentive pay, preferably more. Do not consider incentive dollars as equal to salary dollars. Incentive dollars are cheaper dollars.

They have less equivalent value because (1) they constitute a variable cost to the company, unlike the fixed cost of salary, and (2) they provide contingent income to the person, unlike the certain income of salary. For both employee and company, incentive dollars are worth something less than salary dollars.

OVERRIDE ON TOTAL SALES

The most widely used incentive arrangement for sales managers is the **override**. It pays a flat percentage of subordinates' total sales or total commissions to the manager. It is called an override because the sales representatives receive a commission on their sales and then the manager also receives a commission on those same sales. At first glance, the override on total sales seems to provide a suitable incentive for the manager to build sales through the subordinate sales force. Manager and sales representatives share a common interest in increasing sales. Often, however, the override-on-total-sales falls short of providing strong and appropriate incentive.

The override-on-total-sales may prompt the manager to neglect low producers while providing excessive support to high producers. The manager may see greater short-term potential for added sales from the proven high producers. The manager may tolerate low producers for too long just because they do produce some sales. This type of override sometimes encourages the manager to press for a larger sales force. Added sales through added sales representatives might be good economics for the manager but not necessarily for the company. There are other ways to tie the manager's pay to the results of the subordinate sales force.

OVERRIDE ON AVERAGE SALES

Instead of paying an override on total sales, the company can pay the manager an override on the average sales or average commission of subordinate sales representatives. This approach invites a different direction of effort by the manager. The manager takes a greater interest in the selection and development of trainees. The manager does well if all subordinate sales representatives do well. Low producers must be brought up to standard or be replaced, for they drag down the average commission.

Under this arrangement, the manager may press for a smaller sales force of high producers. That could prove profitable for both manager and company. However, if carried too far, the company could lose potentially profitable sales volume as the small sales force skims only the most easily accessible sales. Once again, a pay plan can support but not replace management.

PAY VARIANCE

A flat percentage override, whether based on total sales or average commission, often fails the test of adequate pay variance for the manager. While any individual salesperson might readily increase sales by some large percentage, the manager over several salespeople faces greater difficulty in raising total sales or average commission by that same percentage. The combined sales force results are dampened by the inevitable averaging effect among low and high producers.

The manager may once have been a highly productive sales representative who could develop strong personal sales. That same person can never hope to develop the entire subordinate sales force to that high level of production. On the other side, total sales will never drop as low as might be the case for a poorly performing or unlucky sales representative. The team's composite sales results swing within a relatively narrow range. Therefore, the manager's incentive pay should be designed to fluctuate adequately within the expected range of results. That usually requires an incentive formula with a larger pay-to-sales multiplier than that applied to the individual salesperson. (See Chapter 6 for further discussion of pay variance.)

A flat-rate override formula typically fails to fluctuate enough to keep the manager excited about the results of the subordinate sales force. However, a set-aside formula often provides the best fit for manager pay objectives—better then either a flat-rate or a progressive-rate formula. As in planning pay for sales representatives, you should design the pay formula to fit the manager's intended pay targets (high, normal, and marginal) and the average pay variance.

MANAGER'S SALES

A manager may be assigned certain accounts or even a regular territory to cover in addition to overseeing subordinate salespeople. When the manager must also function as a salesperson, a chance for conflict arises. If the pay plan rewards the manager for personal sales results, the manager daily faces the decision of whether to support the subordinate salespeople or to concentrate instead on personal selling. Even if the pay plan offers balanced reward opportunities for managing and selling, the manager is likely to devote as much time as possible to personal selling.

In most such situations, the manager has received little or no training in how to manage others. The person was selected as manager because of superior sales skills. That is what the manager does best and feels most comfortable doing. He or she can more readily increase income by selling than by trying to build sales through less-experienced and less-talented subordinates. If given a choice in the matter, the manager naturally gravitates to selling, not to managing.

The result may include disputes over who gets credit for certain sales, skimming of the best leads by the manager, and other crosscurrents of conflict and dissatisfaction within the sales team. Late symptoms may include reduced general selling effort, increased turnover of salespeople, and lower overall sales results. By the time you see such obvious symptoms, the problem has already cost the company dearly and it will be difficult to rectify.

TOTAL TEAM RESULTS

Managerial training and guidance from superiors contribute importantly to the way in which a manager functions. The right kind of pay plan can help keep the manager on the sales team and away from the role of outsider or even competitor. The pay arrangement can provide a strong influence on total sales results, define the manager's responsibilities, and direct the manager's priorities for time and behavior on the job.

If you pay the manager a straight salary, perhaps with a discretionary bonus, you risk sending the message that the manager has risen to a lofty position well above the drudgery of field selling. Add a burden of paperwork and frequent unproductive meetings and you convince the manager that the position calls for concentrating on abstract matters instead of the details of making sales happen through the field sales team. Thus, self-image and imposed distractions can combine to produce a swivel-chair sales manager.

Companies that achieve high productivity within the total sales force usually tie a manager's reward to the results of the sales team the manager directs. The reward is for total team sales results—including the manager's own sales. The manager can then afford to assign accounts and leads where they will be served best. The manager can afford to take the time to coach and support members of the sales team to produce maximum team results.

As with pay for salespeople, the manager's incentive pay (whether override, bonus, or other) may be based on any measure of sales results, including gross profit, and those results may be measured on absolute or relative bases. It may include additional rewards for new-account development, product mix, market penetration, and other factors. The closer the supervisor's pay elements match those of the subordinate salespeople, the closer will be the manager's interest in their selling results.

MANAGEMENT BONUS

The manager is responsible for several management functions in addition to team sales. The manager should receive instruction and coaching in those responsibilities and how they contribute to sales and profits. When making the change from salesperson, however, many newly appointed managers are not made aware of those responsibilities. Such responsibilities seem so obvious to senior executives that the executives may fail either to explain the responsibilities to the new sales manager or to set up a planned program of coaching and follow-up audits.

The manager needs a pay plan that reinforces the management responsibilities of the position, apart from sales results. Although the pay plan may place major attention on generating sales through the sales team, added incentive elements can recognize other management functions. Including too many elements in the plan, however, can create confusion and reduce each element to motivational insignificance. Effective pay plans generally offer incentives for not more than five responsibilities. Here are some common managerial incentive criteria:

- Selecting and training new salespersons
- Assisting on difficult sales
- Controlling costs
- Keeping territories staffed
- Managing gross profit or operating profit

If it is a branch or store manager position, responsibilities may include such as these:

- Branch staff management
- Inventory control
- Accounts receivable
- Customer service
- Operating profit

Such managerial criteria may form the basis for quarterly or semiannual bonuses, rather than being part of the monthly incentive pay for team sales results. Chapter 8 discusses guidelines for setting up a meaningful bonus plan. The same principles apply for manager bonuses as for bonuses to salespersons. Thus, the manager could receive (1) a base salary large enough to recognize the increased scope of responsibility in the position, (2) monthly incentive pay based on total sales team results—and leveraged enough to keep it interesting, and (3) a quarterly or semiannual bonus for results in designated managerial responsibilities. All such elements should be included in a properly drafted document covering the manager's pay plan.

LONG-TERM INCENTIVES

Long-term incentives may add to the manager's compensation package. Such elements as stock options, phantom stock, stock appreciation rights, and participating units (where stock is not available or not appropriate) can help tie the manager to the company. More importantly, long-term incentives give the manager a stake in building the company's future growth and prosperity. Even a basic review of long-term incentives would extend beyond the scope of this book, but the following suggestions may help to avoid some common errors.

Yearly Awards

Plan to award stock options or other long-term incentives annually. Do not commit to an overly generous initial grant. The manager may prove to be worth less or more than you originally hoped. Yearly awards allow you to continually tune the long-term awards to perceived value of the person to the company. Annual grants keep the opportunity for gain constantly rolling forward.

Performance Base

Adjust each year's award to the person's position in the company and the results achieved for the year. Some companies award stock options or other long-term incentives on a formula related to the sum of the year's cash incentive awards earned by the manager. Thus, the manager may receive options with a face value equal to one-half of the person's cash incentives for the year.

Vesting

Five-year vesting is most common for stock options, but participating units commonly vest over three, four, or five years. The plan may provide for full vesting upon a major change in company ownership. Vesting establishes the golden bond that ties the manager to the company. The manager's continued service earns him or her the right to acquire a progressively larger part of the award. It is hoped that the value of the award will grow during the deferral period.

Most plans fit into one of three vesting categories: (1) Cliff vesting gives the manager no rights until the end of the vesting period, such as five years. Then the person suddenly becomes fully vested in the award. (2) Installment vesting establishes the manager's rights in several large steps, such as 20 percent at the end of each year of continued employment. (3) Continual or daily vesting builds the manager's rights steadily and gradually with each day of continued employment during the designated vesting period. Each day makes only a small difference in vested value. Continual vesting avoids the magic-day phenomenon that may prompt the employee or superiors to schedule employment termination decisions around the vesting date.

What, if any, long-term incentives a company provides for sales managers usually depends on a broader plan of management incentives throughout the company. Rarely has a company instituted long-term incentives for sales managers only. However, creative planning for sales manager compensation may trigger changes in thinking about long-term incentives for other managers as well.

CHECKLIST FOR MANAGER PAY

√ Design a pay plan to fit the sales manager's responsibilities.

/ Pay a base salary reasonably above subordinate salaries,

but leave room for incentive pay to provide an important part of total pay.

√ Provide incentive pay based on the team's total or average sales.

√ Include the manager's own sales in the team total for calculating the manager's incentive pay.

√ Design the incentive formula to fit the expected range of total or average sales results, for adequate pay variance.

√ Recognize managerial responsibilities with a management bonus, apart from sales results.

√ Consider long-term incentives to hold the manager and to encourage a long-term growth perspective.

Chapter Sixteen

Special Issues

Miscellaneous notes, consistent principles.

The notes in this chapter address sales pay situations and issues outside the conventional image of field selling. Reviewing the observations and advice of this chapter may add perspective to the unique needs and opportunities of any individual company. These notes show that the sales compensation principles presented elsewhere in this book apply in all sales situations.

RETAILING

They work in department stores, specialty stores, and discount stores. They receive the customer's payment, record the sale on paper or cash register, and deliver the merchandise. They make sales, but should they be called salespeople? Should they be paid as salespeople? Some stores neither call them salespeople nor pay them as such. They may be called clerks, associates, waiters, attendants, cashiers, and so on. Almost all retail store selling depends upon the customer being attracted to the store by location, appearance, advertising, products, prices, and past service. The customer comes to the salesperson, rather than the salesperson having to find the customer. Some field sales managers dismiss the activity as "order taking, not real selling." Some retail salespeople are paid straight salary, for that very reason. Management considers the job as one in which the employee exercises little influence on the sale. However, stores that want their employees to take a positive interest in increasing sales usually pay salary plus commission, and some pay a bonus.

Salary

The term salary is used here to include a regular hourly wage rate, not necessarily a monthly rate. Many retailers have found value in hiring part-time workers. With employees working varied hours, the store pays the designated rate for the hours worked. This avoids problems of compliance with the minimum wage and over-time pay provisions of the federal Fair Labor Standards Act and similar state laws. Sales results, likewise, may be tracked and evaluated on an hourly basis. Thus, the salesperson may receive a salary of $6.50 per hour plus a progressive-rate commission that increases as the person's average sales-per-hour increases within a two-week or one-month incentive period.

Base salary may be scaled up for added length of service. This encourages the salesperson to stay with the store. It also recognizes that a salesperson's value to the store increases over time. Knowledge of the merchandise, sales skills, flexibility of assignment—all of these increase in value up to some point. Replacement of that salesperson would entail added costs of recruiting, training, errors, and lost sales. One prominent department store uses this salary schedule in all departments, with varied commission arrangements added for individual departments:

Service	*Salary*
0 to 800 hours	$5.75 per hour
801 to 1,600	$6.50
1,601 to 2,400	$7.25
2,401 to 3,200	$8.00
3,201 to 4,000	$8.75
Over 4,000	$9.50

Base salary provides survival pay. Retailers commonly offer sales salaries somewhat below the median salary of junior file clerks, junior typists, and messengers—the lowest salary levels among office workers. A retailer lacking competitive pay data for other stores in the area can look into office worker salary surveys to get a general picture of this segment of the labor market. The U.S. Bureau of Labor Statistics publishes Area Wage Surveys for major metropolitan areas. Local employer associations and some state employment offices also provide salary survey data.

Incentive Pay

In addition to the base salary, if any, the retailer may provide incentive pay in any of the forms described earlier in this book. Retailers, especially department stores, face a complex task in planning sales compensation because of the number of different sales jobs. The person selling major appliances or furniture holds a job quite different from that of the person selling candy in the same store. Other departments, such as fine jewelry, children's shoes, men's suits, better coats and dresses, small appliances, and books also differ in the sales-per-hour that may be expected. They may differ also in the experience, knowledge, and selling skills required. Therefore, multiple pay plans are required if the store is to get maximum motivation value from its sales payroll. Each sales job should have a pay plan based on realistic expectations of sales-per-hour and realistic pay targets for high, normal, and low sales results. Because of the multitude of sales jobs, a large department store may have under one roof several different pay formulas: straight salary, straight commission, commission-with-draw, commission-with-guarantee, flat-rate commission, progressive-rate commission, and so on.

Some stores provide a department or store incentive where selling is a team process or where sales cannot be credited realistically and fairly to the efforts of one person. Stores may use a department or store incentive to accommodate the occasional windfall sale. For example, by sheer luck Salesperson A was next up and got the huge sale. Salesperson A receives the regular commission up to some amount. The balance of the commission is allocated among all the department salespeople according to their hours worked in that month. Fairness and employee satisfaction are the aims of that plan.

Criteria

If the retailer wants to encourage selling of related items, the pay plan can provide an increased commission rate for each sales ticket that contains two or more dissimilar items. For example, a purchase of a shirt and tie would receive the extra credit, but a purchase of three shirts would not. To encourage selling higher-priced items, the store may apply a premium commission rate to designated merchandise.

A quota bonus may be paid as a special reward for sales above a specified amount. For example, sales above quota receive 25 percent greater commission. This is another form of a progressive rate commission. An important factor for the pay planner to consider is the appropriate quota. If the aim is to reward high performers, the quota should be adjusted to the sales expectations of the season. The quota for children's shoes should be higher in the back-to-school period than during summer months.

As with other types of sales pay, the planner should include only criteria that will receive a significant value weighting in the total pay package. There is no motivational value in offering trivial increments in pay for certain goals. Each criterion should carry a target value of at least 5 percent of the total pay target, preferably 10 percent or more. Adding criteria may mean reducing the value of the major criterion, such as sales-per-hour. Careful planning of pay targets within the expected range of sales results will keep the plan powerful in its motivational effect and reasonable in cost.

The procedure for planning motivationally effective compensation in retail sales jobs follows the motive power method described in earlier chapters of this book. The incentive period might be one week, two weeks, or one month. The criterion might be average sales-per-hour. Although retail pay targets might seem modest compared to wholesale and industrial pay, and the pay variance might average only 10 to 15 percent, the principles of sales pay planning apply equally to retail selling as to other types of selling.

INDEPENDENT REPS

Managers of companies that sell through independent representatives often wonder about the most effective way to compensate those salespeople. For convenience, we refer here to all nonemployee contracted salespeople as reps. This classification may include representatives, agents, brokers, distributors, and others who sell the company's products but are not employees of the company.

Advantages

The company may gain several advantages in selling through reps. The rep provides immediate sales coverage of a territory, with no immediate, fixed cost to the company. The rep may be highly qualified, with much experience in selling similar or related products to the market that the company wants to reach. In some cases, the company's products can be sold effectively or economically only by a rep who also offers several related products. The rep's contacts and reputation in the market may provide customer access not otherwise available to a lesser-known manufacturer.

Disadvantages

Although many considerations may favor or even require selling through reps, the company also faces some frustrations in this type of selling arrangement. The rep, being an independent contractor, is less subject to direction and control than an employee-salesperson. Both the company and the rep recognize this reality, but only the company sees it as a source of frustration. The company management would like the rep to work harder on behalf of the company and give the company's products a greater amount of time and attention. The rep, however, takes a broader view of the products, market, and earnings opportunity.

Compensation arrangements can help to capture a rep's attention and focus it on the company's marketing strategy and sales goals—sometimes. The first issue for the company to consider is the company's degree of influence with the rep.

Influence

The company may safely assume that it enjoys maximum importance to the rep if the company's products constitute the core of the rep's business in volume or prestige. In that case, the rep looks upon the relationship almost like an employee, and the company can wield much influence through the compensation arrangement as well as through direct communication.

At the other extreme, the company may have little influence on the rep if its products provide only a minor part of the rep's total business. Even in that case, the company's compensation arrangement can bring more attention to the company's products than they would receive otherwise. Companies between those extremes of much influence and little influence also may receive more than their fair share of rep attention through the compensation arrangement. As with employed salespeople, both the amount and the method of compensation contribute to the rep's responsiveness in selling a company's products

Solo versus Organization

If the rep is a self-employed individual, the company may consider the person much like an employee for purposes of designing the compensation plan. If, however, the rep is one of several in a selling organization (brokerage, agency, etc.) the company faces a more difficult problem. The company contracts with and deals through the selling organization's management. The company may find it difficult or impossible to reach and influence the individual rep who makes sales happen. Manufacturers struggle with this problem of isolation and corresponding lack of direct influence.

Some companies offer contests, prizes, and bonuses for special sales results. Even so, the selling organization may frustrate such efforts—intentionally or inadvertently. A distributor of stationery store merchandise carried hundreds of items from dozens of manufacturers. The distributor president regularly destroyed announcements of manufacturers' contests and bonuses. If the distributor organization happened to win any bonus for its sales of a particular product, the bonus went into the organization's revenue and not to the salesperson. The president explained, "We get several special deals every month. It would take all our time to handle the promotion and reporting for those deals. More to the point, we want our salespeople to concentrate on service to the stationery store proprietor and to sell our full catalog. We do not want our people pushing a particular item one month and another the next month." There was no practical way that a manufacturer could influence the individual salespeople of that distributor organization.

Other selling organizations prove more open, especially if they carry only a few lines instead of dozens. When offering prizes or bonuses to salespeople, the manufacturer should consider making the special promotion attractive to sales management also. Then everyone in the organization shares a mutual interest in selling the product.

Method

If the company can reach the individual rep with its compensation arrangement, the company can apply the motive power method as described earlier in this book. The same steps apply to designing compensation arrangements for independent reps—with a few variations.

First, most manufacturing companies will not pay a salary or draw to the rep. The rep's compensation depends upon and follows completion of a sale. That leaves commissions and perhaps bonuses as the available compensation elements. Instead of simply following the industry practice with a me-too flat-rate commission, consider a progressive rate or a set-aside formula.

Planning such arrangements requires a forecast of sales results. From that forecast, you can then design a commission formula. Follow the same procedure explained in earlier chapters for setting high, normal, and low pay targets corresponding to high, normal, and low sales results.

Even if you are pleading with the rep to carry your product line, you might gain some extra attention by proposing a more exciting compensation opportunity than the common practice. The principles of compensation remain the same. Your ability to apply them, however, is subject to a different kind of negotiation when dealing with an independent rep.

LONG CYCLE

How long does it take to sell a jet airplane? A giant power generator? A locomotive? The answer is a long time. Major service and supply contracts may also involve a long sales cycle from initial contact through building confidence, checking references, gaining technical approval, and finally getting the order. Where the normal sales cycle extends from six months to several years, as in the examples above, the company faces a special problem in sales compensation. Such long-cycle selling does not adapt well to conventional sales incentive pay arrangements.

Some companies pay the salespeople straight salary and perhaps a bonus when the sale is made or at year-end. That is simple and may prove adequate. However, most long-cycle selling can be made more exciting and rewarding. The answer lies in looking at the total job of the salesperson, not only at the completed sale.

What should the salesperson be doing? How can we know how well the person is performing? Answering those questions will lead you to identify criteria that can provide a base for an exciting, rewarding pay plan. Those criteria might include various accomplishments or milestones that could lead to a sale.

For example, a company selling executive jet airplanes found certain measurable milestones that lead progressively to a sale. One of the milestones was for the salesperson to take a qualified prospect for a demonstration flight in the plane. To the outsider, that may not seem like much of an achievement. However, in the business of selling executive jet airplanes, the demonstration flight proves to be a key point. The qualified prospect already owns an airplane, and the person leads a busy life. It is difficult for the salesperson to build the relationship to the point where the prospect will take an hour or so to fly in the expensive new airplane. The company's pay plan rewards for such milestones and for the completed sale. Even if the sale is not completed, the salesperson gets the satisfaction of rewards for real achievement within the responsibilities of the job.

A company selling aluminum architectural products found several milestones in their long sales cycle. By providing incentive pay for reaching each of those milestones, the pay plan was made more interesting and rewarding than straight salary.

Even with a very long sales cycle, you can probably find criteria worth rewarding along the way to a sale. In some cases, the salesperson may no longer be involved when the sale is completed. Technical and finance people may take over to complete the sale, while the salesperson moves on to another series of milestones with a new prospect.

RESIDUAL-SALES

Sell an insurance policy and the company receives premiums for many years. Likewise, long-term service contracts, leases, and time-purchase agreements provide income to the company over several years. How should the salesperson be compensated for such sales? Here is a review of key issues to consider in rewarding for residual-sales.

As in other aspects of planning sales compensation, put aside the question of cost and concentrate first on motivation. You need to provide a sales pay plan that will attract and retain the people qualified for this sophisticated selling. You need to keep them excited about building sales. Thus, the basic principles and procedures presented in earlier chapters of this book apply also to residual-sales. The ongoing nature of the customer-company relationship may or may not present a compensation issue.

Not an Issue

If the salesperson's task is completed upon making the sale, there may be no need to extend compensation beyond that point. That would apply where the salesperson cannot influence subsequent collections by the company under the residual-sale. For example, a commercial real estate agent arranges a 10-year lease of a building. The agent sees the deal through to the final signing and receives the commission. If problems arise later between landlord and tenant, the agent's compensation is not affected.

In such situations, the pay plan should reward the salesperson for accomplishing the sale. If subsequent collections or renewals do not involve the salesperson, there is no reason to extend the compensation past the period of the salesperson's contribution.

An Issue

Compensation for the residual portion of such sales becomes an issue of concern where the salesperson can influence subsequent collections. In some cases, the company holds the salesperson responsible for credit evaluation of the customer. If the customer subsequently fails to make payments, the company penalizes the salesperson. (Interestingly, it is almost unheard of for the company's credit manager to be penalized for such collection problems.)

In other situations, the company may expect the salesperson to provide service to the customer during the residual period. Such service may be to keep the customer satisfied or to gain additional sales. In such cases the company should provide extended payment to the salesperson during all or part of the residual-income period. Such extended payments can avoid overpaying for sales that fail to sustain residual-income for the intended period. If the salesperson can select customers or structure the sale so as to enhance the prospects for long-term residual-income, the salesperson should be rewarded as that residual-income is proved. That concept governs the compensation practices of insurance companies.

A Problem

Extending reward for a residual-sale into future years may seem reasonable for both control and financial reasons. However, motivational objectives may be less well served by extended compensation. The accomplishment of making the sale deserves prompt reward, not delayed reward. By extending part of the reward into future years, the initial reward is lessened. The salesperson's income of future years may bear little relationship to the person's selling results in those years. This presents a major problem in the insurance industry. Residual commissions prompt some of the best producers to retire prematurely from active selling as pay variance flattens and the excitement and satisfaction wane.

Moderation

In many residual-sale situations, the company can avoid placing too much money into extended payments for too long a period. If lease or contract renewal is a major objective, the company can reward for such renewals without paying extended commissions between renewals. In many situations, validity of the residual-sale can be established in one year and further service by the salesperson may not be needed. In such cases, the commission period can be limited to one year, even though the residual-sale continues beyond that.

As with other sales pay planning, the company should consider its marketing and motivational aims first. Design the pay plan to provide target pay at target sales levels, with enough pay variance to keep it exciting. Cost should not dictate delayed reward—if you intend to keep a satisfied, productive sales force. Be clear in the sales pay plan document about whether residual commissions will continue after employment terminates.

LIMITED SUPPLY

In some industries, the supply of products occasionally becomes limited. This occurs most often with agricultural products, where planting, weather, or disease may curtail the amount available.

Similar shortages can occur in other industries for a variety of reasons from war to labor stoppages, shipping problems to regulatory controls. Whatever the reason, a limited supply creates a special problem in sales compensation.

The salesperson could sell much but the supply is limited. The company may put its customers on allocations. Where does that leave the salesperson whose pay plan provides low survival pay and high opportunity pay? The opportunity to increase sales has disappeared, at least for now. The salespeople will quickly inform the sales manager of the old adage, "You can't sell from an empty wagon."

The company's top management probably has some idea of how long the shortage will last. They may also be concerned about maintaining customer goodwill during this difficult period. Whether for a few months or a year, the sales job undergoes a radical change. The compensation program must be changed accordingly—if the company is to retain its sales force. Salary or a guarantee must partially replace incentive pay to continue the incomes of the salespeople near their accustomed level. It is seldom necessary or advisable to provide 100 percent replacement income. Fixed income is worth more than contingent income—to both company and salesperson. Therefore, the company may decide to restore 80 to 90 percent of the salesperson's accustomed income during this critical period.

In exchange for the special added salary or guarantee, the salespeople may be assigned to making good-will calls on customers, conducting market research, training, preparing catalogs and manuals . . . anything that can contribute to the company's welfare. This may also become vacation time for all, in spite of individual preferences for another time of year. The aims are to survive and prepare for better days ahead.

NEW PRODUCT

Forecasting sales for a new product presents a most difficult challenge. That, in turn, creates a problem for sales pay design. Much the same difficulty arises in planning for a new company or a new market. Sales pay, to be motivationally effective, must be based on realistic expectations of high, normal, and low sales levels. A totally new product with no related precedents leaves the planner wondering what sales to expect. And that leaves sales compensation equally uncertain.

A large company with many related products will have market research and analyses of prior product introductions to guide its sales expectations. Although the giant company may encounter some surprises, it will have a more reliable sales forecast than does the typical small- to-medium-sized company introducing a new product.

Launching a new product provides uncertainty. Every additional element of newness compounds the uncertainty. The ultimate shot-in-the-dark is a new product being sold by a new sales force to a new market. Whether the sales uncertainty qualifies as mild or severe, the pay planner should keep that question mark in mind. If the planner designs a compensation arrangement that soon proves to provide too little reward, the salespeople will lose enthusiasm and perhaps leave. On the other hand, an overly generous pay plan will cost the company excessively. All things considered, most companies would choose sales success at a high cost over sales failure at a modest cost.

Knowing that sales results cannot be forecasted with reasonable reliability, the planner should expect to change the pay plan frequently as the new product finds its place in the market. In addition to the company executives being prepared for changes in the pay plan, the salespeople also should be prepared. Avoid seeming to back away from a compensation arrangement just because the salespeople have achieved high earnings. Sales force morale and stability will be enhanced if the salespeople are told in advance that the company intends to revise the pay plan after six months to keep it competitive, rewarding, and exciting.

EXCESSIVE PAY

Perhaps earnings have become excessive for some or all salespeople in your company. Such a problem may arise from any of several causes, but usually from inadequate planning coupled with procrastination. As the high-pay situation continues, it becomes more extreme and more difficult to correct.

Too Much Pay?

Some managers and a great many salespeople hold the view that no amount of compensation should be considered as too much for a salesperson. However, when a company finds itself paying $200,000 to accomplish a $50,000 selling job, a question arises. Can carrying excessive cost for selling be justified any more than paying double for warehouse space or other business expenses? When cost far exceeds value in selling, management must make a change. Getting the cost back to a reasonable level will permit expanding the sales force, increasing advertising, or making other business-building investments. Also, a more reasonable level of sales pay better satisfies management's fiduciary obligation to stockholders.

The concern that faces management, and has produced delay to this point, is that of alienating the sales force. Perhaps the problem applies to only a few superstars, but the issue remains the same. You need to bring the pay down, but you do not want to drive away your most productive salespeople. That sounds impossible—and it may be. However, here are a few suggestions drawn from companies that have dealt with the issue of excessive sales pay.

How Many Overpaid?

First, assemble the facts. Compile monthly sales results and sales pay data for each salesperson for the past three years. Determine the scope and intensity of the problem. How many salespeople seem overpaid—by whatever standard you choose? If the problem applies to less than 10 percent of the sales force, it probably can be managed with little risk to the company. If 20 percent of the salespeople seem overpaid, the problem becomes more sensitive because of the wider risk. Beyond 20 percent, it may be classified as a problem of major scope.

Amount of Excess?

The intensity of the problem depends upon the amount and duration of excessive earnings. The size of the pay reduction that may be tolerated varies with the total pay amount. High-income salespeople can accept, at least temporarily, a larger reduction than can those at lower income levels. If the high pay has continued for only one year, you can change it with less upset than if the salespeople have become accustomed to high income for three years or more.

A printing company adopted a new pay plan that reduced the top representative's pay from over $300,000 per year to about $150,000. Management explained the need to control cost, and they granted stock options to the representative. He accepted grudgingly, but continued to sell to his old accounts. Two years later he retired, but by then senior executives had strengthened their relationships with the key accounts.

Ease the Pain

When changing to a pay plan with lower pay targets, try to provide some rationale and some face-saving for the salesperson. Lower pay will mean more than a reduction in income for the salesperson. The change carries negative messages about the person's self-worth. To minimize negative emotional response, try to introduce some positive plan features or other changes at the same time. For example, a wholesaler of tools and shop supplies changed from a straight commission plan to a salary-plus-incentive plan. The company also added a bonus for new accounts. The salespeople experienced a planned reduction in income of 25 percent. However, the new pay was above average for the industry. The change of plan features also allowed the salespeople some rationalization. They could tell themselves and their families that they now receive a regular salary, and the new-account bonus could pay off well for them. The company also reduced some territories, prompting the response, "I may not earn as much as before, but I do not have to work as hard."

If you are planning any improvements in benefits, this is the perfect time to introduce them. When reducing sales pay, give the sales force some other things to think about as well. If those other things are positive elements, so much the better. Reducing pay is never pleasant. When it becomes necessary, plan carefully to minimize the negative effect on morale and customer relations.

AUTOMOBILES

How should an automobile be figured into the sales compensation package? That question has been debated by sales managers and accountants long enough to prove that no single right answer fits every company. Here are some key points to consider.

Company Car

First, should the company provide an auto to the salesperson? Yes, if you require the salesperson to drive a special type of vehicle such as a pickup truck or a van to carry products. Another type of special vehicle sometimes required is a late-model luxury auto. If the company cares about the kind of auto the salesperson drives, the company should provide the vehicle. This ensures that the salesperson has the right kind of vehicle, and it eliminates any question about how the individual will finance it. The company may own or lease the vehicle for use by the salesperson, and the company's regular insurance covers the vehicle. Asking the salesperson to buy or lease a special vehicle could impede the recruiting of new salespeople, and it could be a negative element in future employee relations.

Another reason that some companies provide autos to salespeople is the expectation and perceived value of the auto in the mind of the salesperson. If other companies in your industry generally provide autos, your company could be at a competitive disadvantage in recruiting if it did not provide them. The salesperson who had a company auto in the last job may hesitate to consider a job without one.

When deciding whether to provide a company auto, the issue of its worth in the compensation program should be considered. This is a matter of perception by the salespeople. What value do they ascribe to a company auto? To test this, you can conduct a simple poll, using anonymous ballots. The question is not whether the person wants an auto in addition to regular pay, but how much regular pay the person would exchange for a company auto. If the acceptable exchange rate falls short of the company's cost to provide an auto, the company auto fails to qualify as a bargain for the company. Situations differ, however, and each company should investigate this matter with its own sales force.

Companies that provide autos generally reimburse the salesperson for fuel and other operating and maintenance expenses. Some pay for such expenses through a company credit card.

A recent survey[1] of over 500 companies where salespeople use autos on company business showed the following:

Company provides auto	60%
Employee provides auto	30%
Combination	10%

The pattern of company-provided autos differs among industries, from 70 percent for manufacturing companies to 40 percent for companies in wholesale trade and 30 percent for banks. Companies lease rather than buy autos by a margin of three to one.

Personal, nonbusiness use of a company auto is permitted by 80 percent of companies providing autos. About one-half of those companies charge for personal use of the auto, usually a mileage charge.

In some industries, such as real estate, insurance, and securities, it is rare for any company to provide an auto to salespeople. Many such companies do not reimburse the salesperson for entertainment, parking, tolls, and other expenses. That is typical where

[1] *1991/92 Sales and Marketing Personnel Report* (Fort Lee, N.J.: Executive Compensation Service, Inc., 1991), p. 42.

the salespeople are independent contractors or where the company regards its employee salespeople as virtually free agents. Such distancing between company and sales force also is evident in those companies that exclude or limit the level of participation in retirement plans for salespeople.

Employee Car

Companies that expect the salesperson to provide a vehicle appropriate to the job may require "a midpriced auto in good condition, not over five years old." The purpose of such a policy statement is to ensure reliable transportation and to avoid a negative public image. When the salesperson provides the vehicle, most companies reimburse for business mileage. About 70 percent pay a single rate for mileage, typically the rate allowed by the Internal Revenue Service for income tax purposes. Some reduce that rate for mileage in excess of 15,000 or 20,000 miles in a year. Only about 10 percent pay a flat monthly rate, and 20 percent pay a combination monthly rate plus mileage rate. The most sophisticated approach is to relate the auto allowance to the cost of owning and operating an auto in the particular territory. You may obtain data for this purpose as well as consulting advice on mileage allowances and company autos from

> Runzheimer International
> Runzheimer Park
> Rochester, Wisconsin 53167
> (414) 534-3121

No method, however, will guarantee complete satisfaction of the sales force, short of the company letting each salesperson have a completely free choice in selecting virtually any auto and paying all expenses connected with its use. Although a few do follow just such a policy, most companies dismiss the idea as being beyond their budget objectives and perhaps conveying the wrong message about economy of operations.

Sales pay surveys deserve special attention regarding company autos, mileage allowances, and expense reimbursements. As mentioned in Chapter 3, "Pay Targets," be sure that you compare like with like. If the surveyed companies differ in their practices, with some paying and some not paying for the salesperson's transportation and expenses, that may invalidate any conclusion about cash compensation reported in the survey.

Whatever the sales situation, you can apply the motive power method as presented in this book. It will provide maximum selling power by mobilizing strong motivation in the sales force and coupling that with the company's marketing strategy and sales goals.

Anonymous Company, Inc. Sales Pay Plan

Example of a straight commission sales pay plan, with a progressive-rate commission formula.

SALES PAY PLAN HIGHLIGHTS

This brief summary is not part of the Plan. Please read the Plan for details.

Guarantee

During first four months, based on Rep's experience.

Commission

Paid monthly.

Commission rate:

- 8.0% on sales up to $15,000, plus
- 10.0% on sales from $15,000 to $30,000, plus
- 12.5% on sales over $30,000.

Expenses

Company car.
Company pays fuel, etc.
Company pays other reasonable expenses.

SALES PAY PLAN

1. Eligibility

1.1 All field Sales Representatives (Reps) will be eligible under this Sales Pay Plan (Plan) while actively employed by Anonymous Company, Inc. (Company).

2. Guarantee

2.1 Each Rep will be eligible for a guarantee during the first four months of employment.

2.2 The Sales Manager will evaluate a new Rep's prior experience and will recommend an appropriate guarantee amount for approval by the President. Generally, a Rep with several years of related selling experience will be given a higher guarantee than a Rep with less experience.

2.3 The guarantee will be paid each month if the Rep's commissions for the month are less than the guarantee amount.

2.4 The guarantee is *not* a draw against future commission earnings. If commissions for a month are less than the guarantee amount, no negative balance will be carried forward.

2.5 The company will pay no draws or advances against future commissions.

3. Commission

3.1 Each Rep will be paid commission on sales from assigned accounts called on by the Rep at the assigned frequency for A, B, or C accounts.

3.2 The commission rate will be 8.0 percent of sales up to $15,000 in a month, plus 10.0 percent of sales from $15,000 to $30,000, plus 12.5 percent of sales above $30,000.

3.2.1 Commission calculation examples:

Month Sales	$15,000	
Commission	8.0% × $15,000 =	$1,200
Month Sales	$25,000	
Commission	8.0% × $15,000 =	$1,200
	10.0% × $10,000 =	$1,000
		$2,200

Month Sales $40,000
Commission   8.0% × $15,000 = $1,200
                10.0% × $15,000 = $1,500
                12.5% × $10,000 = $1,250
                                   $3,950

4. Sales Credits

4.1 **Normal Orders:** Sales will be credited to the responsible Rep when the order is billed to the customer. Sales credit will be at the order price, excluding taxes, freight, and other incidental charges.

4.2 **Special-Price Orders:** If an order is taken at other than the usual gross profit—such as a large volume, low price, "brown box" order—the Company may designate the order for adjusted sales credit.

   4.2.1 Such sales credit adjustment will represent approximately the difference in gross profit from a normal order, but in no case will the sales credit be adjusted below 20 percent of the order price. Thus, an order taken at 40 percent of normal gross profit would be credited at 40 percent of the order price, but an order taken at 10 percent of normal gross profit would be credited at the minimum 20 percent of the order price.

   4.2.2 Sales credit adjustments will be recommended by the Estimator for approval by the Sales Manager. The Sales Manager will notify the Rep of the adjustment before the Company accepts the order.

4.3 **Customer Credit:** Any amount credited back to a customer will be deducted from the Rep's sales when the customer credit is granted.

4.4 **Past-Due Accounts:** Any account that becomes 90 days past due will be deducted from the Rep's sales. When collection is made, the amount collected, less collection costs, will be credited to the Rep.

4.5 **House Accounts:** A list of house accounts will be issued by the Sales Manager. No sales credit will be given to a Rep for house account sales, unless the Rep is asked to help service the account on a split-sales basis.

4.6 **Split Sales:** If a Rep shares with another Rep in servicing an account, the Sales Manager will designate the division of sales credit from that account among the Reps involved.

5. **Expenses**

   5.1 The Company will provide an automobile for the Rep's use in business.

   5.2 The Company will reimburse the Rep for fuel, oil, and maintenance of the automobile in business use. Only reasonable expenses will be reimbursed, and the Sales Manager may designate a maximum reimbursement for any Rep.

   5.3 The Company will reimburse the Rep for tolls, parking, telephone, customer entertainment, and other reasonable expenses incidental to the conduct of business. The Rep must submit a monthly statement of such necessary and reasonable expenses, together with receipts for customer meals, parking, and other significant expenses.

6. **Termination**

   6.1 If the Rep's employment terminates for any reason, whether voluntary or involuntary, the Company will settle final payments as follows:

      6.1.1 Guarantee will be prorated through the date of termination and, if any is due, will be paid promptly after commissions are calculated.

      6.1.2 Commissions will be calculated on credited sales, net of any deductions, through two months following the month of termination. The Company will then prorate the calculated commission for the portion of the three-month period (termination month plus two months) actually worked by the Rep. The prorated commission amount will be paid promptly at the end of the three-month period.

7. **Changes**

   7.1 The Company reserves the right to change or discontinue this Plan at any time. The Company intends to change commission rates from time to time as changes occur in sales patterns and in competitive pay.

   7.2 The Company will give written notice to the Rep prior to the effective date of any change or discontinuance of this Plan. Any failure of a Rep to receive such notice will not alter the effect of the change if the Company has made reasonable effort to have the notice delivered.

   7.3 Any change or discontinuance of this Plan will not reduce the rights of any Rep to pay earned under this Plan prior to such change or discontinuance.

8. Limited Rights

8.1 Nothing in this Plan gives any person a right to employment or to receive any pay other than as specified in this Plan.

9. Effective Date

9.1 Prior pay arrangements for Reps will terminate and this Plan will go into effect on January 1, 19xx. This Plan will then remain in effect until further notice.

For Company _____ Date _____

I agree to serve as a Sales Representative under the terms of this Plan.

Signature _____ Date _____

Print Name _____

Address _____

City _____ State _____ Zip _____

Telephone (   ) _____

Sales Pay Example, New Rep
(Guarantee $1,750 for four months)

Month	Sales	Commission	Paid
1	$ 2,000	$ 160	$ 1,750
2	10,000	800	1,750
3	22,000	1,900	1,900
4	16,000	1,300	1,750
5	1,000	80	80
6	18,000	1,500	1,500
7	10,000	800	800
8	22,000	1,900	1,900
9	24,000	2,100	2,100
10	14,000	1,120	1,120
11	32,000	2,950	2,950
12	29,000	2,600	2,600
Year	$200,000		$20,000

Sales Pay Example, Experienced Rep
(No guarantee)

Month	Sales	Commission	Paid
1	$ 16,000	$1,300	$ 1,300
2	20,000	1,700	1,700
3	24,000	2,100	2,100
4	32,000	2,950	2,950
5	10,000	800	800
6	26,000	2,300	2,300
7	30,000	2,700	2,700
8	34,000	3,200	3,200
9	28,000	2,500	2,500
10	30,000	2,700	2,700
11	28,000	2,500	2,500
12	22,000	1,900	1,900
Year	$300,000		$26,650

Sales Pay Example, High Sales
(No guarantee)

Month	Sales	Commission	Paid
1	$ 20,000	$1,700	$ 1,700
2	40,000	3,950	3,950
3	50,000	5,200	5,200
4	10,000	800	800
5	50,000	5,200	5,200
6	80,000	8,950	8,950
7	40,000	3,950	3,950
8	20,000	1,700	1,700
9	40,000	3,950	3,950
10	80,000	8,950	8,950
11	40,000	3,950	3,950
12	30,000	2,700	2,700
Year	$500,000		$51,000

Monthly Sales Compensation Calculation

Rep _____ Month _____ Year _____

Territory _____

Gross sales $ _____

Adjustments (explained below)

   Returns, allowances $ _____

   Below normal GP $ _____

   Accts. past 90 Days $ _____

Net sales credit $ _____

Commission

   8.0% on first $15,000 (to $1,200) $ _____

   10.0% on sales from $15,000 to $30,000 (to $1,500) $ _____

   12.5% on sales over $30,000 $ _____

   Total commission $ _____

   Guarantee (if applicable) $ _____

Adjustments: _____

_____

_____

_____

_____

_____

_____

Approved _____ Date _____

Appendix B

Blank Corporation
Sales Compensation Plan

Example of a commission-with-draw sales pay plan, with a flat-rate commission formula plus a bonus.

SALES COMPENSATION PLAN HIGHLIGHTS

This brief summary is not part of the Plan. Please read the Plan for details.

Coverage

Field Sales Rep.

Commission

Paid monthly.
20% of GM.

Draw

Paid monthly.
Based on experience.
Deducted from commission and bonus.

Bonus

$500 per new account.

Benefits

Regular employee benefits.

Automobile or reimbursement.

SALES COMPENSATION PLAN

1. **Coverage**

    1.1 This Sales Compensation Plan (the Plan) applies to you if you are a Field Sales Representative employed by Blank Corporation (the Company).

    1.2 This Plan does not apply to Telemarketing Representatives, Warehouse Order Processors, or independent Sales Reps.

2. **Commission**

    2.1 The Company will pay you a monthly commission equal to 20 percent of the gross margin (GM) on sales credited to your territory.

3. **Territory**

    3.1 The Vice President of Sales will issue a written definition of your territory. It will include a geographic area, with certain accounts excluded as house accounts.

    3.2 Your territory may be changed upon one month's written notice to you from the Vice President of Sales.

4. **Sales and GM**

    4.1 You will get GM credit for sales from your territory when booked (order received and approved by the Company).

    4.2 The GM credit will be as coded on the current price list, unless sold below list price. If an order is sold at a lower price or a trade-in is taken at a credit above the regular trade-in list, the difference will be deducted from the GM for that order. Every dollar off the list price reduces the GM by one dollar.

5. **Draw**

    5.1 The Company will pay you a monthly draw based on your level of related sales experience:

Experience	Draw
0–1 yr	$2,000
1–3 yrs	2,300
3–5 yrs	2,600
Over 5 years	3,000

5.2 The draw will be an advance against your commission and bonus earnings.

5.3 Any negative draw balance from one month will carry forward to the following months, and must be repaid before any commission or bonus will be paid.

6. Bonus

6.1 The Company will pay you a bonus of $500 for each new account that you open.

6.2 Any account that has not bought $5,000 or more from the Company in the prior 12 months may qualify as a new account.

6.3 The new account becomes established—and you receive the bonus—when the customer buys at least $5,000 in a month and you request new-account status.

   6.3.1 It is your responsibility to send a written note to the Vice President of Sales when you get a substantial order from a customer that might qualify as a new account.

6.4 The Company will assign new-account credit to you if you were primarily responsible for developing the account—even if your supervisor or someone else gave you the lead.

6.5 A division or subsidiary of an active account normally will *not* be considered a new account. However, if you intend to sell to a division or subsidiary that buys independently of the active account, you may request approval to have that division or subsidiary treated as a new account. Such request must be submitted in writing to the Vice President of Sales *before* the Company accepts an order from the division or subsidiary.

7. Split Sales

7.1 A split sale is any sale in which two or more people share primary responsibility for the sale.

7.2 Your supervisor will notify you in writing if a sale is to be treated as a split sale. This notice must be issued no later than five working days after the order is booked, otherwise it will not be treated as a split sale.

7.3 The manager(s) deciding upon a split sale will determine the percentage division of sales credit between the persons involved.

8. Benefits

8.1 You will be eligible for all regular employee benefits of the Company.

8.2 For purposes of calculating any supplemental benefits that are based on pay, your pay will be considered to be your draw amount.

8.3 The Company may supply you with an automobile for business use or may reimburse you for use of your own automobile. This and other direct expense reimbursements are not compensation to you, but are business expenses.

9. Termination

9.1 If your employment by the Company terminates for any reason, voluntary or involuntary, the Company will pay you commission and bonus on sales credited through the date of termination, less any negative draw balance owing.

9.2 All benefits and other rights of employment will cease when your employment terminates.

9.3 In case you are promoted or transferred out of your position, your pay for the old position will end the same as for a termination. The pay for your new position will then start.

10. Limitations, Changes

10.1 Nothing in this Plan shall be construed to (1) give any person a right to be paid any amount except as specifically provided in this Plan, (2) give any person a right to employment by the Company in any particular position at any particular pay for any particular time, (3) limit in any way the right of the Company to terminate any person's employment for any reason or no reason.

10.2 The Company may change this Plan at any time upon 30 days written notice.

10.3 The Company may change your assigned duties, salary, territory, or accounts at any time.

10.4 Any change made by the Company may not reduce earnings correctly credited to you before the date of change.

10.5 This Plan replaces and cancels any prior compensation arrangements for which you may have been eligible. This Plan constitutes your full and only compensation arrangement.

For the Company _____

Effective date _____

I have read this Plan and understand that it replaces any prior compensation arrangements as of the effective date.

Field Sales Rep _____ Date _____

Sales Pay Example No. 1, Low Sales

Month	Sales	GM	Commission Earned	Bonus Earned	Draw Paid	Draw Balance	Total Paid
1	$ 20,000	$ 8,000	$1,600		$2,300	($700)	$ 2,300
2	10,000	4,000	800		2,300	(2,200)	2,300
3	20,000	8,000	1,600		2,300	(2,900)	2,300
4	30,000	12,000	2,400	$500	2,300	(2,300)	2,300
5	30,000	12,000	2,400		2,300	(2,200)	2,300
6	40,000	16,000	3,200	500	2,300	(800)	2,300
7	20,000	8,000	1,600		2,300	(1,500)	2,300
8	40,000	16,000	3,200	500	2,300	(100)	2,300
9	30,000	12,000	2,400		2,300	0	2,300
10	40,000	16,000	3,200		2,300	0	3,200
11	40,000	16,000	3,200	500	2,300	0	3,700
12	30,000	12,000	2,400		2,300	0	2,400
Year	$350,000	$140,000					$30,000

Sales Pay Example No. 2, Good Sales

Month	Sales	GM	Commission Earned	Bonus Earned	Draw Paid	Draw Balance	Total Paid
1	$ 30,000	$ 12,000	$2,400		$2,300	$0	$ 2,400
2	20,000	8,000	1,600	$ 500	2,300	(200)	2,300
3	40,000	16,000	3,200	1,000	2,300	0	4,000
4	30,000	12,000	2,400		2,300	0	2,400
5	30,000	12,000	2,400	500	2,300	0	2,900
6	50,000	20,000	4,000	1,000	2,300	0	5,000
7	20,000	8,000	1,600		2,300	(700)	2,300
8	60,000	24,000	4,800	1,000	2,300	0	5,100
9	60,000	24,000	4,800		2,300	0	4,800
10	70,000	28,000	5,600	500	2,300	0	6,100
11	50,000	20,000	4,000	500	2,300	0	4,500
12	40,000	16,000	3,200		2,300	0	3,200
Year	$500,000	$200,000					$45,000

Sales Pay Example No. 3, High Sales

Month	Sales	GM	Commission Earned	Bonus Earned	Draw Paid	Draw Balance	Total Paid
1	$ 50,000	$ 20,000	$4,000		$2,300	$0	$ 4,000
2	40,000	16,000	3,200	$ 500	2,300	0	2,300
3	60,000	24,000	4,800	1,000	2,300	0	5,800
4	80,000	32,000	6,400		2,300	0	6,400
5	60,000	24,000	4,800	1,500	2,300	0	6,300
6	80,000	32,000	6,400	1,000	2,300	0	7,400
7	50,000	20,000	4,000	500	2,300	0	2,300
8	90,000	36,000	7,200	1,500	2,300	0	8,700
9	80,000	32,000	6,400		2,300	0	6,400
10	70,000	28,000	5,600	1,000	2,300	0	6,600
11	80,000	32,000	6,400	500	2,300	0	6,900
12	60,000	24,000	4,800	500	2,300	0	5,300
Year	$800,000	$320,000					$68,400

Monthly Sales Compensation Calculation

Rep _____ Month _____ Year _____

Territory _____

Sales	$_____	Beginning draw balance	$_____
Gross margin	$_____	Draw paid	$_____

Commission earned	$_____	Net earnings paid
		  Earnings subtotal
		  − Draw Paid
		  − Beginning draw
		    balance
			$_____

Bonus earned	$_____		
Earnings subtotal	$_____	Total paid	$_____
		Ending draw balance	$_____

Adjustments to sales/gross margin: _____

_____

_____

_____

_____

_____

_____

Approved _____ Date _____

Appendix C

Clear Case Company Regional Sales Manager Pay Plan

Example of a salary-plus-incentive plan, with a set-aside formula.

REGIONAL SALES MANAGER PAY PLAN—HIGHLIGHTS

This brief summary is not part of the Plan. Please read the Plan for details.

Salary

Based on qualifications.
Reviewed annually.

GM Award

Paid monthly.
Based on Gross Margin (GM) of region sales.
Calculated on moving 3-month average GM.
GM Award = 5% of average GM over $45,000.
No award if average GM is not over $45,000.

New Account Premium

50% extra GM credit for first 12 months of new account.
New account: credit established, no order of $5,000+ in prior 12 months.

Management Award

Paid every 6 months.

Based on results versus 2 sales management goals.

Management Award:

- 5% of salary for each goal reached.
- More for outstanding results.
- Zero for poor results.

REGIONAL SALES MANAGER PAY PLAN

1. **Purpose**

   1.1 This Regional Sales Manager Pay Plan (the "Plan") is designed to help Clear Case Company (the "Company") to attract, retain, and motivate highly qualified sales people.

2. **Eligibility**

   2.1 Your name on the last page of this Plan indicates that you have been employed by the Company as a Regional Sales Manager.

   2.2 You will be covered by this Plan as long as you continue as a Regional Sales Manager for the Company or until the Plan is changed.

3. **Salary**

   3.1 The Company will pay you a regular salary, with payments made semimonthly.

   3.2 Your salary will be within a range based on your related sales experience. The schedule below is for 1991. The Company intends to review the salary schedule yearly and adjust it as necessary to keep total earnings opportunity in line with competitive pay generally.

   3.3 The Vice President of Sales will evaluate your experience and sales performance to determine your starting salary level. The Company will pay you a salary within the designated salary range. The Company will review your salary 12 months after you become covered under the Plan and annually thereafter.

   3.3.1 Direct sales experience with another laboratory equipment firm will receive full credit, month-for-month. Other types of sales or other experience may receive less credit, depending on the quality of that experience and how closely it relates to selling for our Company.

3.3.2 In no case will outside experience be credited beyond 72 months, that is, six years.

3.3.3 *Example:* A person with six years (72 months) or more laboratory equipment sales experience would start in Level 4 with 72 months' credit. Two years later that person would move to Level 5, providing his/her sales results are satisfactory or better.

3.4 If your sales results are less than satisfactory, the Vice President of Sales will notify you. Your reclassification may be postponed for up to three months. At the end of that time you will be reclassified or your employment will be terminated.

3.5 **1991 Salary Schedule**

	Experience		Salary	
Level	Mos.	Yrs.	Yearly	Semimonthly
1	36–47	3–4	$38,000–$40,000	$1,583–$1,667
2	48–59	4–5	40,000–42,000	1,667–1,750
3	60–71	5–6	42,000–44,000	1,750–1,833
4	72–95	6–8	44,000–46,000	1,833–1,917
5	96–119	8–10	46,000–48,000	1,917–2,000
6	120+	10+	48,000–50,000	2,000–2,083

4. **GM Award**

4.1 The Company will pay you a GM Award each month.

4.2 The GM Award will be based on Gross Margin (GM) for your region, calculated monthly on a moving three-month average.

4.2.1 The Company will list the GM for each item on the price list, using a number code such as:

2 = 20% GM
3 = 30%
4 = 40%
5 = 50%

4.2.2 The GM is an assigned value for the purpose of calculating incentive pay. It need not be the Company's actual gross margin.

4.3 You will receive GM credit for all sales in your region, subject to the provisions in this Plan.

4.4 The GM credit for a sale will be the listed GM less the amount of any price reduction from list price.

4.4.1 *Example:*

Item	List Price		List GM	
334-111	$2,985	20%	$597	
33245-001	+345	40%	+138	
	$3,330		$735	
Sale Price	−2,800		−530	
	−$530		$205	GM Credit

4.5 Your three-month average GM will be the total of your GM credit for the month just ended and the prior two months, divided by three.

4.5.1 *Example:*

Month	Month GM	3-Month GM
Nov.	$40,000	
Dec.	20,000	
Jan.	60,000	$40,000
Feb.	70,000	50,000
Mar.	50,000	60,000

4.5.2 For your first months under this Plan, the "three-month average GM" will be as follows:

Month 1: Month 1 GM
Month 2: Average of Month 1 + Month 2 GM
Month 3: Regular three-month average GM

4.6 Your GM Award will equal 5 percent of your three-month average GM above $45,000 minimum. There will be no award if the average GM is not over $45,000.

4.6.1 *Example:*

3-Month Average GM	$ 85,000
Minimum GM	− 45,000
GM Award Base	40,000
GM Award Rate	× 5 %
GM Award Amount	$ 2,000

5. New Account Premium

5.1 For one year after you establish a new account, the Company will give you 50 percent extra credit for GM from the new account.

5.2 A new account is an account that has established credit with the Company and has not placed an order of $5,000 or more in the prior 12 months. The new account GM credit period starts with the first order of $5,000 or more and continues for all orders shipped and billed within 12 months after the first order as a new account.

5.3 *Example:* XYZ, Inc. bought from the Company in earlier years, but not recently. The last sale to XYZ was shipped July 5, 1990. You reactivate the XYZ account. On August 15, 1992, we ship XYZ an order for $15,000. No sale was made in the prior 12 months, therefore XYZ is a new account. You get 50 percent additional GM credit from that sale and from every sale to XYZ from August 15, 1992, through August 14, 1993.

6. Management Award

6.1 The Company will pay you a Management Award every six months or less.

6.2 Your Management Award will be based on your achievement of certain regional sales management goals for the award period.

6.2.1 Your goals will be developed by the senior sales executive in consultation with you. Normally, two goals will be designated in writing for an award period. The goals may be quantitative or qualitative. They should be specific, and they should include indication of how results will be rated against the goals.

6.3 At the end of the award period, the Vice President of Sales will rate your results against your goals according to this schedule:

Results versus Goals	Management Award per Goal
Outstanding: Far better than expected in quality, quantity, and/or time.	7.5%
As expected: OK, satisfactory, good.	5.0%
Marginal: Less than satisfactory, but better than poor—even if a good effort was made.	2.5%
Poor: Clearly disappointing in quality, quantity, or time—even if a good effort was made.	0%

6.4 Your Management Award will be the rated percent of salary for the incentive period for each goal.

6.4.1 *Example:*

Award period: 6 months
Salary for the period: $24,000

Goal 1   results as expected   5.0%   = $1,200
Goal 2   results outstanding   7.5%   =   +1,800

Total Award
for 6-month period $3,000

7. Split Sales

7.1 The Vice President of Sales may designate any order for split credit among two or more Regional Sales Managers who may contribute to making a sale or to providing subsequent local support to a sale from another region.

7.2 Normally, split-sales credits will total 100 percent of the regular GM value of the sale. However, in some cases, the split-sales credits may total more than 100 percent. In no case will split-sales credits total less than 100 percent unless the sale is to a house account.

8. House Accounts

8.1 The Vice President of Sales will designate in writing any accounts that will be considered as house accounts.

8.2 You will not be expected to call on house accounts, and you will receive no GM credit for sales to house accounts *unless* the Vice President of Sales specifically assigns a split-sales partial credit to you for helping to make or support a house account sale.

9. GM Credits & Adjustments

9.1 *When Credited:* The GM for a sale will be credited when the order is booked for shipment within 90 days. If shipment is scheduled for longer than 90 days from booking, the GM will be credited when shipped.

9.1.1 *Example:*
An order is booked January 25 for shipment in two parts on June 1 and August 1. The GM value shipped on June 1 will be credited in June, and the GM value shipped on August 1 will be credited in August.

9.2 *Adjustments:* Corresponding GM values will be deducted from your account when any of these occurs: return-for-credit, negative price adjustment, slow-pay account (customer fails to pay amount due within 90 days after billing). GM values will be added to your account when and as any of these occurs: positive price adjustment, payment of a slow-pay account. No GM will be credited on interest or collection charges.

9.3 *Territory Change:*

9.3.1 The Vice President of Sales will assign you to a sales territory of a certain geographic area and/or designated accounts. Your territory may be changed at any time.

9.3.2 If there is a change of territory, the GM credit from a changed account will be phased out for the losing Regional Sales Manager and phased in for the gaining Regional Sales Manager as follows:

	Losing RSM	*Gaining RSM*
Month 1*	100%	0%
Month 2	50%	50%
Month 3	0%	100%

* Includes the month in which the change occurs plus the first full calendar month after the date of change.

9.3.3 If the losing or gaining Regional Sales Manager position is not filled, the Vice President of Sales may assign all GM credit to the Regional Sales Manager who is available to serve the account.

10. Expenses

10.1 The Company will reimburse you for reasonable and necessary business expenses, as approved by the Vice President of Sales, up to a limit set by the Company and subject to federal income tax limitations on deduction of business expenses.

10.2 To collect this reimbursement, you must submit a detailed statement of expenses and receipts (where available) for each month. Show date, place, type of expense (bridge toll, parking, etc.). If you pay for a meal, also show names of those present, place, and purpose.

10.3 The Company believes that these expense reimbursements will not be includable in your taxable income. However, you should retain copies of your expense reports in case federal or state tax officials request such information.

11. Employee Benefits

11.1 You will be eligible to participate in the Company employee benefit programs under the same conditions as other employees.

12. Termination

12.1 If your employment with the Company terminates for any reason, voluntary or involuntary, the Company will pay you according to the following sections.

12.1.1 *Salary:* Your salary will be prorated through date of termination and paid promptly after termination.

12.1.2 *GM Award and New-Account Premium:* These incentive payments will be credited through date of termination. Awards will be calculated at end of month, subject to the regular terms. Awards will be paid at the end of the second month following your termination.

12.1.3 *Management Award:* A Management Award will be paid only if you have been an active employee through the end of the award period. No Management Award will be paid for less than a full award period, even if results meet goals.

12.2 You must return any Company-owned equipment supplied to you (such as telephone equipment, computer, and demonstration equipment) promptly upon termination. Failure to do so could result in charges to you at full price and deduction from your final pay.

12.3 If you are transferred to a position other than Regional Sales Manager, the Company will complete your pay as a Regional Sales Manager under the terms of this section, the same as if your employment terminated.

13. Rights and Limitations

13.1 *Only Agreement:* This Plan is the only agreement governing compensation matters between the Company and you. This Plan supersedes any prior agreement or understanding regarding compensation.

13.2 *Only Pay:* Nothing in this Plan shall be construed to give any person any right to be paid any amount other than under the terms of this Plan, or ensure employment to any person for any period of time.

13.3 *Employment at Will:* Your employment by the Company is at will. This means that either the Company or you may terminate the employment at any time for any reason or for no reason.

13.4 *Employment Limitations:* While employed by the Company, you may not engage in any business that competes with the Company. You may not do so either directly or indirectly. You may not serve as an employee, employer, consultant, agent, officer, or representative for any organization, product, or service that competes. While employed, you may not accept employment with any other employer without prior approval from the President. If you have any question about a proposed situation, please consult with the President.

13.5 *Secrets:* As an employee, you will learn Company trade secrets. These secrets include such things as: identification of customers and prospects; prices; products and services; selling methods; and details of conducting the business. The law recognizes these things as the property of the Company. Even though you learn about these secrets or help in developing them, they belong only to the Company. You may never use or disclose these secrets outside the Company. This restriction applies while you are an employee of the Company and even after you leave the Company. To avoid the embarrassment and cost of possible legal action against you, always treat information that you learn in the Company as confidential.

13.6 *Plan Changes:* The Company may change or terminate this Plan upon one month's written notice to you. The notice may be delivered in person or sent by mail to your last known address.

13.6.1 Any change or termination of this Plan may not reduce earnings properly credited to you prior to the change or termination.

13.6.2 If the Company changes or terminates this Plan, your earnings will be prorated as in the case of employment termination.

13.7 *Arbitration:* Any controversy or claim arising out of or relating to this Plan or the breach thereof, shall be settled by arbitration in accordance with the Commercial Arbitration Rules of the American Arbitration Association. Judgment upon the award rendered by the Arbitrator(s) may be entered in any Court having jurisdiction. The law of the State of California shall apply.

13.8 *Effective:* This Plan will be in effect from the date signed until the Plan is changed or terminated.

I have read, understand, and agree to serve as a Regional Sales Manager under the terms of this Plan.

Level _____ Experience Credit _____ Salary $ _____ semimonthly

Signature _____ Date _____

Print Name _____

Address_____

City _____ State _____ Zip _____

Telephone ( ) _____

Witness _____ Date _____

For The Company _____ Date _____

Clear Case Company
1234 Fifth Street
Anycity, CA 94403
(415) 555-4321

EXHIBIT A

GM Award *(5% of 3-month average GM over $45,000)*

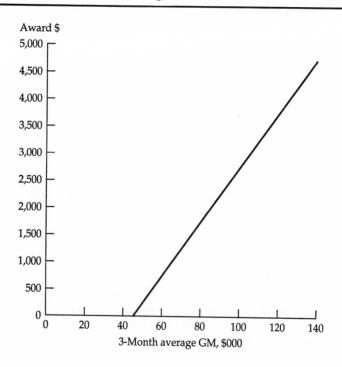

Regional Sales Manager Pay, Example 1 *(Low bookings, low gross margin. Amounts booked and GM in $ 000, pay amounts in $.)*

Month	Book	GM (%)	Mo. GM	New Acct.	Avg. GM	GM Award	Mgt. Award	Salary	Total Pay
1	$ 100	28%	$ 28		$28.0	$ 0		$ 4,000	$ 4,000
2	200	33	66		47.0	100		4,000	4,100
3	150	27	41		44.8	0		4,000	4,000
4	50	27	14		40.0	0		4,000	4,000
5	200	34	68		40.7	0		4,000	4,000
6	150	39	59		46.7	83	$2,400	4,000	6,483
7	250	20	50	5	60.5	775		4,000	4,775
8	50	35	18		43.7	0		4,000	4,000
9	50	40	20		30.8	0		4,000	4,000
10	100	35	35	2	24.8	0		4,000	4,000
11	100	20	20		25.7	0		4,000	4,000
12	100	33	33		30.0	0	2,400	4,000	6,400
Year	$1,500	30%	$450			$958	$4,800	$48,000	$53,758
						% of book			3.6%
						% of GM			11.9%

Regional Sales Manager Pay, Example 2 *(Good bookings, good gross margin. Amounts booked and GM in $ 000, pay amounts in $.)*

Month	Book	GM (%)	Mo. GM	New Acct.	Avg. GM	GM Award	Mgt. Award	Salary	Total Pay
1	$ 200	36%	$ 72		$ 72.0	$ 1,350		$ 4,000	$ 5,350
2	150	35	53		62.3	863		4,000	4,863
3	150	40	60	5	63.2	908		4,000	4,908
4	50	40	20		45.8	42		4,000	4,042
5	300	30	90	2	59.0	700		4,000	4,700
6	400	38	152	10	91.3	2,317	$2,400	4,000	8,717
7	100	38	38	5	99.0	2,700		4,000	6,700
8	300	35	105		103.3	2,917		4,000	6,917
9	50	40	20		56.0	550		4,000	4,550
10	300	35	105	6	78.7	1,683		4,000	5,683
11	150	40	60	4	65.0	1,000		4,000	5,000
12	100	36	36		70.3	1,267	2,400	4,000	7,667
Year	$2,250	36%	$811			$16,296	$4,800	$48,000	$69,096
						% of book			3.1%
						% of GM			8.5%

Regional Sales Manager Pay, Example 3 *(Good bookings, low gross margin (compare Example 2). Amounts booked and GM in $ 000, pay amounts in $.)*

Month	Book	GM (%)	Mo. GM	New Acct.	Avg. GM	GM Award	Mgt. Award	Salary	Total Pay
1	$ 200	30%	$ 60		$60.0	$ 750		$ 4,000	$ 4,750
2	150	38	57		58.5	675		4,000	4,675
3	150	32	48	5	56.7	583		4,000	4,583
4	50	28	14		41.3	0		4,000	4,000
5	300	24	72	2	47.0	100		4,000	4,100
6	400	32	128	10	75.3	1,517	$2,400	4,000	7,917
7	100	28	28	5	81.7	1,833		4,000	5,833
8	300	28	84		85.0	2,000		4,000	6,000
9	50	34	17		44.7	0		4,000	4,000
10	300	30	90	6	65.7	1,033		4,000	5,033
11	150	30	45	4	54.0	450		4,000	4,450
12	100	32	32		59.0	700	2,400	4,000	7,100
Year	$2,250	30%	$675			$9,642	$4,800	$48,000	$62,442
						% of book			2.8%
						% of GM			9.3%

Regional Sales Manager Pay, Example 4 *(High bookings, high gross margin. Amounts booked and GM in $ 000, pay amounts in $.)*

Month	Book	GM (%)	Mo. GM	New Acct.	Avg. GM	GM Award	Mgt. Award	Salary	Total Pay
1	$ 300	40%	$ 120	7	$127.0	$ 4,100		$ 4,000	$ 8,100
2	200	42	84		105.5	3,025		4,000	7,025
3	300	38	114	10	111.7	3,333		4,000	7,333
4	100	36	36	2	82.0	1,850		4,000	5,850
5	400	44	176	5	114.3	3,467		4,000	7,467
6	400	45	180	15	138.0	4,650	$2,400	4,000	11,050
7	100	39	39	10	141.7	4,833		4,000	8,833
8	200	35	70		104.7	2,983		4,000	6,983
9	200	40	80	5	68.0	1,150		4,000	5,150
10	300	35	105	7	89.0	2,200		4,000	6,200
11	150	40	60	6	87.7	2,133		4,000	6,133
12	100	36	36		71.3	1,317	2,400	4,000	7,717
Year	$2,750	40%	$1,100			$35,042	$4,800	$48,000	$87,842
						% of book			3.2%
						% of GM			8.0%

Monthly Sales Compensation Calculation

Reg. Sales. Mgr. _____ Month _____ Year _____

Region _____

		GM award	
Sales booked	$ ____	3-month avg. GM	$ ____
Gross margin	$ ____	Less minimum	$ 45,000
New acct. premium	$ ____	GM award base	$ ____
Adjustments (see below)	$ ____	GM award @ 5%	$ ____
Month GM credit	$ ____	Management award	$ ____
Month-1 GM	$ ____	Salary	$ ____
Month-2 GM	$ ____	Total pay	$ ____
3-month avg. GM	$ ____		

Adjustments to gross margin credit: _____

_____

_____

_____

_____

_____

_____

Approved _____ Date _____

Glossary

Sales compensation terms and their meanings as used in this book.

account An entity that buys or may buy from the company. Usually applied to businesses rather than to individuals.

bluebird An unusually large sale. Also called a windfall.

bonus Cash incentive award based on some special or sustained achievement. Usually paid quarterly, semiannually, yearly, or upon completion of a goal.

commission Variable incentive pay based on sales results. Usually paid weekly, biweekly, semimonthly, monthly, or quarterly.

company Used here to mean any organizational unit with common marketing objectives. May be a corporation, subsidiary, division, or product group.

customer Someone who buys from the company. May be applied to businesses as well as to individuals.

draw Amount paid by the company to the salesperson as an advance or loan against future incentive earnings.

full-line selling Selling all types of items offered by the company, in contrast to restricting sales effort to one or a few items.

gross profit Selling price less cost of the item. Companies differ in what costs they include for calculating gross profit. Same as gross margin.

guarantee A minimum amount of assured incentive pay. If actual incentive earnings for a pay period (such as a month) are less than the guarantee, the company pays the difference, with no balance carried forward to later pay periods. Same as a nonrecoverable draw.

incentive pay A general term meaning any or all variable pay elements. Includes commissions and bonuses.

learning curve The typical, expected level of sales at increasing periods of time from date of hire.

leverage The multiplier relationship between sales results and incentive pay.

milestones Discernible points of progress in the selling process.

nonrecoverable draw A draw that will be offset against incentive earnings only for the current pay period (such as a month), with no balance carried forward to later pay periods. Same as a guarantee.

override A manager's commission calculated as a percentage of the sales or commissions of subordinate salespersons.

pay variance Month-to-month fluctuation in a salesperson's total pay, calculated as the absolute percentage change each month and averaged over a year.

productivity Sales results (sales volume, gross profit, or other measure) divided by cost-of-selling. Term sometimes applied to sales results per salesperson.

prospect An identified potential customer. Also, as a verb, to search for customers.

quota Target or expected level of sales results for a certain time period.

recoverable draw A draw that the salesperson must repay before collecting future incentive earnings.

salary Base pay, paid regularly (such as weekly, biweekly, or semimonthly), not based on current sales results.

sales Used here as a general term meaning whatever the company wants the salesperson to accomplish, usually bookings, shipments, billings, or receipts. May be measured in dollar volume, units, gross profits, percent increase, percent of quota, etc.

spiff An added commission for selling certain items such as overstocked, out-of-season, or obsolete.

split Sales credit divided between two or more salespersons who are involved in making a sale or in providing after-sale service.

territory Geographic area and/or accounts assigned to a salesperson.

threshold A minimum or dividing point that separates two categories or conditions.

total pay Sum of all cash compensation received: salary, draw, commission, and bonus. Does not include reimbursement for automobile, travel, and expenses.

turnover Employee separations as percentage of average number of employees for the period, either monthly or yearly.

windfall An unusually large sale or exceptionally high total sales volume in a short period. Also called a bluebird.

Index